vintage
jewelry
design

To Joanna and Clive

Library of Congress Cataloging-in-Publication Data

Cox, Caroline.
  Vintage jewelry design : classics to collect & wear / Caroline Cox.—1st ed.
      p. cm.
  Includes index.
  ISBN 978-1-60059-714-5 (hc-plc : alk. paper)
  1. Costume jewelry—Collectors and collecting—Catalogs.
2. Costume jewelry—History—20th century—Catalogs. 3.
Jewelry—Collectors and collecting—Catalogs. 4. Jewelry—
History—20th century--Catalogs. I. Title.
  NK4890.C67C695 2010
  739.27075—dc22
                                                2010030858

10 9 8 7 6 5 4 3 2 1

First Edition

Published by Lark Crafts
An Imprint of Sterling Publishing Co., Inc.
387 Park Avenue South, New York, NY 10016

Distributed in Canada by Sterling Publishing,
c/o Canadian Manda Group, 165 Dufferin Street
Toronto, Ontario, Canada M6K 3H6

The Five Mile Press Pty Ltd
1 Centre Road, Scoresby
Victoria 3179 Australia
www.fivemile.com.au

Design and special photography
copyright © Carlton Books Limited 2010
Text © Caroline Cox 2010
Foreword © Gerda Flöckinger 2010

ISBN 13: 978-1-60059-714-5

For information about custom editions, special sales, premium
and corporate purchases, please contact Sterling Special Sales
Department at 800-805-5489 or specialsales@sterlingpub.com.

For information about desk and examination copies available to
college and university professors, requests must be submit-
ted to academic@larkbooks.com. Our complete policy can be
found at www.larkcrafts.com.

Printed and bound in Dubai 5 4 3 2 1

Senior Executive Editor: Lisa Dyer
Managing Art Director: Lucy Coley
Designer: A&E Design
Illustrations: Adam Wright
Copy Editor: Jane Donovan
Picture Researcher: Jenny Meredith
Production: Kate Pimm
Special Photography: Russell Porter

PREVIOUS PAGE Gold and Swarovski crystal cuff bracelet, circa 1950s.

RIGHT A necklace from Alan Andersen uses vintage stones in a new design.

PAGE 4 A model wearing white gloves and a choker, New York, 1948.

vintage
jewelry
design

*classics to
collect & wear*

Caroline Cox

LARK
CRAFTS

An Imprint of Sterling Publishing Co., Inc.
New York
WWW.LARKCRAFTS.COM

Contents

Foreword by Gerda Flöckinger CBE

ABOVE Here an 18-karat gold ring with a cabochon matte white topaz and a single grey diamond, left, and an 18-karat gold ring with a dark opal and dark diamonds, right, are both from 1986. Gerda Flöckinger's work has been called 'a subtle blend of abstract form and Eastern splendor, with a distant echo of the flowing elements in Art Nouveau' by David Thomas of the City of London's Goldsmiths' Company.

Jewelry probably predates most other human fashioning, possibly even clothing, certainly writing and perhaps even speech. It must surely originate in the realm of the instincts, close behind food, shelter and sex. Ancient artifacts in the form of wearable objects made of materials such as stone, horn, bone, seashells, wood, cloth, fossils and metals are known to have existed and examples have been found that date back to prehistoric times. The modes of adornment have changed enormously through time and place and the purposes of personal adornment have also not remained the same, which accounts for the many and varied styles of ornament and adornment. None of these thoughts had surfaced in my own mind when I suddenly decided to make jewelry in a very different way than anything seen in the London of 1952.

As part of my studies I traveled in Europe, had been in Paris, at the Louvre already at the age of eight, and later saw many other treasures. In 1951, at the Musée d'Art Moderne, I first saw the wonderful Deco jewelry of George Fouquet with my mother (she was a fashion designer and took me also to see fashion collections in Paris). I traveled in Italy in the early 1950s, where—in spite of the terrible destruction of the Second World War—it was already possible to see both Modern design in the applied arts as well as the incredible

historic treasures, and still without being overwhelmed by tourism. In order to see the collection of Etruscan jewelry at the Villa Giulia in Rome, I was locked into the room with the jewels for as long as I wanted; I was the only visitor.

It was in Ravenna in the summer of 1952, one evening, that I knew I wanted to make jewelry, in a modern way, in a way which at that time did not exist in England at all, and I had barely even begun to glimpse myself. My determination to master unknown skills to carry out my own ideas certainly overcame my fears as to whether I would ever dare to do such work. I was extremely lucky in my choice of college because in 1952 the Central School of Arts and Crafts still gave students a considerable amount of freedom to dispose over their own studies as well as having a number of hugely interesting artists working with the jewelry students specifically. This meant that I was able to work on my own ideas from the beginning.

Most of the techniques I have developed over the years are self-invented. They have evolved through time and experience though the work has certainly never become easier. Fusion remains the foundation of my work, but really it is the ideas in play which have the most importance: technique for its own sake is of no interest at all.

ABOVE A 1998 bracelet in 18-karat gold with a golden moonstone, dark pearls and colored diamonds. Her work often includes tourmalines, topaz, aquamarines, moonstones, opal and amber, which she mosty cuts herself, mixed with subtly colored pearls and diamonds.

RIGHT, TOP TO BOTTOM An 18-karat gold ring with a cabochon beige quartz and two small pink cabochon tourmalines, 1969; an 18-karat gold ring with oval pink cabochon tourmaline and two dark diamonds, 1989; an 18-karat gold ring with colored diamonds, 2006.

'Gerda Flöckinger is one of the key pioneers of the revival of jewelry-making in this country. Without her imagination, innovation and inspiration as an example much of what has followed may never have happened. She blazed a trail for the distinguished women jewelers who followed. With her we light the blue touch paper of a renaissance.'

Sir Roy Strong, *writer and historian*

'OOs–'IOs   *'IOs*   *'20s*   *'30s*   *'40s*

Introduction

Whether it's the fire and ice of a Harry Winston diamond, the milky glow of an Akoya cultured pearl, the warmth of a Victorian rose-gold ring or the chill of an Art Deco platinum parure, the desire to decorate the body with fabulous jewels has always been a natural human preoccupation. Body ornament excites our imagination and, when mixed with the mysterious alchemy of gems and jewelry, magic is made. The beauty of precious gemstones has been lauded since the beginning of civilization. Pliny the Elder, Roman author and philosopher, penned an ode to the opal after being dazzled by the array of colors encapsulated in a single stone:

> *For in them you shall see the living fire of a ruby, the glorious purple of the amethyst, the sea green of the emerald—all glittering together in incredible mixture of light. Some by their splendor rival the colors of the painters, others the flame of burning sulphur or of fire quickened by oil.*

The magical opal also mesmerized Art Nouveau designers such as Georges Fouquet and Murrle-Bennett who, as this book shows, tapped into the same mystical properties that it seemed to possess many centuries later.

Jewelry may once have been our oldest form of currency but it is much more than a symbol of wealth and social status. From the pagan belief that a string around the neck kept the soul from flying away from the body to the ostentatious flaunting of jewelry won from a succession of rich paramors by the *grand horizontales* of the *belle époque*, jewelry has always been a potent expression of the zeitgeist. Marilyn Monroe's paen to the rock, 'Diamonds are a Girl's Best Friend,' fused our cultural obsession with the jewel on film in *Gentlemen Prefer Blondes* (1953), while Grace Kelly's elegant string of pearls was a symbol of her cool patrician beauty. The ups and downs of the love affair between Elizabeth Taylor and Richard Burton were made manifest in the huge gems he gave her, including the celebrated La Peregrina pearl. More recently, the couple's modern-day counterparts, Brad Pitt and Angelina Jolie, did things differently—in 2009 they collaborated with Asprey of London on the Protector, a collection designed to benefit the Education Partnership for Children in Conflict.

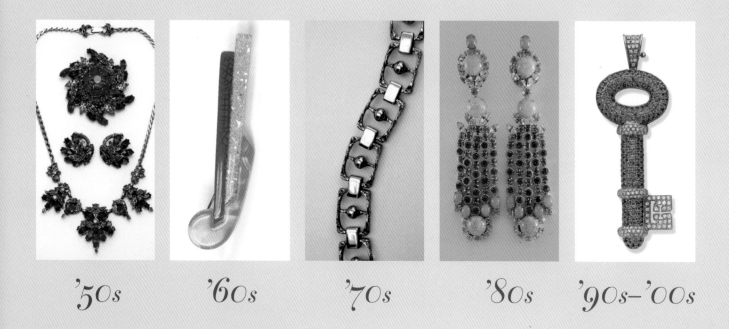

'50s   '60s   '70s   '80s   '90s–'00s

We have a lexicon of jewelry forms to dip into; rings, for instance, have evolved from being symbols of ownership to a dazzling expression of status, from the industrial-sized gems worn by the ace-faces of hip-hop in the 1990s through to the work of innovative designers such as Catherine Provost and Marie-Hélène de Taillac, both renowned for using gems in very contemporary ways. The brooch, the only piece of jewelry that necessitates the wearing of clothes, is perhaps the most idiosyncratic in its subject matter. Queen Victoria loved brooches and had a set of three in the shape of bows made by Garrard, which are still occasionally worn today by Queen Elizabeth II; in 1949, maverick artist Salvador Dalí designed a pair of ruby-encrusted lips with pearl teeth looking as if set to jump from a lapel to give a vicious nip. Earrings are playful—at their lengthiest, it seems, when hair fashions are short and leave a lobe as an optimum site for display. With the chic flapper bobs of the 1920s, triangles and trapezoid earrings reflected the dynamism of metropolitan life, making women seem like beautiful machines; in the 1980s a logo mania took hold and a huge double-C-emblazoned Chanel clip in faux gold gave instant cachet.

In the twenty-first century jewelry has never been more inventive and one of the most exciting areas of development is in *haute joaillerie* produced by fashion's most prestigious houses. Labels such as Versace, Gucci and Dior challenge the role of companies such as Cartier and Bulgari, which have dominated the luxury market for generations. Avant-garde designers such as Shaun Leane for McQueen parlay their catwalk experiments into ranges of wearable and desirable jewelry that are clearly the collectables of the future, and if you need a quick fix from the privacy of your own home, Butler & Wilson—who have produced some of the sparkliest of costume jewelry since the 1970s—can now be purchased with a click of a remote from shopping TV.

This book charts over 100 years of jewelry history and is a celebration of the best designers and houses of fine jewelry through to key costume jewelry manufacturers and the most exciting of the craft and avant-garde. The result? A luscious tome chock-full of the visual tools needed to identify each significant style and designer, and to help you know in which direction your collecting passion lies. Enjoy!

1890–1910:
Divinely Decadent

Cartier, Fabergé, Tiffany & Co., Boucheron…fabulous names that conjure up the glitter of diamonds, the sheen of pearls and the glint of emeralds and rubies—and names that could never have achieved their evocative power in the early twentieth century before the rise of the industrialists, middle-class metropolitans with bottomless pockets of 'new money.'

The notion that a jewelry house could have its own signature piece or that a designer could craft an object of beauty to commission is an invention of the modern world. Traditionally the most fabulous pieces belonged to aristocratic dynasties who passed the 'family jewels' down from generation to generation, having the stones re-set or cut according to changes in taste and fashion. With the rise of a new *haute-bourgeoisie* who had money to burn and a taste for the trappings of status, jewelry became desirous not just for the stones in the settings but also for the magical maker's name.

During this period the most prestigious firms consolidated their reputations both at home and abroad, becoming mighty brands that continue to dominate the market today. In the same era came others whose approach was revolutionary: René Lalique, Philippe Wolfers and Josef Hoffmann, innovative artist-jewelers who were also to gain a global following, albeit on a smaller scale.

Such jewelry was worn against limpid silks, soft crepe de chine and pintucked lace, giving Edwardian fashion a sensuality that had barely existed before. A woman's body may have been rigidly encased in heavy corsetry to gain the required S-bend silhouette or 'pouter-pigeon' look, but it was also swathed in a variety of flirtatiously beribboned garments. The look was one of a lascivious gift, ready to be unwrapped by a besotted beau, who had been bewitched by the sound of *froufrou*, the name given to the rustling sound of taffeta petticoats brushing against the underside of a heavy outer skirt. Cream, grey and lavender were perfectly accented by white on white jewelry, making diamonds set in platinum mounts popular. Queen Alexandra introduced one of the key looks of this period when she wore several rows of pearls set into a *collier de chien*, or dog collar, stunning when worn against her pale swan-like neck. Fashion became more fluid during this decade, anticipating the more liberated styles of the 1920s, clearly reflected in the switchback curves of Art Nouveau design.

La Belle Epoque

During this period Paris became notorious as a city of glittering extravagance and *belle époque* decadence; a center of erotic pleasure before the cataclysmic carnage of the First World War. Italian writer Edmondo de Amicis, overwhelmed by the *grandes boulevards*, wrote of, 'Windows, shops, advertisements, doors, façades (which) all rise, widen and become silvered, gilded and illumined. It is a rivalry of magnificence which borders on madness. The eye finds no place on which to rest' and concluded that it was a place 'of coquetry and pride—a great opulent and sensual city, living only for pleasure and glory.'

Paris was the backdrop to the international celebrities and queens of the demimonde La Belle Otero, Liane de Pougy and Emilienne d'Alençon, women collectively known as the *grandes horizontales,* who used their wit and guile to amass huge fortunes from a series of wealthy, if unwary suitors. Spanish dancer Caroline Otero (1868–1965) in particular was a talented performer, both in and out of bed, and had a list of lovers that included Edward, Prince of Wales, King Alfonzo XIII of Spain and Nicholas, Czar of Russia, who showered her with a collection of jewelry that was world-renowned. As Otero put it, 'no man who has an account at Cartier's can be regarded as ugly,' and she was duly welcomed at 13 rue de la Paix where the elegant and discreetly luxurious premises of Cartier were situated, one of the most prestigious names in the history of jewelry.

It was Cartier who created the most extraordinary breast ornament for Otero, the name given to a huge looped pendant that reached entirely across the torso to hang in shimmering swags below. Otero's was fashioned out of 10 million francs worth of precious stones set into a pure gold frame. Along the bottom hung a series of 30 enormous diamonds, appearing, as one observer put it, 'like huge tears' and heavy ropes of diamonds were arranged across the front to be secured in the center with a large diamond clasp. An object of desire such as this had to be kept in a bank vault, but whenever Otero chose to wear it, it had to be delivered to her dressing room via a reinforced carriage accompanied by two fully armed gendarmes. Otero's Cartier piece gave out a rather unsubtle message—she could be bought, but only by the very richest, and her magnificent jewels represented her sexual prowess.

Otero's choice of ornamentation also displays the more mainstream attitude to jewelry that began to emerge during this period. Art Nouveau may have suited an artsy crowd, but the Edwardian sensibility was far more interested in the stones rather than the settings. A lust for big diamonds coincided with advances in diamond-cutting technologies that improved the prismatic qualities of the stone and thus allowed a more showy sparkle when a woman chose to sashay through Maxim's, the famed haunt of many a woman of pleasure. The Omnibus Bar, in particular, had every wall covered with mirrors deliberately designed to intensify the flash of a diamond-encrusted aigrette arranged in a coquette's blue-black hair. It was here that one of the most celebrated encounters of the demimonde took place, between two rivals in love—La Belle Otero and Liane de Pougy. Otero made a dazzling entrance wearing her entire collection of jewels plus a daringly plunging gown. Precious gems blazed across her entire body from her hair down to her ankles, including three pearl necklaces, one of which had belonged to the Empress of Austria, and ten cabochon-ruby clips. Liane, however, had been tipped off in advance and appeared in a simple white gown, a diamond pendant at her throat, and followed by a maid carrying the rest of her jewels on a black velvet cushion. Otero was instantly transformed into a vulgar vision of boastful spite.

PAGE 10 Queen Alexandra set the vogue for the pearl and diamond *collier de chien* in the Edwardian period. She sports a style that accentuates her swan-like neck in 1889.

OPPOSITE, BELOW Georg Jensen (1866–1935) was one of the new band of artist-craftsmen who transformed jewelry design in the early twentieth century. These two brooches of sterling silver, one set with amber, malachite and chrysophase, 1904, and the other set with pearl and coral, 1909, are examples of Jensen's rejection of historicism.

RIGHT La Belle Otero, the infamous Spanish dancer and courtesan, amassed a fortune in jewels from her numerous lovers, which she flaunted at every public opportunity.

Jewelry as Art

Women like La Belle Otero may have surveyed the effects of the Industrial Revolution with cynicism, however William Morris, founder of the Arts and Crafts movement, was filled with abject loathing. He was one of many involved in the applied arts who feared that the rise of mechanical production could banish skilled artisanship forever—in its place the conveyor-belt production of shoddy, if affordable, junk. Accordingly, Morris and a number of other similarly minded artists, set up their own workshops in order to produce beautifully crafted goods by hand, including the most exquisite of early twentieth-century jewelry. They truly believed there would always be a place for good craftsmanship—even in the teeming streets of the modern metropolis.

Since the Renaissance, a strict hierarchy of cultural production had placed fine art and architecture at the pinnacle of creative attainment and the applied arts, such as jewelry, lower down the scale. The popular notion ran that true art had a purely aesthetic, rather than utilitarian, function and any image created for fashionable use was ineffably inferior to that conveyed on canvas. The Arts and Crafts movement and its inevitable by-product Art Nouveau negated those assumptions. Art didn't have to have a gallery wall; it could be small scale, fashionable and exquisite, taking the form of a beautiful parure of shimmering opals or a brooch fashioned into a moonstone-bedecked *femme fatale*. For these designers, the aesthetics of an object were considered more important than the intrinsic value of the materials used, so in Art Nouveau design in particular, semiprecious stones like amethyst, citrine, peridot and freshwater pearls can be seen in abundance. Designers believed the pursuit of the perfect setting and the flashiest gem had driven creativity out of mainstream jewelry design and they were determined to instigate a change.

Such ideas had incredible effects for twentieth-century jewelry as many a talented artist moved into its sphere, thereby changing the status of the occupation from that of a mere setter of stones for a client's approval into a true artist capable of creating *bijouterie,* a personal vision in precious metal and luminous gems.

ABOVE This 1898 poster in the Art Nouveau style by graphic artist Adolfo Hohenstein advertises Calderoni jewels. The long-running Italian firm, established in Milan in 1840, was bought by Damiani in 2006.

L'Art Nouveau

The whiplash curling lines and elaborate arabesques of Art Nouveau ran rampant over jewelry design in the period known as the *belle époque* **(1890–1910).** Art Nouveau, or 'new art,' was seductive and sinuous, derived from an essentially exoticized nature with recurring motifs such as dragonflies, peacocks and death's-head moths combined with the hallucinatory experimentation of French symbolism, the heady seduction of the work of artist Aubrey Beardsley and the *femme fatales* of Czech artist Alphonse Mucha. It was the first truly international design movement of the twentieth century, and is called, variously, *Jugendstil* in Germany, *Sezessionstil* in Vienna, *Arte Joven* ('Young Style') in Spain and, owing to its close association with the work of Louis Comfort Tiffany, the Tiffany Style in America. The curvilinear aesthetic of Art Nouveau was equally at home in the large-scale architectural projects of Antoni Gaudí in Barcelona or Victor Horta in Brussels and in the more intimate jewelry designs of René Lalique in Paris and Philippe Wolfers in Brussels.

What marked Art Nouveau jewelry out was the way it broke away from the revivalist styles of the nineteenth century and what was considered 'the tyranny of the diamond.' Artists began to concentrate on nature, above all else, as a source of inspiration. The discovery of Japanese art in the mid-nineteenth century opened many a designer's eyes to the beauty of asymmetry, simplicity of composition and economy of line; when combined with the decadent mysteries of Baudelaire's symbolism, a new aesthetic was born.

Many Art Nouveau pieces incorporated organic forms *à la Japonisme* combined with the use of small stones studded over the whole rather than the more showy single gems of the Victorian period. Baroque or river pearls were much sought after for their irregular shape and opals were favored because of their milky bloom, so different from the ice-cold glint of diamonds. New combinations of metals and semiprecious stones were used to emphasize color with enamel providing lustrous hues and pastel shading. This vitreous material, a mix of powdered silica, potash and metallic oxide colorants, was a feature of traditional Japanese art, in particular the *inro*, a compartmented box for personal effects. The discovery by Art Nouveau designers led to its use in the metal surfaces of jewelry employing a variety of revivalist techniques such as:

* *Basse-taille*, in which glass enamel is applied to a metal surface that has been engraved deeply enough to hold the enamel when heated, and with sides high enough to keep each color separate.

* *Champlevé*, where the metal background is etched or carved and then filled with enamel and polished to produce a flat surface.

* *Cloisonné*, where the sections of enamel are defined by wire, as in a stained glass window.

The subjects of this new type of jewelry were organic in the extreme, such as vines, water lilies, irises and anemone, all chosen for their ability to be rendered as the most sinuous of tendrils, full of rhythmic energy. The animal kingdom was similarly depicted in all its emotionally charged complexities to reflect the duality of nature. Fauna could be serene and life-affirming, such as swans, swallows and peacocks, or fraught with danger, such as serpents, bats, mythological fire-breathing dragons, sinister vultures and wasps.

ABOVE In this 1899 poster, *La Plume,* by Alphonse Mucha, the enigmatic Art Nouveau femme fatale is depicted as an elemental force of nature, whose swirling tresses find echo in the whiplash lines of early twentieth-century jewelry design.

Philippe Wolfers

Brussels was the most Art Nouveau of cities with a prodigious output of the style in all its forms. Architects Victor Horta and Henri van der Velde found enthusiastic patrons for the most avant-garde of projects, including the Tassel House, and the country's booming industrial economy meant money was readily available for *bijoux de luxe*.

Son of master-goldsmith Louis Wolfers, Philippe (1858–1929) entered his father's workshop as an apprentice in 1875 where he received extensive training in jewelry-making techniques. In the 1880s he began crafting a series of ewers in gold and silver decorated with asymmetrical floral motifs that anticipated the Art Nouveau style and influenced the jewelry he began producing from 1890 in his own workshop, culminating in a successful collection exhibited at the Paris Salon in 1900.

Much of the jewelry created by Philippe Wolfers transforms the languid lines of Art Nouveau into theatrically decadent excess. He had a particular penchant for the *femme fatale*, a key motif in Symbolism, that retained its popularity in Art Nouveau design. The *femme fatale* was a woman of such dazzling beauty that she became a harbinger of death to any man enraptured by her mesmerizing, yet ultimately fatal beauty—a stereotype of femininity, stretching back to Eve and her forbidden fruit in the Garden of Eden. The fatal woman gained currency in the new century as men looked on with alarm at the vociferous movement for women's suffrage and the fight for the right to vote. This was a very different woman to the one who had dominated most of the nineteenth century as a domesticated keeper of hearth and home; as women discovered themselves socially, politically, and above all sexually (as documented in the work of the father of psychoanalysis, Sigmund Freud, based in Vienna), so men retreated, their minds beset by ancient fears. The *femme fatale* was back, mysterious and seductively dangerous—a woman who could lure men to their doom.

The *femme fatale* is used in many of Wolfers' jewelry designs such as his Medusa pendant, on which she is depicted surrounded by a menagerie of her peculiars that take the uncanny forms of bats, insects and serpents. Brooches shape-shift into pearl-studded dragonflies; diamond- and ruby-encrusted orchids act as exotic hair ornaments fashioned from enamel and gold. Notably, Wolfers was one of the first modern designers to use ivory, in plentiful supply due to Belgium's presence in the Congo. His work is marked by incredible technical virtuosity, especially in the use of *plique-à-jour* enameling, considered the most difficult of enameling techniques. Thin veins of silver or gold filigree wire are fused into a vitreous enamel with the backing metal removed after firing. The resulting translucent effect is designed to evoke the effect of light glimpsed through a stained-glass window—hence the name *plique-à-jour,* or 'glimpse of day.'

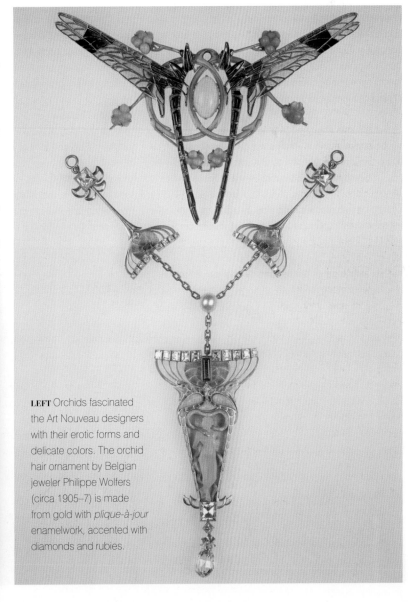

LEFT Orchids fascinated the Art Nouveau designers with their erotic forms and delicate colors. The orchid hair ornament by Belgian jeweler Philippe Wolfers (circa 1905–7) is made from gold with *plique-à-jour* enamelwork, accented with diamonds and rubies.

René Lalique

Known today as a master of glass, Lalique (1860–1945) is one of the greatest exponents of Art Nouveau jewelry. He was born in Ay, a village situated in the region of Marne, France, in 1860. In 1874, after the death of his father, he was indentured as an apprentice to the goldsmith Louis Aucoc in Paris, where he began his training as a jeweler, opening his own business in 1885. He was an innovator, already renowned for his liberal use of the Art Nouveau aesthetic by the time entrepreneur Samuel Bing set up his showcase boutique La Maison l'Art Nouveau in 1895. Bing duly commissioned work from Lalique that helped spread the style across the global marketplace, influencing a whole generation of young jewelers, including Lucien Gaillard, who became known for his innovative use of patination.

Lalique's work is luxurious and sensuous, and incorporates combinations of glass, silver, enamel, gold and milky pearls. Poppies, the source of opium and a gateway to the world of dreams, recur in his work as a motif, especially adorning the heads of the ubiquitous *femme fatale*, such as in a pendant design that portrays a baleful face of opalescent glass with swirling hair dressed with four poppy heads. In much of this jeweler's work long hair is almost fetishized, acting as a trap for the unwary man and echoing poet Swinburne's popular poem, *Laus Veneris*. In these lines the malignant sexual force of the *femme fatale* found an expressive power:

> *Ah, with blind lips I felt for you and found*
> *About my neck your hands and hair enwound*
> *The hands that stifle and the hair that stings*
> *I felt them fasten sharply without sound.*

Lalique was also known for his pectorals or necklaces with pendants that hung over the breastbone, a form of jewelry that originated from ancient Egypt. One of the most flamboyant comprises nine serpents, cleverly entwined to form a knot from which their bodies emerge, mouths agape with fangs exposed.

Innovation followed innovation in the designer's work and he was one of the few twentieth-century jewelers able to fashion horn into extraordinary shapes. Lalique loved horn because it was light and translucent yet durable. After buying small quantities from the local abattoir, the designer found he was able to transform one of the cheapest and humblest of materials into objects of great beauty, such as his horn hair-combs studded with amethyst and chrysoprases (a type of chalcedony quartz gemstone containing nickel, which gives it a distinctive apple-green color) and in 1900 a stunning horn and diamond tiara depicting a simple wreath of autumn leaves. At the International Exhibition (Exposition Universelle) held in Paris in the same year, Henri Vever, a contemporary of Lalique's, described how he felt on seeing the jeweler's showcase for the first time: 'I felt a shudder. You thought you were dreaming when you saw these beautiful things... a cockerel holding an enormous yellow diamond in its beak; a huge dragonfly with a woman's body and diaphanous wings; enameled country scenes sparkling with diamond dew-drops; ornaments like pine cones.'

Georges Fouquet

Le Maison Fouquet was one of a number of rather grand Parisian jewelers at the turn of the century founded in 1860 by Alphonse Fouquet (1828–1911) and was known for setting gems into heavy Renaissance Revival settings. As the vogue for Art Nouveau took hold, the firm began to adopt the central motifs such as the *femme fatale* and the dragonfly, but the first pieces were a little

OPPOSITE Theatricality of expression, which can be seen in Lalique's serpent pectoral in enameled gold, found a willing audience in the notorious actress Sarah Bernhardt. A second version had chains of pearls hanging from the creature's open mouths.

BELOW Two jewelry designs by René Lalique from 1898–1900. On the left, a typical hair ornament in horn takes nature as a source of inspiration to transform an everyday object into a miniature work of art. The pendant on the right is in black patinated silver with a spectral face in opalescent glass surrounded by poppy heads—the source of opium.

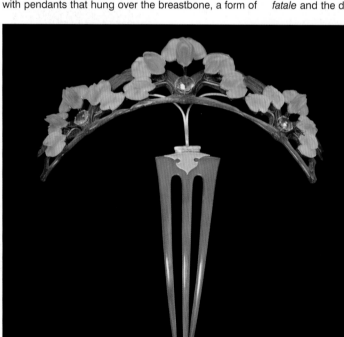

unconvincing and lacked the style's deft lightness of touch. This was to change dramatically when Georges Fouquet took over as director of La Maison Fouquet in 1895. He immediately dropped all the retrospective styles that had originally established the firm's name and wholeheartedly embraced Art Nouveau.

Georges Fouquet (1858–1929) was a jeweler of incredible technical expertise with an impeccable eye for detail. In the main, he worked in gold and employed Etienne Tourette to produce the fashionable *plique-à-jour*, to which Tourette gave a unique twist by adding paillon or tiny flakes of platinum, silver or gold for a little extra glitter. Semiprecious stones such as opals, moonstones and pearls feature in pendants, sautoirs and lavalier, which combine exotic orchids, dragonflies and snakes with floral scrolls and fluttering butterflies.

Fouquet rose to prominence in the Art Nouveau movement as a result of a three-year partnership from 1899–1901 with the sublime Alphonse Mucha, the Czech graphic artist whose work now epitomizes the deluxe and decadent Art Nouveau style. Fouquet fell in love with the fantasy jewelry and headgear with which Mucha adorned the female subjects of posters such as *The Brunette* (1897), many of whom were the ferocious *grandes horizontales* of ignominious renown.

Together Fouquet and Mucha created an array of fantastically theatrical Byzantine-inspired pieces combining cabochon, ivory and baroque pearls with detailed miniatures by Mucha set into enamel plaques. The work was displayed at the 1900 International Exhibition in Paris to great acclaim. So successful was the partnership that, in the following year, Fouquet commissioned Mucha to design the frontage and interior for the jewelry firm's new premises in the rue Royale, the only large-scale commission ever executed by the artist. It was temple to Art Nouveau merchandising; a riot of bronze fittings, carving and stained glass, with a huge relief sculpture of a peacock over one wall and wall cabinets in the shape of bubbles. When the shop was remodeled in 1923, this fabulous interior was removed and rebuilt in the Musée Carnavalet.

Mucha and Fouquet's most famous piece was a huge articulated armlet and hand ornament in the shape of a writhing snake, designed for the great actress Sarah Bernhardt, the toast of *tout* Paris. She was a lover of jewels, graciously accepting a diamond brooch from Alfonso XII of Spain, a necklace from Emperor Franz Josef, and even a bicycle from Tiffany's studded with diamonds and rubies. After her stirring performance in his play *Hernani*, Victor Hugo wrote to Bernhardt: 'I wept. That tear...is yours' and enclosed a tear-shaped diamond.

Mucha had collaborated with Bernhardt before, having designed sets, costumes, even hairstyles for her productions, and the bracelet was designed to commemorate her triumph in the role of Cleopatra in 1890. The ruby-eyed articulated snake's head was fashioned from opal mosaic, the body worked in enamel, and from the jaws of the reptile hung a series of fine gold chains that ended in a diamond and emerald ring. Legend has it that Bernhardt lacked the funds to pay for such an expensive piece so Fouquet was required to go to the theater every night to collect the money in installments.

BELOW The outstanding Art Nouveau interior of Georges Fouquet's Magasin Fouquet (circa 1900) in the rue Royale, Paris, designed by Alphonse Mucha. On the far right between stained-glass windows, the peacock roundel stands guard over the store.

BOTTOM A Fouquet brooch in matte and burnished gold with enamel, pearls and diamonds. By the time this brooch was produced in 1903, the firm was situated in the Mucha-designed shop on the rue Royale, with a workshop on the upper floor.

OPPOSITE *The Brunette*, a 1897 poster designed by Alphonse Mucha and one of a pair of Byzantine heads. The luxuriously fantastical headpiece is intended to conjure the splendor of Byzantine culture and exemplifies high Art Nouveau style.

Louis Comfort Tiffany

Son of Charles Lewis Tiffany, the founder of Tiffany & Co., Louis (1848–1933) became a world-renowned proponent of Art Nouveau in America. European Art Nouveau derived its magic from nature—so did Tiffany's but from a more American point of view: lilies and poppies were replaced with wild carrot flowers, and garnets used to form blackberries and grapes. Metals were mixed into combinations of silver, gold and platinum, providing the sumptuous settings for soft enamelwork developed by Julia Munson Sherman, and Tiffany's use of understated gemstones such as opals, tourmalines, moonstones and pink sapphires followed the color palette he had developed while training as an Impressionist painter. The designer also put to good use the extensive travels he had undertaken after rejecting a position in the family firm in favor of studying fine art. When appointed design director of Tiffany & Co. after his father's death in 1902, Louis' personal collection of *objects trouvés* from his travels in Europe, Africa, Asia and the Middle East—including Benin armbands and bead necklaces plundered from the tombs of Egyptian mummies and folk jewelry from the Indian sub-continent—provided the inspiration for many designs.

Such influences can clearly be seen in his Egyptian Revival chokers with their oversize, multi-hued cabochon-cut gemstones, as well as pieces inspired by the royal jewels from the Mughal court of India. As in the work of other Art Nouveau designers, nature remained a source of influence and the designer used an array of brightly colored fruits, flowers, birds and insects in both his stained-glass design and such jewelry as his 1904 St Louis World's Fair Dragonfly brooch. In this naturalistic piece, black opals and green garnets form the body and the wings are executed in gossamer-thin platinum and gold filigree work.

Tiffany's use of enameling was masterful. He built up layer upon layer of translucency in naturalistically shaded hues, which were then applied to a gilt surface. His techniques included *champlevé*, *cloisonné*, *basse taille* and *plique-à-jour* (see also page 14), and he placed drops of gold in the enamel for added lustre. Gemstones included pink sapphires, peridots, moonstones and demantoid garnets in a striking bright green. Tiffany also revived the cannetille settings originally used in Georgian jewelry, which imitated fine lace enriched with leaf, rosette and berry motifs.

RIGHT This 1910 leaded glass lamp pendant from Tiffany Studios is made in the shape of the ubiquitous Art Nouveau butterfly. The iridescent Favrile glass, in which the color is ingrained in the glass, was Louis Tiffany's trademark.

OPPOSITE The pale colors of much *belle époque* jewelry flattered the softer fashions of the pre-war woman, a decorative and pampered femininity that was to be swept away in the 1920s. This seed pearl parure by Tiffany (circa 1890), comprises a pin and earrings.

BELOW This platinum pendant watch by Tiffany & Co., circa 1900, has a gold and diamond-set fob with an openwork foliate, surmount set with pearls.

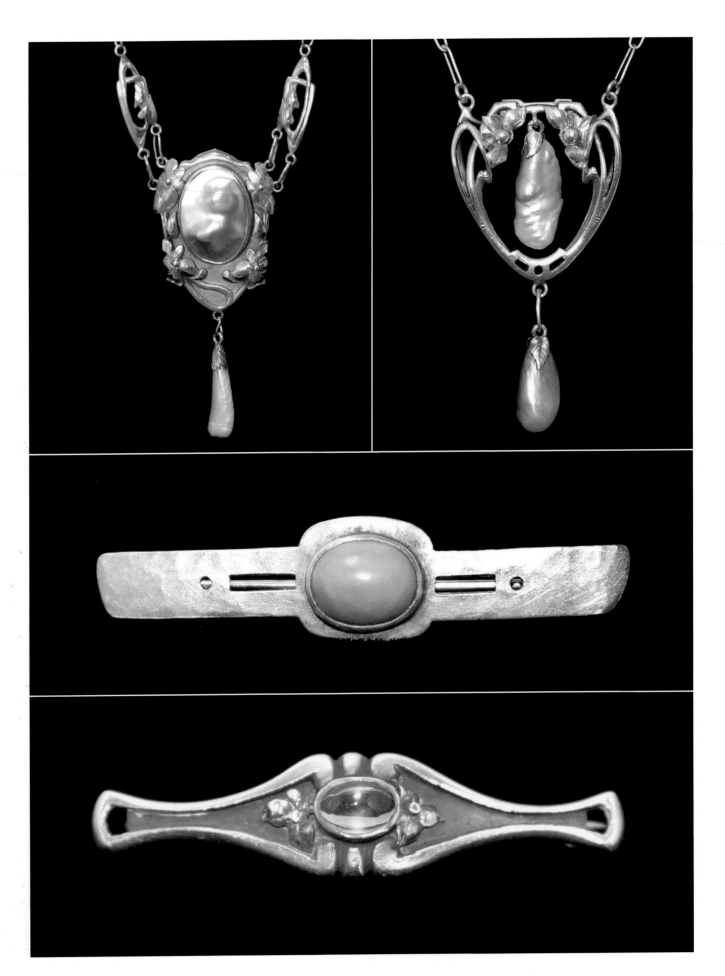

Clara Barck Welles

Chicago was a city at the center of the Art Nouveau style having already a flourishing Arts and Crafts community that included celebrated silversmiths Janet Payne Bowles and Jessie M Preston. What marked out the work of designers such as Clara Barck Welles was a marriage of North American Indian motifs and earth colors with the prairie landscape's distinctive grasses and flowers. Brooches, rings and necklaces incorporating moonstones, aquamarines, opals and lapis lazuli were sold at the Kalo Shop founded in 1900 in Park Ridge, Illinois, by 32-year-old Barck (1868–1965), who named it after the Greek word for beauty. Barck's first output included Arts-and-Crafts-inspired textiles, leatherwork, pyrography, baskets and copper items, but in 1905 after she married amateur silversmith George Welles, the Kalo Shop began to focus exclusively on hand-wrought metalwork following her personal aesthetic of 'Beautiful, Useful, Enduring.'

Kalo work is recognizable by its use of subtly convex or 'puffy' saw-pierced oval forms of chased and repoussé fruit such as cherries or pineapples and arrangements of flowers, leaves and vines. Pieces are usually bezel-set with amethysts, baroque pearls, lapis, bloodstones, moonstones and citrines.

Welles was an astute businesswoman from the outset, eschewing a small-scale 'boutique' business in favor of a large commercial concern—at one point she employed over 25 female silversmiths called the 'Kalo girls' as designers allowing her output to continue during the First World War, when many male silversmiths were sent overseas. Welles retired to California at the age of 40 and turned the shop over to four of its craftsmen—Robert Bower, Daniel Pederson, Arne Myhre and Yngve Olsson—in 1959. When Pederson and Olsson died in 1970, the doors of Kalo finally closed.

OPPOSITE, TOP LEFT
A Kalo pendant on a silver paper-clip style chain with a gold shield containing a blister pearl is surrounded by flowers and trailing vines and a baroque pearl drop.

OPPOSITE, TOP RIGHT
A Kalo pendant on a silver paperclip chain features two oversized baroque pearls, one dangling in a frame surmounted with Art Nouveau detail and the other in a drop at the bottom. The chased and hammered detail is typical of Kalo jewelry.

OPPOSITE CENTER In many ways, Kalo's muted Art Nouveau anticipates the Art Deco style of the 1920s. This can be seen in this simple brooch from Chicago, made from gold with a bezel-set oval coral cabochon and flanked by small cutouts.

OPPOSITE, LEFT A Kalo bar brooch features a bezel-set oval cabochon citrine with simple flower detail.

RIGHT AND BELOW The almost Scandinavian restraint of many Kalo pieces shows links with the work of George Jensen and the Wiener Werkstätte. These simple silver designs – a ring with its delicately carved coral rose, and a bangle with a bezel-set oval coral stone – are examples.

LEFT Clara Barck Welles, pictured here in 1906, was the pioneering founder of Chicago's influential silversmith group and the Kalo Shop. She was also one of the few independent businesswomen working in the early twentieth-century jewelry trade. The shop had many customers, who were persuaded to have their old-fashioned jewelry rejuvenated by having stones taken out of their heavy settings and set into new ones.

Liberty Style

Britain had been at the forefront of the Arts and Crafts movement in the nineteenth century and there is a clear overlap between the jewelry produced in this style and that of Art Nouveau. Henry Wilson, Archibald Knox, C R Ashbee, Sybil Dunlop and Harold Stabler all used interlaced and knotted decorative motifs of Celtic origin which had their roots in William Morris' romantic obsession with the mythology of Britain's ancient past. Religious iconography from the Renaissance and Gothic period, together with motifs from Scandinavian folklore also featured heavily. Silver was the material of choice in much of British jewelry at the turn of the century. Expertly crafted into brooches, belt buckles, hatpins and lavalier, it was retailed through outlets such as Liberty of London, a store established in 1875 by Arthur Lazenby Liberty to sell goods such as silk and porcelain from the East Indies and Japan. Such was Liberty's commercial success that Art Nouveau, which had barely entered the architectural annals of England, became surprisingly popular. Restrained yet rhythmic pieces in silver and gold set with turquoise and tiny river pearls by Knox, among others, retailed at the store under the name Cymric from 1899 on. Knox designs can be instantly recognized by his distinctive use of peacock or blue-green colored enamel set into patinated silver, a style copied and mass-produced by a number of other firms.

Charles Horner

From the late 1850s, Charles Horner (1837–96) of Halifax had been a prosperous firm supplying mass-produced jewelry for local retailers. In 1905, after the death of the founder, Horner's sons opened modern premises in Halifax, Yorkshire, and began to churn out jewelry in the Liberty Style, from the initial design right through to the finished product, including pendants, hatpins, earrings, thimbles and brooches with an emphasis on distinctive iridescent peacock-blue enamel set in silver. Despite being mass-produced, an efficient quality control meant that each piece was of a high standard and the company gained a huge following as a result of their jewelry being sold in major department stores, including Liberty.

LEFT A comprehensive collection of silver, gold and enamel British Art Nouveau and Arts and Crafts brooches, including designs by Charles Horner, Murrle Bennett and William H Haseler, circa 1908–11. Motifs from nature were popular at this time, including the dragonfly that was used by designers all over the world. Stones are incorporated as part of the overall design of the piece, rather than an overtly flashy focal point.

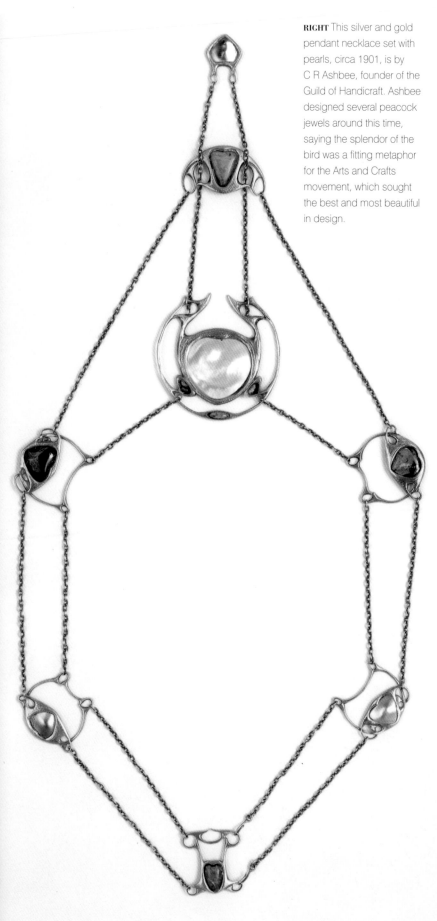

RIGHT This silver and gold pendant necklace set with pearls, circa 1901, is by C R Ashbee, founder of the Guild of Handicraft. Ashbee designed several peacock jewels around this time, saying the splendor of the bird was a fitting metaphor for the Arts and Crafts movement, which sought the best and most beautiful in design.

LEFT This delicate gold pendant from 1902 is set with mother-of-pearl and opals and is typical of the much sought after work of Archibald Knox. Born on the Isle of Man, which is famed for its carved stone crosses, the island's Celtic influence informed much of Knox's work for Liberty & Co.

Austrian Art Nouveau: Wiener Werkstätte

Vienna was a cultured city of understated elegance at the turn of the century, enjoying a period of industrial prosperity, unprecedented in its history. The patronage of newly rich middle-class sophisticates made the city a magnet for the avant-garde, drawing artists from all over Europe to participate in an atmosphere of discrete Bohemianism, which in turn made the city one of the cradles of twentieth-century Modernism. Traditions were challenged by artists such as Gustav Klimt and Egon Schiele, founder members of the Secessionist group who gave the work of psychoanalyst Sigmund Freud a new visual language that revealed the intimate secrets of the human unconscious. Into this heady mix came a band of artisan-artists known collectively as the Wiener Werkstätte, essentially a cooperative of craftspeople founded in 1903 and dedicated to the elevation of the applied arts, including jewelry design. Leaders Josef Hoffmann and Koloman Moser were keen to pursue the concept of *gesamtkunstwerk* or 'total work of art,' in which every object in every home should be desirable and designed to display the pinnacle of avant-garde taste.

Funded by art collector and businessman Fritz Waerndorfer, the Wiener Werkstätte drew together a band of young jewelry designers—Carl Otto Czeschka (1878–1960) and Dagobert Peche (1887–1923), who ran the workshop from 1910–23, and Lotte Calm and Editha Moser, who worked in a spirit of artistic collaboration. In Vienna, the curvilinear Nouveau mode was given a harder edge and a more restrained geometry became the order of the day. The use of silver, copper and semiprecious stones blurred the boundaries of jewelry and sculpture. Flowers became cubic, brooches rectilinear; shapes reflected the concerns of the Wiener artists and architects such as Adolf Loos and Charles Rennie Mackintosh in Scotland, and forms of their designs permeated art, architecture and jewelry. Within the geometry of Werkstätte jewelry one can still see the long curving lines of European Art Nouveau, and the use of silver and gold set with mother-of-pearl had the same lightness of touch, but increasingly geometry began to prevail: cabochon agates, malachite and darker hues of enamel were set in linear forms that anticipated the cool, sleek lines of Art Deco. Hoffman seemed enamored of silver-gilt squares, in particular, and the use of monochrome enamel and hammered metal.

For some time, the Wiener Werkstätte enjoyed great success, setting up outlets in Paris, Zurich and New York, but the looming threat of war caused the slow decline of this Bohemian style. The idealistic and uncompromising Hoffmann refused to go more down-market by using cheaper materials and mechanical modes of production and, in 1914, a bankrupted Waerndorfer was forced to emigrate to America. Even so, Werkstätte jewelry stands the test of time, appealing to an audience of modern collectors with its emphasis on restrained luxury, sophistication and the subtle taming of the excesses of Art Nouveau.

OPPOSITE Josef Hoffmann's work at the Wiener Werkstätte forms a clear visual link between Art Nouveau and Art Deco by using forms from nature in a geometric, rather than overly flowing, style. This 1910 pendant is made from gold set with mother-of-pearl and semiprecious stones.

BELOW LEFT A superbly composed silver pendant by Hoffmann, circa 1905, achieves its effect from the bold composition of brightly colored semiprecious stones.

BELOW RIGHT This austere design by Koloman Moser shows the transition to Modernism that was transforming visual language in the twentieth century. Fashioned of brass and enamel, the geometric brooch dates from 1912.

▶ Semiprecious stones

Semiprecious stones are favored in Art Nouveau jewelry, over the ostentatious glitter of diamonds, rubies and emeralds. The softer color schemes of the new aesthetic required stones such as opal, moonstone and river pearl for their effects. This enameled silver pendant with semiprecious stones is by Ernestine Mills.

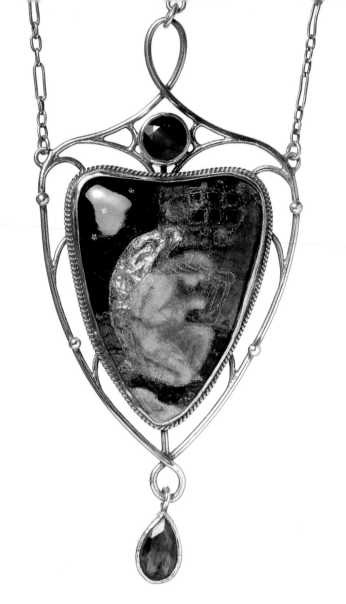

▲ Enamel

Art Nouveau is recognizable by the use of enamel work on metals, such as pewter or silver, rather than gold or platinum. In this enamel and pressed steel marcasite brooch the ornamentation comes from shades of navy, light blue and yellow enamel rather than an emphasis on the effects of light on sparkling gemstones.

Key looks of the decades
1890– 1910

Bijouterie

Highly decorated designs incorporating the use of smaller gemstones with a variety of other techniques, all worked in an integrated piece, took prominence over large showy gemstones in settings.

Celtic knots

The Celtic knot was both a fashionable and desirable decorative format during the later Arts and Crafts and Art Nouveau periods, promoted by such jewelry designers as Archibald Knox and Liberty of London.

◀ Opals and moonstones

The moonstone was used by many designers in this period including Danish jeweler Georg Jensen, as seen in this silver brooch. Moonstone is a translucent gemstone with a blue-white sheen and is said to bring good luck to the wearer. The misty dream-like effects it produced suited the spirit of Art Nouveau.

▼ Themes from nature

Nature was the main source of inspiration in Art Nouveau jewelry as its adherents tried to break the shackles of Victorian design that looked backwards rather than forwards. Eschewing any sort of revivalism, designers used flora and fauna for their motifs, as clearly seen in this selection of brooches from 1901.

▲ The *femme fatale*

Art Nouveau jewelry featured the *femme fatale*, a mysterious woman whose erotic appearance was beautiful but potentially deadly. This Belle du Nuit brooch, circa 1900, depicts a bat-like female figure carved from ivory with *plique-à-jour* enamel wings scattered with diamond collets set against a crescent moon.

1910s:
The Edwardian Era

While Art Nouveau attempted to evade retrospection in its style, striving for an ahistorical mystical modernity, many of the leading jewelry firms were looking backward to eighteenth-century French Rococo for their motifs. Rococo was a style that was intimately connected with the French courts at Versailles, its name derived from *rocaille*, or 'rocks,' specifically the small rock or shell formations found in grottoes. In design terms it meant delicacy, elegance and a profusion of gilding applied to feminine forms derived from nature— a light, dexterous style that can be seen at its most accomplished in the paintings of court favourites François Boucher (1703–70) and Jean-Honoré Fragonard (1732–1806).

The Rococo Revival style was the one that announced wealth and social status, perfect for a newly emerging middle-class of industrialists, entrepreneurs and bankers who loved the symbolic association with the great royal dynasties of the past. Mrs Cornelius Vanderbilt was but one member of many American families who attempted to channel the pomp and splendor of Versailles into the salons of New York, taking her place in society in the guise of a modern Madame de Pompadour. She bought many of her jewels from Cartier, the popularizer of the Rococo Revival look. The firm specialized in eighteenth-century decorative motifs such as swag, bow, cartouche and wreath shapes, and many a gold tassel hung from brooches, collars and pendants. The use of the flower garland was so ubiquitous at Cartier that this type of early Edwardian jewelry is now referred to as the Garland style. Even to this day floral swags adorn the lids of Cartier's evocative red-and-gold boxes.

Cartier

This magical name has its origins in a business set up by Louis-François Cartier in 1847 to sell high-end jewelry and luxury goods. Customers soon included the wealthiest scions of aristocratic Europe, among them the Empress Eugenie, renowned worldwide for her spectacular dresses designed by the great couturier Charles Frederick Worth. The subsequent revenue generated by the firm and the increased confidence inspired by the name led to Cartier creating its own pieces in-house by the late 1880s.

By the early twentieth century Cartier was already an institution, helped by the accolade of becoming the official supplier of jewelry to royalty, including King Edward VII and King Zog of Albania, and also because the firm was not afraid to experiment with new techniques of gem cutting and stone setting. For instance, Cartier pioneered the use of platinum, a metal that was harder than silver or gold, and which made articulated settings for fabulous gems much lighter, brighter and deluxe. The strength of platinum also meant that designs could be more delicate as very little metal was needed to hold a stone in place. Such 'invisible' settings were, as Louis Cartier put it, 'embroidery rather than armor-plating,' and this approach led to Garland-style festooned necklaces in which the diamonds appeared to be floating over the surface of the skin. Cartier's filigree settings complemented the Edwardian fashion for pale lace and frothy tea-gowns, and saw-piercing techniques completed the airy look.

The discovery of gigantic deposits of diamonds in South Africa by the De Beers Mining Company and new cuts, such as marquise, baguette and briolette, together with an international clientele with pots of money, was a winning combination for many prestigious jewelers in Paris, including, Louis Aucoc, Bernard and Charles Mauret. Cartier had the edge, though, and many a language barrier was swept away when a visiting mogul or foreign dignitary was confronted with tray upon tray of glittering gems in the premises in the rue de la Paix. Wearing a spectacular piece designed by Cartier was one of the myriad ways of gaining social respectability in the Edwardian *demimonde*

PAGE 30 The Edwardian period called for a heightened femininity in dress that was reminiscent of the Versailles court. The extreme décolletage of gowns led to an emphasis on jewelry for the neck and shoulders, such as sentimental lockets, velvet chokers and pendants.

BELOW From 1899 the Cartier boutique was situated on the same street in Paris as the prestigious House of Worth, which resulted in an inextricable link between fine jewelry and haute couture.

SIGNATURE EDWARDIAN FEATURES

* Platinum and white gold in 'invisible' or millegrain settings. Light decorative jewelry matched the fashions of the time.
* Rococo Revival—or Garland style—decorative effects, such as bows, tassels, swags, stars, wreaths and floral garlands.
* Elaborate 'negligee' necklaces with pendants, such as two stones or pearls hanging at different lengths from a central diamond.
* Diamonds and pearls—Edwardian diamond jewelry is still considered the best of its time.
* Filigree rings, including engagement rings, of white gold, set with a single diamond.

and Mrs Ogden Mills and Doris Duke tried to outdo each other at society functions with their diamond and emerald brooches, tiaras and rings sparkling from every finger. (Duke gained the upper hand when her husband bought her the flawless Tiffany Diamond, the largest yellow diamond in the world, weighing in at a massive 128.54 carats). Such was the fashion for Cartier diamonds in New York, given a further push by the opening of a store on Fifth Avenue in 1909, that when the 35 boxes were fully occupied at the city's Metropolitan Opera House it was dubbed the 'Diamond Horseshoe.'

Cartier was one of the first firms to understand the relationship between jewelry and fashion, not least because, from 1899 on, they were situated on the same shopping street as the House of Worth, the leading couturier of the day, and were canny enough to realize that rich women would want to coordinate their new wardrobes with matching gems. The upswept hair and low necklines of the Edwardian era called out for extravagant necklaces and Cartier responded with *colliers de chien* (dog collars), sautoirs (rope-style necklaces with a tassel or pendant) and a new design, the lavalier. Named after the popular actress Eve Lavallière, one of the first women in Paris to bob her hair, the lavalier was essentially a double pendant, one suspended from another. The vogue for a graceful swan-like neck was further exaggerated by the use of Cartier chokers with a black velvet or moiré base that acted as a foil to intricate openwork of diamonds and pearls. Bracelets fell out of favor as the fashion for long sleeves took hold, so bodice jewelry was *de rigeur* with brooches worn in multiples with huge strings of pearls.

RIGHT Olga Karnovich was the second wife of Grand Duke Paul Alexandrovich of Russia. Pictured here in 1912, she is wearing diamond Cartier jewelry. The wealthiest Edwardian women did not just wear jewelry on their bodies; it was also spectacularly incorporated into their couture gowns.

Fabergé

Known as the purveyor of luxury bejeweled eggs for the Russian Royal Family, Peter Carl Fabergé (1846–1920) was also a jeweler of international renown, particularly for designs that combined the most painstaking hand-enameling with machine-made guilloché metal backgrounds and the use of the new rose-cut diamond. In 1885 the firm employed the talented Mikhail Perkhin as Fabergé's head designer and Peter and his brother Agathon became the most assiduous of quality controllers, rejecting anything that was not of the highest of standards. By the early twentieth century, Fabergé was the jeweler of choice for all of the Russian aristocracy, creating jewels by commission and offering an array of precious objects including bejeweled flowers, opera glasses, parasol handles and the ubiquitous Imperial eggs—the ultimate expression of jewelry as art.

These opulent yet ultimately useless items are today rare pieces of astronomical value, a literal embodiment of the aristocratic excess overthrown by the Russian Revolution of 1917. Fabergé eggs were commissioned from 1885 on by the Russian royal family as commemorative gifts and became something of a family tradition. The first egg set the style and was ordered up by Tsar Alexander III for his wife, Maria Fedorovna, as a special gift for Easter, the most significant date on the Russian Orthodox calendar. The Hen Egg, the moniker by which it is known today, opens to reveal a ruby set within a miniature crown, contained in a gold chicken sitting in a yolk of pure gold. Miniature eggs were popular gifts at Easter and would be worn on a neck chain either singly or in groups.

International recognition soon followed and, in 1900, Peter Carl Fabergé was awarded the Légion d'Honneur at the International Exhibition in Paris for his enameled objects. Stores were opened to admiring crowds in London and Paris only to close when the Russian government repatriated its citizens and capital during the First World War. After the Revolution and the assassination of the royal family, the firm's production effectively stopped. In 2009, Tatiana and Sarah Fabergé, great-granddaughters of the company's original founder Gustav Fabergé, launched the first jewelry collection for 90 years, Les Fabuleuses. Famed Parisian artist-jeweler Frédéric Zaavy designed the new collection with creative director Katharina Flohr, and is faithful to the original aesthetic of the brand, with prices starting at £26,000 for the diamond pavé-set Ludmila ring rising up to a staggering £6 million.

OPPOSITE Eighteenth-century French court style is the inspiration for this Rococo Revival pendant brooch of gold, set with diamonds and made by the Fabergé workshop in St Petersburg, circa 1900.

ABOVE Fabulous Fabergé Easter Egg of 1899 in the form of a trompe l'oeil vase contains flowers fashioned from enameled precious metal and gemstones. The eggs were designed for the Russian tsars as annual gifts for their consorts, with many taking up to a year to be crafted.

Boucheron

In 1858 this family dynasty was founded in Paris by Frédéric Boucheron, who reputedly chose the sunniest side of the Place Vendôme to situate his business so that the diamonds in the windows would glitter all the more seductively. La Belle Otero and actress Sarah Bernhardt were customers of the day. Boucheron's fame in the Edwardian period rested on the patronage of the heiresses of the plutocratic dynasties of the New World, wealthy American families such the Astors and the Vanderbilts. Emancipated American heiresses, whose wealth derived from the new railway, oil and steel industries, were invading Europe in the hope of obtaining a title through marriage to one of the members of the impoverished aristocratic dynasties. They were dubbed 'buccaneers' by novelist Edith Wharton and successful matches included Jennie Jerome to Lord Randolph Churchill; May Goelet, daughter of a New York real-estate tycoon, to the ninth Duke of Roxburghe; and Maude Burke from San Francisco, who married Sir Bache Cunard, the shipping magnate. Consuelo Vanderbilt was one such 'dollar duchess,' brought into Britain to rescue a fiscally ailing aristocracy: due to marry the Duke of Marlborough, she described the excessive amounts of jewels judged appropriate for entry into English society:

It was the fashion to wear dog collars; mine was of pearls and had 19 rows, with high diamond clasps which rasped my neck. My mother had given me all the pearls she had received from my father. There were two fine rows, which had once belonged to Catherine of Russia and to the Empress Eugenie, and also a sautoir, which I could clasp around my waist. A diamond tiara capped with pearl-shaped stones was my father's gift to me and from Marlborough came a diamond belt. They were beautiful indeed, but jewels never gave me any pleasure, and my heavy tiara invariably produced a violent headache, my dog collar a chafed neck. Thus bejeweled and bedecked I was deemed worthy to meet English society.

Boucheron's heavy diamond floral designs were legendary among this group, but the house was also a purveyor of the finest pearls and innovative design features that are still with us today. In 1889, Boucheron's legendary designer, Paul LeGrand, hit upon the idea of stringing pearls alongside diamond rondelle separators. Diamond-cutter Bordincx, who collaborated with the house for many years, had dared to pierce diamonds and cut them into round flat shapes resembling a wheel or doughnut shape, called a rondelle. LeGrand combined 28 diamond rondelles with 29 large natural pearls realizing that the subtlety of a pearl would be in perfect position next to the more brash sparkle of a diamond—it was an instant success and has become a design classic in jewelry today.

A BEAUTIFUL DUCHESS.

THE DUCHESS OF MARLBOROUGH

Wife of the 9th duke, whom she married in 1895. The Duchess of Marlborough, who before her marriage was Miss Consuelo Vanderbilt, has two sons—the Marquis of Blandford and Lord Ivor Charles Spencer Churchill. She is a strong supporter and active helper of many deserving charities.

1910–19: The Edwardian Era 37

Hair Ornaments

Hair was the focal point of a woman of fashion and the feminine ideal called for enormous hairdos requiring the administrations of a maid throughout the day. A complex language was attached to the ornamentation of hair: shells were used for dinner or the theater; ribbons with flowers and lace for balls and parties; fancy feathers and diamonds for gala and royal festivals. Women required an assortment of hair accessories and combs, despite being functional, could still be stylish when made in tortoiseshell with filigree silver openwork. Aluminum or mock tortoiseshell set with rhinestones was a cheap popular alternative. In 1918, *The Delineator* magazine advised on the appropriate use of hair ornament for the Edwardian gentlewoman, thereby giving a modern audience a flavor of the myriad of types to hand:

In combs, barrettes, bandeaux and other
accessories there are many varieties, and
a judicious selection is of no small importance
in the general effect of the hairdressing.
Too ornate or too numerous ones are in
bad taste, and detract from, rather than add
to, the beauty of the coiffure. The large hairpins
of shell with the tops inlaid with gold filigree or
set with brilliants are very attractive and modest
ornaments. Two or three may be used at the sides
of the coiffure and prove of very effective service
as well as decoration.

The Aigrette

Derived from the plumage of the egret, the aigrette took the form of a huge gem, from which plumage emerged to create a headdress in the manner of an Indian maharajah.

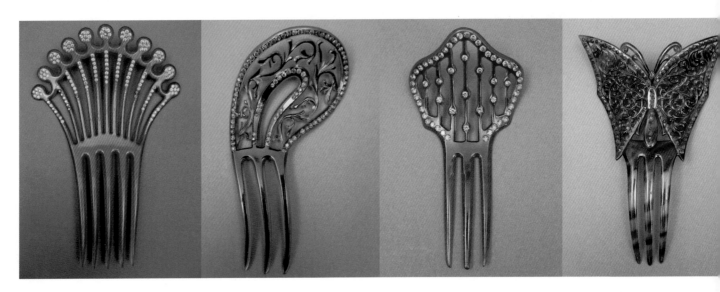

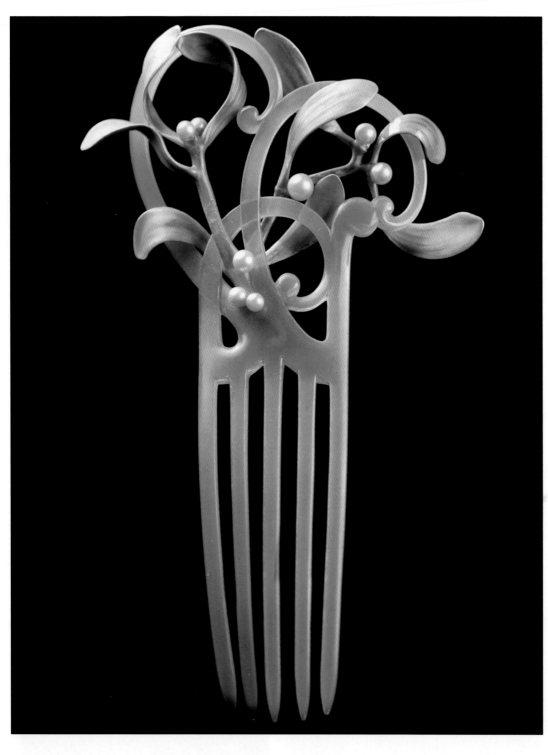

OPPOSITE TOP An Edwardian portrait, said to be of Mata Hari, showing the bandeau worn with an attached aigrette. An exotic dancer of Dutch descent, Mata Hari posed as a princess from Java while pursuing a double life as a courtesan and spy. She was executed by firing squad in 1917.

OPPOSITE BELOW Decorative updos of the Edwardian period led to a huge market for hair-related jewelry. To emphasize the decorative shape that sat above the hair, this selection of celluloid hair combs from the 1910s are all outlined and set with colored rhinestones. From left: tall back comb in salmon-colored celluloid over yellow with spokes and roundels at the ends; side comb in an asymmetrical Art Nouveau shape with scrollwork and an outline of blue rhinestones; standard-shaped hair comb in amber; back comb in the shape of a butterfly in faux tortoiseshell celluloid with red rhinestones.

LEFT An exquisite hair comb set with pearls in the shape of mistletoe, by the leading Paris jewelry firm Vever. The characteristic shape of European mistletoe inspired many Art Nouveau designers who considered it an ancient and sacred plant; according to folklore, mistletoe was believed to bestow life and fertility.

It became extremely fashionable after the exoticism promoted by Diaghilev's production of *Scheherazade,* featuring costumes by Leon Bakst, in 1910 fired the imagination of many designers, including couturier Paul Poiret. Wide-brimmed hats gave way to turbans and aigrettes were worn with semi-transparent harem trousers or the new hobble skirt. The Countess Uvarov had a Cartier aigrette shaped like a Chinese gong with a border of diamonds and calibre-cut rubies, and Tiffany & Co. designed an aigrette that incorporated real peacock feathers.

The Bandeau

A derivation of the tiara, the bandeau has one or two rows of gems but they do not complete a full circle and have no upright elements. The bandeau derived from the neo-classical fantasies of Paul Iribe, fashion illustrator for Paul Poiret, and it perfectly suited the maverick couturier's empire-line gowns. Inspiration was taken from the portrait of Pauline Borghese by Robert Lefèvre (see page 40), which depicted the princess wearing a simple muslin gown and a flat bandeau of opals and cameos rimmed with diamonds.

The Tiara and Diadem

One of the oldest jewelry types, the tiara was found in ancient Egypt and the classical civilizations of Greece and Rome, where its shape is derived from the gold laurel-leaf wreaths worn by those of the very highest rank or victors from the battleground. By the nineteenth century, the tiara was a prestigious ornament associated with royalty, in particular the rise of the Bourbons, but during the Edwardian era it became less associated with rank and more of a fashion accessory. The tiara became a signature piece for a woman of means due to the practice of the bride's parents of bestowing one upon their daughter as a wedding present. Tiaras perched perfectly in the overblown dressed updos of the period, puffed out with the use of postiche, and were intricately fashioned into neo-classical acanthus leaves, wheat sheaves, stars and trefoils.

In 1889 Henri Vever created one of the first sun tiaras, designed to represent a sunburst, a style of tiara that depends on a huge gem at the centre from which smaller gems radiate to imitate the rays of the sun. The quality of the central stone determines the sparkle and Cartier, and others, were prepared to use the largest and rarest of pink, with smaller stones symmetrically decreasing on both sides and matching emeralds situated toward the base of the sunburst. In the later Edwardian period, winged tiaras became popular after Debut & Coulon fashioned one in the shape of doves' wings.

Tiaras were essential for formal balls but had no function out of the season. Cartier hit upon the idea of creating a tiara that could be disassembled to be converted into more wearable brooches or pendants. After two world wars and the move to more relaxed fashions to match, many tiaras were melted down and the stones sold or reassembled. A convertible Edwardian tiara dating from 1910 hit the headlines in 2000 when Madonna wore one loaned from the London jewelers Asprey & Garrard on the occasion of her wedding to film director Guy Ritchie. The Madonna Tiara, as it is now known, is of platinum and consists of nearly 800 diamonds weighing 78 carats plus two larger diamonds at 2.5 carats set into scrolls that form seven floral garlands connected by swinging festoons.

The Hatpin

Immensely collectible, yet no longer of any modern use, are Edwardian hatpins, items of jewelry beloved of a hat-obsessed era. Lady Violet Harvey wrote of 'Enormous hats,

often poised on a pyramid of hair, which if not possessed was supplied; pads under the hair to puff it out were universal and made heads unnaturally big. This entailed innumerable hatpins.' The bigger the hat, the longer the pin, and some measured up to an incredible 14 inches (35.5 cm), causing some American states such as Oregon to legislate against them, deeming the long hatpin an offensive weapon. Suffragettes were also divested of their hatpins in court in case the more militant of the group used them to attack the unwary male. Accidents could occur, as was reported in *The New York Times* in 1911, when a Mrs Robert Cartwright, chairman of the public safety committee for the Federation of Women's Clubs, described seeing a man at the Waldorf Hotel 'who had a scar from his nose to his ear across his face. He will wear that scar until his death.' She went on to add, 'It's alright for women to wear hatpins but they needn't stand out so far.'

During the Edwardian era thousands upon thousands of hatpins were produced in sober Whitby jet, Italian micro-mosaic and Japanese Satsuma porcelain through to high-end designs by Lalique that took the form of moths in flight or mysterious scarab beetles rendered in emerald and jade, as if from ancient Egypt. One of the most popular outputs from Charles Horner was the thistle hatpin in silver with the flower represented by a soft purple amethyst. Many had personal meanings attached: a lady golfer could have one in the shape of a club; a huntswoman may have favored a fox's head; and during the First World War young soldiers attached a tunic button to a pin and sent it as a memento to their sweetheart back home. By 1926, however, the fad was truly over. Shingled and bobbed hair and cloche hats needed no anchor and more functional fashion began to see the light of day.

The War Years

For obvious reasons, very little significant innovation in jewelry occurred during the war years of 1914–18, save the introduction of white gold alloy used as a less-expensive alternative to other precious metals, especially as the use of platinum was restricted. Thus metals were added to pure gold to vary its color—white gold had a proportion of silver or palladium added to its content and copper was added to create a hybrid metal, called rose gold. Both these alloys were used in the production of significantly cheaper pieces. Jewelry design, which was labor-intensive, suffered, as in the case of Art Nouveau, and the essential impracticality of the pieces made them unsuitable for wartime wear. The movement's legacy was an emphasis on color and form, rather than karats, and the notion that creating a unique piece was pandering to the vague whim of a wealthy parvenu. Design need no longer look backward for inspiration.

BELOW An array of Edwardian hatpins, one of the few jewelry types that has been entirely out of fashion for decades. The Edwardian fashion for huge hats atop puffed-out hairstyles created a demand for hatpins used as anchoring devices.

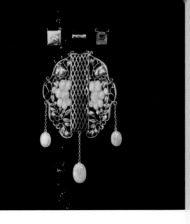

▲ Lavalier

The lavalier was a rather delicately constructed necklace popular in the Edwardian period and made up of several linked components set with gemstones in a trellis. The name is said to derive from Louise La Vallière, a celebrated mistress of Louis IV. This one is fashioned from gold and opals by the Wiener Werkstätte, circa 1915.

▶ Bandeaus and aigrettes

Popularized by couturier Paul Poiret, the evening bandeau in the Edwardian era had an attached aigrette, a jeweled hair ornament that included the feathers of the egret in the manner of a maharajah's turban. In and out of fashion since the seventeenth century, the aigrette appears in military ceremonial dress today.

Key looks of the decade
1910– 19

Bows and swags

The graceful bow and swag designs first used in the late eighteenth-century became a recognizable feature in Edwardian design appearing in earrings, pendants and brooches. Also the simple circular brooch, often representing a wreath or garland, is typical of the period.

◀ Tiaras and headpieces

A heavily jeweled headpiece attributed to Charles Riffault for Boucheron. Riffault was a master of gold openwork and revived the technique of unbacked or translucent *cloisonné* enameling.

Colliers de chien

Chokers, known as *colliers de chien* or dog collars, first became popular in Edwardian times in emulation of Queen Alexandra, who is said to have worn multiple rows of close-fitting pearls to conceal a scar on her neck. They usually comprise of several rows of pearls or a wide ribbon decorated with gemstones or brooches.

◀ Cameos

The cameo enjoyed a fresh wave of popularity. The most coveted were carved out of shell with the outer layers cut away to leave the design in relief against the darker background. The cameo was then set in a silver, gold or base metal frame. Many of the most rare are carved in Italy from volcanic lava.

▼ Garland necklace

A garland necklace is shorter than a standard necklace length, thus sits closer to the neck, and is decorated with a series of ornamental drops or pendants. The upswept hairstyles of the early 1900s laid emphasis upon the neck, which became an important area for the display of jewelry.

▲ White on white

The white on white style dominated fine jewelry, with silver and platinum settings taking over from gold. The style is most associated with Cartier, whose 'invisible' settings made diamonds appear as if they were floating over the surface of the skin.

1920s:
Streamlined and Chic

Modernism transformed the look of the twentieth century arising like a phoenix from the ashes of the First World War to sweep away both the febrile swirls of Art Nouveau and the Rococo tracery of High Edwardian style. The first generation born in the twentieth century felt a deep-seated need to reject the cult of the past and the revivalist styles of jewelry that they associated with their parents. Modernism was clearly the appropriate aesthetic for the age of the machine: hard-edged, clean-cut and pared down to purity.

Such innovation of line and form first surfaced in the architecture of Adolf Loos in Vienna and Le Corbusier in France. Loos was garrulous in his antipathy to any overly decorative form in design, intoning, 'Ornament is Crime' in his polemical writings. He continued, 'We are approaching a new and greater time. No longer by an appeal to sensuality, but rather by economic dependence earned through work, will women bring about her equal status with man. Then velvet, silk and ribbons, feathers and paint will fail to have their effect. They will disappear.'

Fashion did undergo a transformation, but perhaps not as radically as Loos would have liked, and the more youthful streamlined *garçonne* silhouette—with its dropped waist, perfect for showing off long strings of beads, sleeveless shift dresses and shortened skirts —reflected the new opportunities for women that were emerging professionally, socially and politically. The new woman or 'flapper,' as the popular press dubbed her, had hair newly bobbed or shorn into an Eton crop, all the better for showing off a pair of huge drop earrings in ivory or Cubist cloisonné. Such 'bright young things' made the old sartorial rules redundant; softly dimpled faces no longer flirted behind fans but were vividly painted, scarlet red lips drawn into a Cupid's bow amid lashings of stark white face powder. Socialite and novelist Violet Trefusis, daughter of Alice Keppel (the mistress of Edward VII) and lover of Vita Sackville-West, wrote of the new 'brittle' goddesses with 'bones of joss sticks, eyes by Fabergé and hearts made out of Venetian glass' such as the fictitious character, Terpsichore van Pusch who wore, 'a hat with two little mercury wings specifically designed for her by Lucienne' with matching diamond wings on her ears.

Art and Industry

The actual application of Modernist principles to smaller-scale design took place at the Bauhaus, a German design school that operated from 1919 onwards under the auspices of director Walter Gropius, its influence continuing even when the school was forcibly shut by Hitler's Nazi forces in 1933. The Bauhaus philosophy of 'form follows function' was applied to all the products emanating from this influential think tank of avant-garde teachers and students. Bauhaus design had to have a 'fitness for purpose' and found visual expression in pure ergonomic lines, such as in the tubular steel and canvas chair by Marcel Breuer, a clear break from the overstuffed comfort and cosy domesticity of the traditional fireside seat, and the glass and steel Constructivist tables by Modernist visionary Ludwig Mies van der Rohe.

The Bauhaus instigated a radical concept into the designer's oeuvre—designing for industry. William Morris had proposed the unification of art and design but his ideas were essentially romantic and small-scale, and no amount of lovingly crafted pseudo-Gothic objects created in medieval-inspired guilds and workshops could meet the demands of a world hungry for cheap consumer durables. The Bauhaus was an urban operation embracing the world of industrial processes and mass production, seeing industry as the utopian route to good design in every home. The romantic and aesthetic complexities of nineteenth-century Art Nouveau were also to be wholly rejected in favor of a style of design based on bare essentials. Life was now being lived too fast for any bourgeois visual distraction.

PAGE 44 A Cartier necklace and matching earrings in emeralds and pearls create Modernist elegance in 1924. The Art Deco dress pin and cabochon headband were re-interpreted by many fine and costume jewelers.

BELOW LEFT Modernism was a new aesthetic for the twentieth century. René Boivin's silver choker collar necklace, made of two rows of narrow, pointed acorns, makes geometry out of nature in 1928.

BELOW Jean Fouquet used loosely twisted bands of 'grey' gold to create a collar, scattered with diamonds that appear to orbit around the neck. It was created in 1928 for Princess Jean-Louis de Faucigny-Lucinge, a friend of Salvador Dalí.

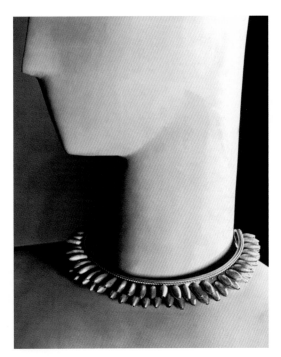

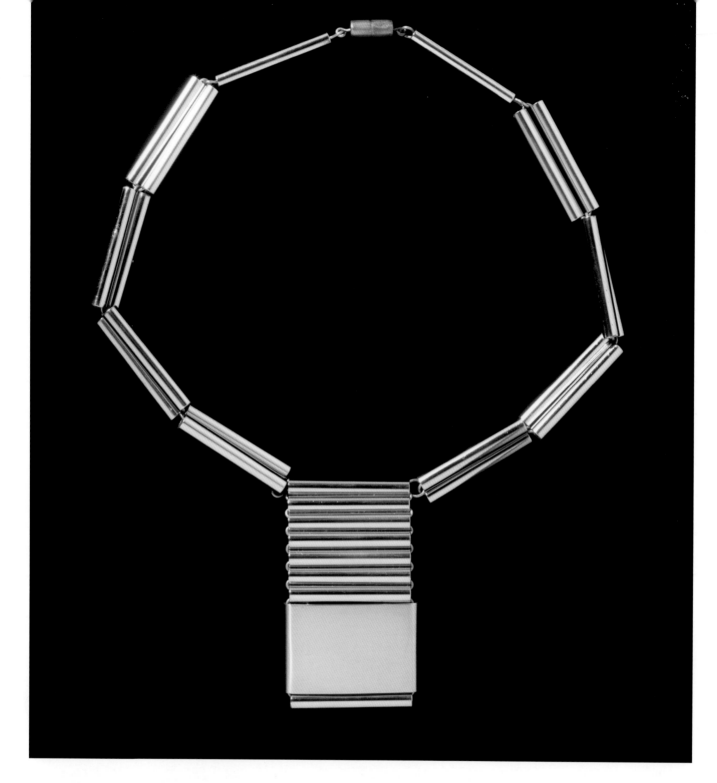

Naum Slutzky

Born in Kiev to goldsmith Gilel Slutzky, Naum (1894–1965) trained in Vienna under the jeweler Anton Dumant before working for a short time at the Wiener Werkstätte in 1912. After studying engineering, the young Slutzky was invited by Walter Gropius to join the Bauhaus at its inception as assistant in the metal and goldsmithing workshops, where he became master goldsmith in 1922. His jewelry designs in steel and brass are an extreme embodiment of Bauhaus philosophy; monastic in their austerity, every unnecessary detail is stripped away to leave an almost elemental elegance—reinforced with

the complete refusal to apply any historical references. Slutzky's work may appear simple yet it is superbly engineered, instantly recognizable by its futuristic use of steel with a gleaming chromium finish. Bracelets and neckpieces have an abstract geometry that relates to the visual language of the Russian Constructivists and the De Stijl group, in particular the planar play of architect and furniture designer Gerrit Rietveld's Red Blue chair of 1923. When the Bauhaus closed, Slutzky moved to England, where he became professor of industrial design at Ravensbourne College of Art.

ABOVE Pure, pared-down Modernism in jewelry design was seen at its most austere in the work of Naum Slutzky at the Bauhaus in the 1920s. Here the designer has fashioned a pendant necklace out of chromium-plated brass tubing.

The Rise of the Gemstone

By the 1920s Bauhaus Modernism had infiltrated jewelry; a significant moment occurred when the institution Fouquet & Sons refitted in a controlled, sleekly modern style. French jewelers Cartier and Boucheron injected a more palatable glamour into the originally austere Bauhaus style and the Exposition Internationale des Arts Décoratifs held in Paris in 1925 popularized this new French deluxe version of Bauhaus Modernism to an international audience. Its huge jewelry pavilion in the Grand Palais showcased work by Aucoc, Boucheron, Van Cleef & Arpels and Mauboussin, among other fine houses, all set against draperies of the palest dusky-rose crepe de chine.

Geometric settings were given a deluxe high-end feel with huge gemstones to create *joaillerie*—jewelry that focused on high-impact gemstones rather than Art Nouveau *bijouterie* with its emphasis on metalwork. New advances in machining rather than hand-cutting, such as the rectangular-shaped baguette, gave gems a sharper line and edge that complemented the geometric Deco settings. Large citrines, amethysts and chunks of rock crystal found favor during this period, their translucency played against opaque materials such as coral and jade—and the juxtaposition of a diamond set against onyx gave a stark visual contrast in monochrome black that seemed an absolute fit with the dynamic feel of the times. Hematite, the principal ore of iron was used for its hard metallic shine. Its dark crystal formations complemented the polished surface of silver and grey gold or super-shiny black lacquer, particularly stunning in the work of Raymond Templier. Clashing shades of emerald and tango, inspired by the Ballets Russes of 1909–29, also enjoyed a vogue among the bohemian set in Paris. The opening of Tutankhamen's tomb in 1922 led to a mania for Egyptian motifs such as winged scarabs and pharaoh's heads—the Castellani workshop in Rome was famed for its luxurious interpretations of the ancient Egyptian style.

ABOVE The magnificent jewelry pavilion at the Exposition Internationale des Arts Décoratifs in Paris, 1925, introduced the key names of French Art Deco design to an international audience.

OPPOSITE In the 1920s simple forms were given visual drama with innovative color combinations, as in the small box in gold and black enamel by Boucheron from 1930, top right. A bright orange color infiltrated all types of jewelry production and is here seen at its most luxe in a Boucheron cigarette case of 1920, left, and a powder compact in silver, coral and diamonds, 1925, by Cartier, bottom right.

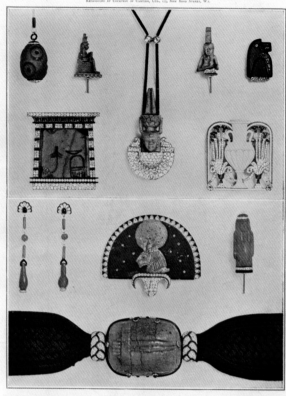

THE "TUTANKHAMEN" INFLUENCE IN MODERN JEWELLERY.

REPRODUCED BY COURTESY OF CARTIER, LTD., 175, NEW BOND STREET, W.1.

EGYPTIAN TRINKETS FROM 1500 TO 3000 YEARS OLD ADAPTED AS MODERN JEWELLERY: BROOCHES, PENDANTS, EARRINGS, AND HAT-PINS SET WITH REAL ANTIQUES, AND A TUTANKHAMEN REPLICA.

Women interested in Egyptology, who desire to be in the Tutankhamen fashion, can now wear real ancient gems in modern settings as personal ornaments. We illustrate here some typical examples, by courtesy of Cartier, the well-known Bond Street jewellers. Taken in order from left to right, beginning at the top, the objects are described as follows :— (1) A head of glazed faience of the Twenty-second Dynasty (about 900 B.C.). Its deep colour shows its age. (2) A figure of Isis and child in glazed faience (Twenty-sixth Dynasty, 600 B.C.) set as a hat-pin. (3) A faience head of Isis (600 B.C.) set as a pendant. (4) A faience bust of Isis (600 B.C.) set as a hat-pin. (5) A glazed faience head of Hapi, the monkey-god of the Nile (Twenty-second Dynasty, 900 B.C.) set as a hat-pin. (6) A miniature temple in glazed faience (900 B.C.) set as a brooch. (7) This is the only object on the page which is not an actual Egyptian antique. It is a miniature replica of the most beautiful alabaster vase found in Tutankhamen's Tomb. (8) Ear-rings of lotus seeds and glazed faience tubes (Eighteenth Dynasty, 1500 B.C.) set with diamonds and onyx. (9) A sacred cam in glazed faience (600 B.C.) set as a brooch. (10) A figure of Ta-urt, protecting goddess of women, in sardonyx (Thirtieth Dynasty) set as a hat-pin. (11) A scarab (Twenty-first Dynasty, 1000 B.C.) set in coloured stones as a clasp for a twisted silk belt.

UNE BROCHE ET DES BOUCLES D'OREILLE

BIJOUX, DE CARTIER

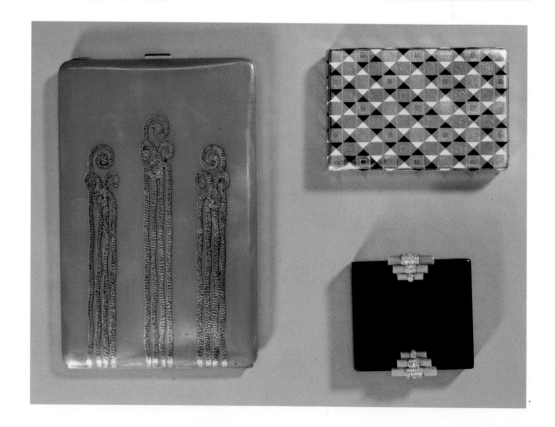

ABOVE LEFT The discovery of Tutankhamen's tomb in 1922 created a short-lived craze for Egyptian-style jewelry. Cartier went one step further by setting brooches, pendants, earrings and hatpins with ancient Egyptian artifacts.

ABOVE RIGHT A brooch and earrings, circa 1924–25, designed in the Egyptian style by Cartier. Motifs taken from hieroglyphics had a two-dimensionality that fitted with the vogue for Modernism.

THIS PAGE The romance of the machine and the speed and dynamism of modern metropolitan life was reflected in 1920s jewelry design. A ring by Alexandre Marchak of Paris, circa 1920–30, combines platinum with coral, diamonds and innovative black plastic, right, while a gold and chrome ring set with diamonds by Jean Desprès, circa 1930, is achieved in the ball-bearing style, below.

The Machine Aesthetic

The jewelers associated with French Art Deco include Jean Fouquet, Gérard Sandoz, Suzanne Belperron and Raymond Templier—all of whose work experimented with the basic geometry of circles, the smooth surfaces of squares and sharp-edged rectangles reflecting the general vogue for what design historian Bevis Hillier dubbed 'domesticated Cubism.' Raymond Templier made full use of the chevron, a particularly popular shape in Art Deco jewelry, having originally appeared on the canvases of the Italian Futurists who were operating as an avant-garde group in the cities of Milan and Turin just before the First World War.

Speed transfixed these Italian mavericks, conveyed pictorially by the use of sequenced diagonals, planes, angles and interpenetrating forms. Artist Giacomo Balla, in particular, used the chevron to convey a sense of wonder at the technology that was changing the world, such as the 1909 electrification of Milan in *Street Light* (1909–10), a painting in which multicolored chevrons are used to depict the dynamism of a street lamp's cosmic glow. The machine aesthetic can also be seen in the paintings of Tamara de Lempicka, who painted a self-portrait in 1929 that is the epitome of Art Deco glamour: the artist as a heavy-lidded Russian émigré posed in a shiny green Bugatti racing car with leather gloves, a metallic leather driving cap

and a billowing scarf. The perfect woman for Jean Fouquet, for instance, who began to design bulkier rings in the 1920s using frosted rock crystal, cabochon moonstones and faceted amethysts set into platinum, correctly believing that 'the female hand holding the steering wheel would not be able to adorn itself with too fragile a ring.'

This glamorous modern woman would surely have been the customer for the most extreme examples of machine-inspired style such as the jewelry constructed out of ball bearings by Charlotte Perriand, Jean Després and Gérard Sandoz. Ball bearings were commonly used to eliminate friction in mechanical parts, specifically axles, and took the form of simple chromium-plated brass balls—a fabulous shape for invention. These perfect silver spheres were threaded onto lengths of steel or copper wire to make the most Modernist of necklaces and sautoirs (a type of long necklace with a pendant or tassel hanging from the end) or were trapped between cases of ebonite and displayed on the arm. It would have taken a woman of great presence to wear this kind of jewelry when her contemporaries complacently flashed their diamonds. In 1920, film star and celebrated bisexual Marlene Dietrich was spotted in a silver bracelet created by Cartier that was decorated with small gold spheres in the ball-bearing style—reputedly a present from her lover, Jean Gabin.

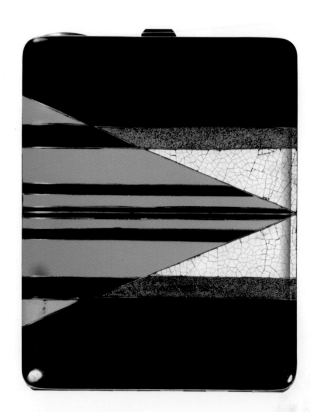

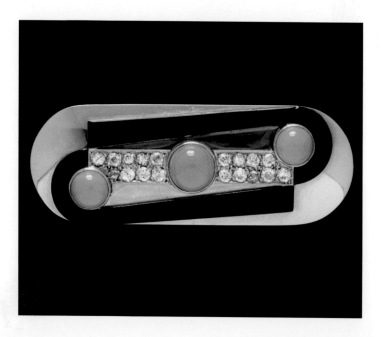

The Barbaric Bangle

Each decade has an item of covetable jewelry that chimes with the times and resonates with the stylistic credo of the era. There is always a hierarchy of desire—for particular items of jewelry may not be equally in vogue. It was the bangle, a rigid circle that could be fashioned out of materials from precious metal to the more prosaic Bakelite, which achieved unprecedented heights of popularity in the 1920s. Emancipated flappers—the seductive sirens of new Jazz Age—were no longer fettered with corsets and ostentatiously dressed hair. Freed from the constraints and restrictions of the pre-war Edwardian period, the bangle became the ultimate expression of modernity.

Much Deco jewelry referenced the geometry found in the paintings of Pablo Picasso and Georges Braque. Protagonists of one of the most influential art movements of the twentieth century, these iconic Cubist artists were profoundly influenced by the formal simplification and expressive power of African sculpture, clearly expressed in Picasso's *Les Demoiselles d'Avignon* (1907), in which the women appear to be wearing African masks. Within intellectual circles in Paris, collecting African art was extremely fashionable and African culture seen as a paradigm of a life lived free from the constraints of a dull and bourgeois society. Some members of the European avant-garde went even further, appropriating aspects of African dress, including the wearing of African-inspired jewelry—Jean Dunand's giraffe multi-ringed necklaces in red and black lacquered gold were all the rage. Josephine Baker, a dancer who wowed Paris in *La Revue Nègre*, exemplified the popularity of this style. On stage she performed stripped to the waist with glossy brilliantined black hair by celebrity coiffeur Antoine de Paris and flashed huge, lacquered cuff bracelets by Jean Dunand.

OPPOSITE An illustration from the fashion magazine *Le Gazette du Bon Ton* by Georges Barbier show the rampant appropriation of global culture inherent in 1920s fashion; the 'barbaric' color palette of red and green from Africa and arm of 'tribal' cuffs and bangles is mixed with a Japanese floral arrangement and a French Rococo table.

BELOW LEFT The bangle has become a ubiquitous symbol of the 1920s, a simple Modernist loop that could be fashioned out of a variety of materials and matched the freedom of contemporary fashion. Like Picasso and Braque before him, sculptor and designer Jean Dunand found inspiration in African culture, as seen in this lacquered brass bangle from 1925.

BELOW Orientalism enjoyed a vogue in jewelry design in this decade. Here a jade, onyx and diamond brooch by Fouquet, dating from the 1920s, is in the form of a Chinese mask.

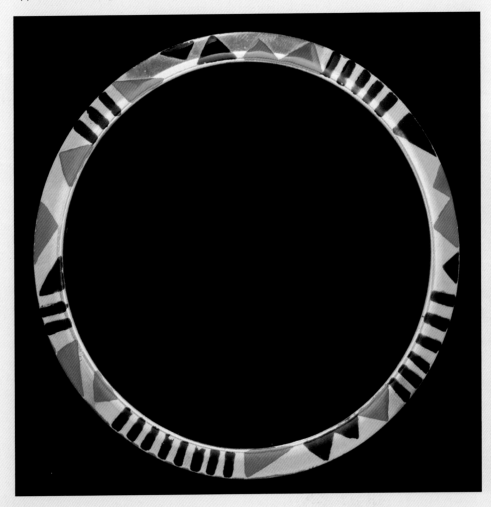

GEORGE BARBIER 1925

Jean Dunand

Swiss-born Dunand (1877–1942) was an accomplished sculptor who had studied at the School of Industrial Arts in Geneva, traveling to Paris as a scholarship student around the turn of the twentieth century. Here he worked as an apprentice to the sculptor Jean Dampt for five years and was encouraged by his mentor to realize his ambition to become an interior designer. It was in *dinanderie* that Dunand really found his forte; the name given to work in brass derived from the Flemish city of Dinant, which had been an important center for the production of this type of metalwork in the fifteenth century. Dunand's *dinanderie* caught the attention of the critics in 1905 when he exhibited three softly hammered brass vases at the Salon la Nationale. One review at the time ran: 'This brilliant artist seems to have drawn from copper all that this metal has to offer by way of full and subtle form.'

In 1912, once he had learned the techniques of Japanese lacquer from artist Seizo Sugawara and recognized how such skills could be used to enhance the work he had been producing in wood and metal, his career really took off. He collaborated with the great furniture designer Emile-Jacques Ruhlmann to apply luxurious lacquer finishes in a Cubo-Japanese style to his designs and was a successful creator of a whole series of stunning Art Deco lacquered screens. One of Dunand's most important commissions was for the interior of the first-class dining room of the great ocean liner *Alantique* in 1930 and panels for the smoking room of the *Normandie* in 1935. It was not long before Dunand was applying his experimental lacquer techniques to jewelry, such as metal buckles and clips, an interest sparked off in the 1920s by his friendship with the couturier Madeleine Vionnet, for whom he

BELOW Jean Dunand was a master craftsman in Japanese lacquer, having originally learned the skill from Japanese artist Seizo Sugawara. This jungle-themed panel was created in 1930 and Dunand went on to use jewelry as a vehicle to experiment with new lacquer techniques.

produced a lacquered panel depicting three panthers, a popular 1920s motif.

Dunand's Art Deco jewelry is created from copper inlaid with silver or combinations of lacquered wood and metal. One of his most distinctive stylistic devices is a striking checkerboard effect, most commonly of red and silver, that manages to combine the pure lines of Modernism with an uninhibited 'barbaric' luxury. Huge metal Cubist earrings recall the thrusting New York skyscraper and his trademark bracelets are fashioned from huge rectangular metal plaques, big enough to serve as a micro-canvas for a miniature Cubist painting and joined together with sturdy rings or hinges. Rigid bangles and cuffs are molded from nickel, copper and brass, and lacquered with Cubist patterns.

Shipping heiress Nancy Cunard (1895–1965) personified the flamboyant excess of Dunand's look. Born in 1896 to an American mother and an English baronet, she frequented the cafes of Paris with her 'corrupt coterie' of fellow bohemians—Iris Tree, Osbert Sitwell, Ezra Pound and Augustus John. In 1928 she founded Hours Press, which published writers such as George Moore, Samuel Beckett and Robert Graves. Her long and languid form and etiolated limbs, emphasized by the newly bobbed and shorn hair, required a different type of jewelry. She adopted the wearing of outsize African ivory bangles that stretched from elbow to wrist on both arms or Cubist cuff bracelets to express her solidarity with black struggles against social injustice. To achieve such a performance of rather patronizing 'primitivism,' she was reputed to own several lacquered abstract designs by Dunand that she wore with long necklaces of heavy wooden beads wound around her neck and shimmering scarves wrapped into a turban, anticipating the radical chic of the 1970s.

In 1929 *The New York Times* called these back-to-nature artifacts of wood, bone and ivory 'jewelry for the new barbarians.' In wearing the jewelry Cunard was, by analogy, investing herself with the stereotypical notions of the primitive sexuality of African women. Her relationship with the African-American jazz musician, Henry Crowder, scandalized society and, after being ostracized by her parents, confirmed her status as an outsider. By the early 1930s the so-called 'barbaric' look had lost its avant-garde status and was being produced by many of the high-end jewelry firms. Boucheron, for instance, exhibited a large African cuff bracelet at the Exposition Coloniale in 1931, which combined ivory, green malachite and purpurite, a manganese phosphate mineral with a striking purple color, interspersed with polished gold beads.

THE LADY OF THE BROBDINGNAGIAN BANGLES: MISS NANCY CUNARD.

The vogue for wooden jewellery is here seen in all its glory and lavishness. Miss Nancy Cunard, the poet daughter of Maud Lady Cunard, and owner of the Hours Printing Press, was evidently fascinated by the beautifully painted and enamelled wooden bracelets and beads sold in that Mecca of the *chic*—Paris—as she bought some of the very largest ornaments she could find. Painted in all colours, they certainly become her extraordinarily well, and, well supported by the imposing background of polka-dots, they give a remarkably handsome and baroque effect to this portrait of her.

PHOTOGRAPH BY CECIL BEATON, EXCLUSIVE TO "THE SKETCH."

ABOVE Heiress, poet and political activist, Nancy Cunard, poses in her trademark outsized African ivory bangles that stretch from elbow to wrist, and a huge 'barbaric' wooden necklace.

Fashion and Jewelry Combine

The links between the houses of fashion and jewelry have always been eminently exploitable. Louis Cartier, the man at the helm of the Paris-based jewelers in the early twentieth century, married Andrée Worth, daughter of Jean-Philippe Worth and grand-daughter of Charles Frederick Worth, the grande couturier. Another link in the proverbial chain was forged when jeweler René Boivin married couturier Paul Poiret's sister Jeanne. It was in the 1920s, however, when clearer collaborations were cleverly marketed to the haute-couture crowd. Several fashion houses and jewelry firms joined forces to display their wares; in 1927, Jean Patou showed dresses accessorized with the color-matched jewels of Georges Fouquet (significantly both names had equal prominence in the program) and in 1931, Jeanne Lanvin showed with Boucheron.

Coco Chanel and Costume Jewelry

It was not long before astute designers realized they could parley out their brands by applying their own name to branded jewelry that would provide a direct visual link with their couture gowns. Coco Chanel, always a canny operator, understood the power of her moniker after the unmitigated success of what was dubbed her poverty de *luxe* look. The understated chic of Coco's little black dress moved the language of fashion from the vulgar and showy to something a little more sophisticated and harder to define, a must for the more discerning post-war customer who wanted to distance themselves from the Edwardian past. Fashion was no longer about the overt flashing of cash; it was about being to able to navigate your way as a modern woman in the city without being seen as a rich man's plaything or a mere working girl. The color black had formerly only been used for mourning dress; Chanel made it elegant and wearable anyplace, any time. The simple, uncluttered lines of a garment of such streamlined efficiency (almost the sartorial equivalent of the Ford motor car) was also a perfect background to jewelry and it was here that Chanel hit upon a groundbreaking idea. She cast aside the use of real gemstones substituting the much cheaper glass in their place. Her explanation? 'Because they were devoid of arrogance in an atmosphere of too-easy luxe.'

In one fell swoop Coco kickstarted the whole trend for what became known as costume jewelry. From 1921, Chanel boutiques sold pieces in an Art Deco style that appeared somewhat derivative of the other Parisian jewelry firms, but in 1924 showed a breakthrough collection designed with the Maison Gripoix, who were renowned as the leaders in glass jewelry. *Harper's Bazaar* greeted the resultant gems in poured glass as

ABOVE This 1924 illustration is a modern take on the Judgement of Paris from classical mythology. Fashion and jewelry are perfectly matched as long strings and circlets of pearls offset the pale draped satin of the evening gowns. The center gown incorporates jewelry in its construction.

OPPOSITE A sleeveless satin draped dress by couturier Jean Patou, accessorized by a triple strand of pearls and a large turquoise pin in the Egyptian style by Fouquet, circa 1928.

'the most revolutionary designs of our time' and they were produced in a whole host of styles that ranged from Indian, Baroque and Renaissance to the more obvious Art Deco. The most recognizable piece is the pearl or faux pearl necklace, sometimes interspersed with other metal and crystal beads and the signature use of red and green poured glass, influenced by the Byzantine treasury of St Mark's in Venice. The couturiere and her models were walking advertisements for this new look, seen at the races or the Bois de Boulogne swathed in ropes and ropes of pearls and glittering gewgaws as a theatrical counterpoint to the simplicity of the clothes. In 1929 Chanel affixed a huge brooch to her beret and the fashion house persuaded other women to follow suit by showing huge gold-tone pins in the shape of Maltese crosses with a faux pearl at the centre and ruby red poured-glass hearts surround by diamanté.

Another of Chanel's innovative ideas was to set fabulous gems in informal settings, a result of her collaboration with designer Duke Fulco di Verdura. The Duke of Westminster, the incalculably wealthy lover of Chanel, who was described by diarist Sir Henry

Channon as a 'mixture of Henry VIII and Lorenzo Il Magnifico,' had reputedly given Chanel some precious stones and she had asked Fulco what she should do with them. He had responded with a languorous, 'The thought of designing something for all these different stones is *too* enervating,' and his solution was to treat the precious gems with simplicity rather than showiness—as if they were mere baubles. Fulco's design comprised a single chain containing all the different colored stones in restrained understatement, an approach that blurred the boundaries between costume jewelry and 'the real thing.'

Chanel's new approach was irreverent and appeared democratic, but her work was still prohibitively expensive for any woman of standard income. It wasn't until the invention of injection-plastic molding in 1934 that such brightly colored pieces could be available to all. Yet it was through Chanel that modern techniques infiltrated the design of precious jewelry, a journey that was to have profound effects in the decade of the Depression, a time when women wanted aspirational fantasies very much on the cheap.

ABOVE In 1929, Coco Chanel pinned a huge brooch to her beret and thousands of women followed suit. Here she sports the same look in 1937, together with swathes of pearls and a Maltese Cross cuff by Fulco di Verdura.

COCO CHANEL TALKS JEWELRY

* Costume jewelry is not made to give women an aura of wealth, but to make them beautiful.
* If you want to start a collection, start with a brooch because you will find most use for it. It can be pinned on a suit lapel, collar or pocket, on a hat, belt or evening gown.
* My jewelry never stands in isolation from the idea of women and their dress. And because dresses change, so does my jewelry.
* A woman should mix fake and real. To ask a woman to wear real jewelry is only like asking her to cover herself with real flowers instead of flowery silk prints. She'd look faded in a few hours.
* I love fakes because I find such jewelry provocative, and I find it disgraceful to walk around with millions around your neck just because you're rich. The point of jewelry isn't to make a woman look rich but to adorn her; not the same thing.
* I couldn't wear my own pearls without being stopped on the street, so I started the vogue of wearing false ones.

ABOVE LEFT A Murano glass bead necklace in the typically 1920s color combination of red, black and white, which has its roots in the experimental color palettes of the Russian Constructivists, Agitprop artists of the Russian Revolution.

LEFT Not all 1920s jewelry is uncompromisingly Modernist in design. Here, a Venetian glass bead necklace shows that the Rococo revival was still popular, especially among more conservative women.

Egyptian and ethnic motifs

Inspiration came from Oriental, Indian and Egyptian art. Following Howard Carter's discovery of Tutankhamen's tomb and artifacts in 1922, Egyptian motifs became all the rage.

▼ Bangles and cuff bracelets

Silent-screen star Olga Baclanova, aka the 'Russian Tigress,' models the cuff bracelet, a popular jewelry design in the 1920s. The cuff could be simple when molded in Perspex; avant-garde and 'barbaric' when sported in armfuls or the height of luxury when fashioned out of gold and studded with diamonds.

Key looks of the decade
1920s

▲ Venetian beads

Beads enjoyed a vogue as they could be produced in a variety of vivid colors and intricate designs. Venetian beads incorporated floral features that today are prized by collectors all over the world. They are created by heating and stretching glass rods, which are then thinly sliced and molded into beads.

▼ Art Deco

Many women wore fan-shaped Spanish-style hair combs as not everyone had a bob in the 1920s. The fan, together with the chevron, was one of the most popular motifs of this period and appears in architecture and interior as well as jewelry design. These celluloid combs from the mid 1920s are outlined in blue and green rhinestones.

Tasseled necklaces

Long necklaces made of glass beads and ending in a tassel, originally called sautoirs, were re-named 'flapper beads.' They were accompanied by tassel earrings that dangled below newly shorn bobbed hair and tasseled shimmy dresses that created an energetic sense of movement when participating in new dance crazes like the Charleston.

Machine-cut gemstones

High-quality cutting and polishing with the aid of machines took over from the traditional hand work. This meant that more facets and complicated new cuts could be introduced. Plastic also suited the new mechanical processes and was available in a wide variety of colors and finishes.

▲ Geometric settings

Edwardian floral designs seemed desperately outmoded to a new generation of young women who were forging ahead to find their place in a modern post-war world. The *garçonne* look of the 1920s need a new kind of jewelry to match and geometric settings held sway, as in this diadem and collar by Cartier from 1926.

◀ Glass and crystal

Glass and crystal combined with silver was a combination that could achieve sparkling effects when matched with beaded flapper dresses. Here a silver necklace is given a visual lift with the insertion of carved red glass tablets.

1930s:
Hollywood Glamour

Panic hit the world as the American Stock Market collapsed in 1929 after years of unscrupulous gambling by banks, corporations and city financiers. An economic slump followed, dubbed the Great Depression, which lasted until the end of the 1930s and affected the lives of most people in the Western world. The sudden disappearance of the rich American consumer caused great concern in the luxury industries; Cartier immediately sent employees across the Atlantic to pick up any pieces that had not yet been paid for and Coco Chanel dramatically halved her prices.

The silver screen gave much-needed respite in such troubled times and created a hunger for glamour among the decade's consumer, as people dreamed of a better time to come. Established fashion houses soon found that their monopoly on style was being usurped by film stars, who became the new celebrities – their every moment documented in the pages of fan magazines. The fashionable silhouette moved away from the androgynous *garçonne* to a more womanly voluptuousness and clothes were cut in the round to cling to every curve, a style popularized by Madeleine Vionnet in Paris and on screen by Jean Harlow. The star's platinum blonde hair and white satin gowns inspired a vogue for 'blondeness' that infiltrated almost every aspect of design. Interior designer Syrie Maugham had a house with white walls, white satin curtains, white velvet lampshades and white lilies in white vases. Cecil Beaton wrote of 'Mayfair drawing rooms being turned into albino stage sets' and in Evelyn Waugh's cynical novel *Decline and Fall* (1928) brittle socialite Margot Beste-Chetwynde demolishes an untouched medieval country pile and builds in its stead a Modernist monstrosity with colonnades of black glass and contrasting aluminium balustrades. Accordingly the 'white on white' style made a spectacular comeback in jewelry design re-marketed as *le note blanche* and white gold and platinum became the favored metals used in Art Deco designs. Gems were there to sparkle above all, offering up prisms of light to catch the eye – an aesthetic that was effortlessly effective when captured on black and white film. The camera lingered over every glint and glitter seeming to absorb the white heat of every shard of 'ice' including Harlow's infamous diamond-studded cigarette holder in *Public Enemy* (1931).

The coming of sound to the movies also led to a dramatic change in jewelry. The heavy beads and clattering bangles that had added such exotic drama to the theatrical gesturing of the silent film had no place on the sound stage. Designers experimented with rubber jewels to little effect and simply turned to tighter-fitting necklace and bracelet styles. This new aesthetic was readily noted and copied by the movies' adoring audience.

Art Deco Goes American

French Art Deco designers led the way at the beginning of the decade and their geometric designs grew ever bigger. Suzanne Belperron (1900–83) embarked on a very successful business in 1933 with the financial backing of pearl dealer Bernard Herz; her customers included Elsa Schiaparelli the celebrated couturier and Mrs Reginald Fellowes, a Franco-American heiress of immense wealth and fashionable *savoir-faire*. Belperron's work was austere and monumental, incorporating huge chunks of rock crystal or quartz into heavy settings inspired by Modernist architecture or the stepped silhouettes of Mayan temples.

As the decade progressed, the dynamic motifs of Art Deco—such as zigzags and chevrons—remained *de rigueur* but were given a little extra luxe with American streamlining. This design affectation emanated from a society obsessed by speed and efficiency and had its origins in the field of hydrodynamics, where it described the path of least resistance taken by water when encountering an object. Originally applied to boats, airplanes and cars, by the 1930s streamlining was being used as an aesthetic on almost every object to give it a modern, almost technological touch, as can be seen in the work of industrial designers Norman Bel Geddes and Raymond Loewy. The hard angles of Art Deco became sleekly curved and rounded, well suited to the new generation of plastics that were becoming increasingly acceptable in domestic design. Jewelry designers

BELOW LEFT A matching set of a smoked crystal bracelet and ring encrusted with yellow diamonds by Suzanne Belperron for Herz, from 1935, in the Streamline Moderne style.

BELOW Jewelry by Herz from 1934. The model wears a nine-strand agate bracelet, black pearl ring, diamond-studded brooch, and leaf earrings with diamond veins.

PAGE 62 In the 1930s a Hollywood-inspired glamour was evoked in jewelry editorial. Gems were there to sparkle, as in this photograph by Horst P Horst of 1939.

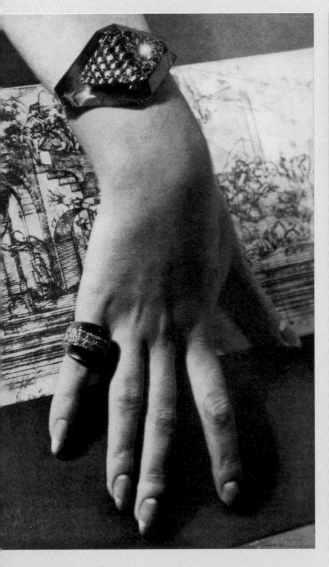

RIGHT A dress clip and cocktail ring by Suzanne Belperron circa 1934, showing how geometric Art Deco motifs in jewelry were streamlined and monumental.

BELOW A selection of fashionable bracelets, bangles and cuffs from 1935. From top left, counter-clockwise: a minimalist disc bangle by Schiaparelli; a Max Boinet gold cuff set with aquamarines; a metal bracelet of flattened balls by Schiaparelli; a Boivin coil bracelet; a Schiaparelli bracelet inspired by a factory cogwheel. The model wears geometric bright gold and black cuffs by couturier Maggy Rouff.

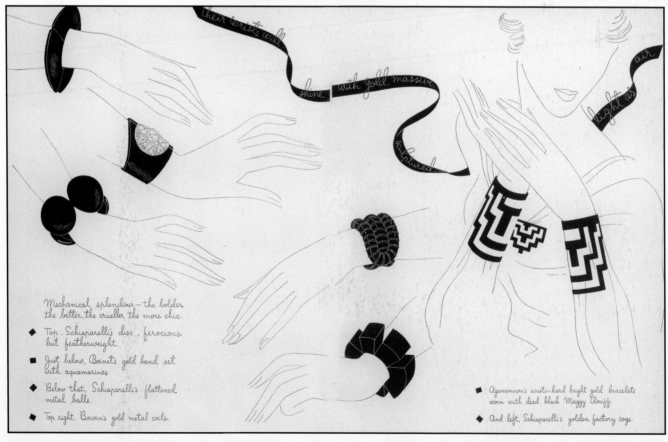

Mechanical splendour – the bolder the better the crueller the more chic.

◆ Top. Schiaparelli's disc, ferocious but featherweight.

■ Just below, Boinet's gold band set with aquamarines

◆ Below that, Schiaparelli's flattened metal balls

■ Top right, Boivin's gold metal coils

■ Agamemnon's wrists – hard bright gold bracelets worn with dead black Maggy Rouff.

◆ And left, Schiaparelli's golden factory cogs

embraced the clean, flowing lines of the streamlined look and the sleek curves of molded plastics such as Bakelite were accented with horizontal chrome bands, perfectly complementing the clinging contours created by bias-cut fashion. Svelte styling was definitely in vogue and 'Streamline Moderne' was the new name to describe it.

In this decade Cartier created a range of jewelry in the Moghul style that had been inspired by an earlier visit by Jacques Cartier to India in 1911. Moghul was a highly decorative aesthetic that dated from the eponymous empire that controlled the country from the sixteenth to the nineteenth century. It was a sumptuous style that combined rich color with exuberant carving, its goal to create a sense of paradise on earth. During the long years of the Moghul Empire, brightly colored precious gems such as rubies and emeralds were carved into the form of leaves and fruit, particularly berries. Cartier acknowledged their uncanny beauty and began to collect the stones on his travels among the Indian elite. The carved Moghul stones were then interspersed with brilliant-cut diamonds and ribbed and smooth beads, and invisibly set in platinum. Christened 'tutti-frutti,' this impactful style became very much in vogue with Hollywood stars and royalty in the early 1930s including Edwina, Lady Mountbatten, who bought a £900 sapphire, emerald and carved Indian ruby bandeau from Cartier. In 1936 Daisy Fellowes commissioned Cartier to create a huge flexible collar, dubbed the Hindu necklace, that incorporated emeralds, sapphires, diamonds and rubies set in platinum with two huge sapphires at its center that could be converted into a brooch.

RIGHT A selection of day jewelry from 1931. On the left a diamond and ruby brooch in the shape of a basket of flowers by Mauboussin is worn on the shoulder. On the right, a white cloche hat is decorated with a feather brooch of carved red and green arabe, set with diamonds and worn with a necklace of egg-shaped beads in deep red coral from Goldsmiths and Silversmiths Co.

ABOVE A collection of cabochon-ruby jewelry by Cartier, featuring a sumptuous necklace with matching earrings and bracelet in an Indian-inspired style circa 1930.

Such overt luxury notwithstanding, the majority of women had little spare cash to fritter away on overly expensive baubles, bangles and beads. Cheap costume jewelry began to dominate the market with marcasite (silver inlaid with small stones of iron pyrite), diamanté and Bakelite becoming popular. New plastics appeared on the market such as Resinox, Plaskon and Catalin, which was described as 'the gaudy brother of Bakelite,' and were used to create brightly colored gee-gaws dubbed 'Dime Store Deco.' Designers were liberated by such inexpensive materials and became incredibly experimental, whimsical or just plain surreal.

This decade is also marked by the vast quantities of glass jewelry that were imported from Czechoslovakia, a country that had been renowned for its glass production since the nineteenth century. High-quality glass bead pieces came from three towns—Jablonec, Harrachov and Liberec—where skilled workers set glass and crystal stones into white and yellow metal alloy settings in floral filigree designs. Stylistically out of step with Art Deco, the jewelry found an audience who wanted something a little less severe than the prevailing fashion for Moderne. Faceted glass necklaces in pale pastel colors or deep cranberry and purple shades combined a simplicity of design with stunning use of color and have become increasingly collectable. Towards the end of the decade refugees from Czechoslovakia fled from the rise of Fascism, many of them skilled workers, who added their talents to costume jewelry firms in 1940s America.

By the 1930s cheap and cheerful Dime Store Deco was readily available on most high streets—here an Art Deco pin of apple green Bakelite and blue enameled chevron detail has a center circle of chrome. A jade green Bakelite pin is mounted in a chrome setting faceted to mimic marcasite. A reverse-carved apple juice Bakelite features a row of rectangular rhinestones at the center— pieces of this quality are increasingly collectable. A removable carved buckle in metal and black Bakelite— buckles such as this were popular fashion accessories as they could be affixed to the cloth belt of any dress. A peach Bakelite and chrome pin shows the influence of Belperron's simple shapes combined with a 1930s touch—the Greek key motif.

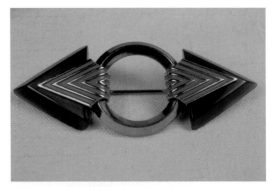

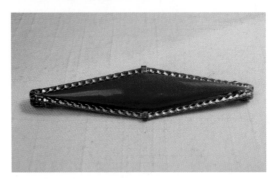

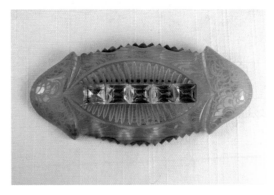

ABOVE A carved red Bakelite dress clip of 1931 shows how naturalistic forms were simplified in this era to echo the fluid minimalism of the 1930s fashion silhouette.

LEFT An illustration from the 1931 edition of *The Delineator*, a popular American women's magazine that was published from 1873 until 1937. It provided an in-depth coverage of contemporary fashion with tips on how women could achieve the latest looks. This editorial shows how wearing many jewelry items at once was acceptable in the 1930s.

BELOW LEFT A dress clip and brooch combination, called a 'Duette pin,' is fashioned in clear round and emerald square-cut rhinestones. The innovatory design mechanism, attributed to Coro, allows dress clips to slide into a pin from the sides, latching with a pushdown tab.

BELOW A Czechoslovakian glass bead, celluloid and rhinestone necklace shows why Czech craftsmen have had a reputation for high-quality glass jewelry since the late nineteenth century. Settings are of commonly of yellow metal alloy.

ABOVE A spectacular pair of Moderne collars from the 1930s shows how French Art Deco became big, bold and glamorous during the Hollywood years. On the left French jet and paste are combined to create a glittering monochromatic effect and on the right raw and enameled steel links end in a dangling triangular pendant of green glass.

RIGHT A pair of early, circa 1940, Trifari fur clips feature a Hollywood-style Baroque leaf and flower design entwined with a navy blue enamel ribbon.

The Cultured Pearl

The 1920s vogue for long strings of pearls was supplanted by a new shape in the 1930s: a short, double row of pearls, fastened with a diamanté clip at the back, was within reach for many women because of the availability of the cultured pearl from Kokichi Mikimoto. This Japanese jeweler had devoted his life to one ambition, saying 'I would like to adorn the necks of all the women of the world with pearls,' and by the 1930s his perfectly spherical cultured pearls had achieved global recognition. Decades earlier, in the 1890s, Mikimoto knew that the oysters around his hometown of Ise-Shima were being critically over-harvested, bringing an important local industry to its knees. Mikimoto realized that the formation of a pearl occurs purely by chance when a foreign object such as a fragment of shell or piece of grit becomes accidentally lodged in the soft tissues of an oyster's inner body. To ease this irritant, the oyster takes protective action by secreting nacre, a crystalline substance around the invasive object that builds up layer upon layer over time, thus creating a lustrous and translucent pearl.

Mikimoto decided to replicate this essentially random act by inserting a piece of shell or metal into the oyster's body to create an irritant. After years of experimentation (following on from the initial research done by William Sackville-Kent in Australia) marred by tidal flow, typhoons and changes in water temperature, the breakthrough came on 11 July, 1893. Mikimoto raised one of his creaking bamboo oyster baskets out of the water's depths, opened an oyster and nestling inside the shell was a milky, if slightly misshapen, pearl. His first perfectly spherical pearl was eventually cultured in 1905. Following Mikimoto's developments, the Japanese pearl industry underwent a rapid expansion and by 1935 there were 350 pearl farms in the country.

COLLECTING PEARLS

* Cultured and natural pearls have thick coatings (nacre), which make them more durable than faux pearls, but all pearls are more fragile than most other stones.
* Faux pearls can be made from Lucite, other plastics or glass; the glass versions are higher in value.
* All pearls can scratch, crack or stain easily, so look for signs of wear when collecting.
* Real pearls are drilled from both sides to meet in the center. Fake pearls will often have 'flaking' at the entry—a sign that they are not real.

ABOVE The dangling pearls of the 1920s were supplanted in the 1930s by a shorter multistrand collar that fit the neat, chic style of the decade. This eight-strand pearl necklace from 1934 is by Richelieu.

OPPOSITE Actress Kay Francis, one of the highest paid actresses in 1930s Hollywood, is bestrewn with pearls in 1935. Her pearl-encrusted bandeau, multistrand bracelet, ring and necklaces conjured up a fantastic vision of glamour for women in the depths of the Depression.

TYPES OF PEARL NECKLACE
The traditional way to buy a pearl necklace is by length.

Collar: The most popular length sits at the base of the neck and measures 10–13 inches (25–33 cm). This pearl necklace was considered suitable for both formal and casual occasions.

Princess: A longer version of the choker, this version hangs just below the collarbone and is 17–19 inches (43–48 cm) in length.

Matinee: The standard length for daytime at 22–24 inches (50–60 cm) is designed to fall just above the décolleté.

Opera: A longer length at 30–32 inches (70–90 cm), usually twisted and worn looped at formal events, hence its name.

Rope: Any string of pearls that measures over 32 inches (90 cm), an example most famously worn by film star Louise Brooks in the celebrated photographic portrait of 1928 by Eugene Robert Richee.

Haute Hollywood

During the Depression many jewelry designers were forced out of business, but those who remained were prepared to be innovative and create for new markets; Paul Flato, for example, opened a boutique in Los Angeles specifically to cater to the Hollywood elite. Los Angeles took over from Paris as the new capital of glamour and Harry Winston, Trabert & Hoeffer, Van Cleef & Arpels and Cartier were among an astute few who recognized the value of product placement and lent their best gems to the movie industry free of charge—as long as their name was in the credits. Throughout the 1930s other established jewelers set up shop in Hollywood to cater to the demands of the cream of the acting crop.

Joseff of Hollywood

Eugene Joseff's (1905–1948) career as jeweler to the stars began in 1930 after the former advertising man made a move from Chicago to Hollywood. His reputation rocketed after persuading the costume designer Walter Plunkett that the sixteenth-century Italian costumes used in *The Affairs of Cellini* (1934) should be complemented with jewelry that had some kind of basis in historical fact, rather than the modern baubles that were in use. Joseff's skill was to marry vintage detail with enough glitzy glamour to satisfy the demands of a modern audience and he went on to make jewelry for many of Hollywood's most extravagant productions. All Joseff of Hollywood designs were made in-house, from the drawing board to the finished piece, and he would rent them out to each movie rather than selling them outright. As a result of this astute policy the firm now possesses an extensive archive of its most famous work, which is regularly displayed in traveling exhibitions. Iconic Joseff pieces still owned by the company include Rhett Butler's cigar case and Scarlett O'Hara's necklaces and rings from *Gone with the Wind* (1939). Other major film work includes: *Mary Queen of Scots* (1936), for which Joseff designed Katharine Hepburn's crown; *Marie Antoinette* (1938), in which Moira Shearer appears resplendent in a glorious headpiece of trembling diamond stars; and a nine-strand bib of pearls and rubies created for Bette Davis in *The Private Lives of Elizabeth and Essex* (1939).

Any star dressed in such fantastic pieces on set wanted the same caliber of jewelry for the red carpet, and Joseff was persuaded to design pieces for the personal use of Joan Crawford, Marlene Dietrich and Bette Davis, among others. A successful high-end retail line was sold at department stores all over America. It can be recognized by its size (many pieces are huge) and its figural Hollywood Baroque style, which combines decorative floral scrolls, tassels and faux gems with a soft, Russian, antique gold finish that worked particularly well under studio lighting. Trademark motifs included owls set into chatelaine-style brooches, sun-face pins with diamanté eyes and swagged pendants incorporating cherubs, bees or cats.

RIGHT Joseff of Hollywood showing three figurative snake pieces of 18-karat gold set with emerald, ruby and diamonds worn by Rita Hayworth in *Down to Earth* (1947) and *Gilda* (1946). The large rhinestone and topaz necklace was worn in several movies in the 1940s by Ona Munson, Alice Faye, Tallulah Bankhead and Linda Darnell.

ABOVE Dramatic wing-shaped brooches of bead-set rhinestones with sapphire centers, by Joseff.

RIGHT, TOP TO BOTTOM A jet and rhinestone parure in full Hollywood Baroque style worn by Greta Garbo in *Camille* (1936). A leaf-spray brooch in aquamarine with brilliant bead-set rhinestone worn in *The Libeled Lady* (1936). A cocktail bracelet set with aquamarine and clear rhinestones in 10-karat gold worn in *Lady of the Tropics* (1939). All by Joseff.

JOSEFF TALKS JEWELRY
Joseff gave this following jewelry advice in Movie Show *magazine, February 1948.*

* If you want to acquire a collection, start with a brooch because you will find most use for it. It can be pinned on a suit lapel, collar or pocket, on a hat, a belt, or an evening gown.
* Remember, gold can be worn with more things than silver and topaz is a good stone that looks smart with almost every type of costume.
* Earrings should be the next jewelry investment. They also have many uses. You can wear them on your hat, cuffs, shoes, as well as your ears.
* A ring comes next in your collection and I'd suggest finding a bold ring with a large stone, something massive and distinctive.
* A bracelet and a necklace come last in importance because they can so seldom be worn with all your costumes or for all occasions.

Hobé Jewelry

Founded by William Hobé in 1927, the firm was active in Hollywood in the 1930s designing for both the studios and the stars with a popular store situated in Beverly Hills. Originally a design house for stage costumes and jewelry in late nineteenth century France and renowned for its production of high-quality fine jewelry, the new version of Hobé entered the American theatrical scene in 1925. It was in this year that the legendary Florenz Ziegfeld commissioned Hobé to create bugle-beaded costumes and flashy fake jewelry for his showgirls, as he could not afford real gems.

Hobé made jewelry that aspired to be as high quality as the best fine jewelry, hence the tagline 'Jewels of Legendary Splendor' and the firm is said to have included real gems among the fake—perhaps the reason why it is one of the most highly sought-after labels by vintage jewelry collectors today. Regular clients at its Beverly Hills boutique included Barbara Stanwyck, Carole Lombard, Betty Grable, and Maureen O'Hara and William Hobé had a close working relationship with Oscar-winning costumier Edith Head, who was said to be so demanding he would have to work night and day to finish many last-minute commissions.

Paul Flato

A humble watch salesman in 1920s New York, Paul Flato (1900–99) went on to become one of the most flamboyant jewelers in America, whose diamonds were worn by the shiniest of Hollywood stars including the divine Greta Garbo, Rita Hayworth and Merle Oberon. His first jewelry business opened on East 57th Street in Manhattan and was an instant success selling 'white on white' brooches, necklaces and bracelets in the form of flowers, ribbons and scrolls to Hollywood clients as well as New York socialites. Ten years later he opened on Hollywood's Sunset Boulevard and, through his annual fashion shows, Flato jewels took on a starring role of their own appearing, in 1941, on Merle Oberon in *That Uncertain Feeling*, Garbo in *Two Faced Woman* and Rita Hayworth in *Blood and Sand*; in the film *Holiday* (1938) Katherine Hepburn sported an unlikely diamond toe-ring and a stunning sunburst brooch of canary-colored diamonds. One of his most extravagant pieces was a necklace of cascading apple blossoms worn by the opera singer Lily Pons.

Known for his humor above all else, Flato's designs included the Corset bracelet, based on Mae West's hourglass shape and rendered in rubies and diamonds, and the Golddigger bracelet, complete with miniature pickaxe. The Hand of God, a brooch worn by Joan Bennett for an RKO publicity shot, took the form of a 18-karat gold palm-reader's hand with diamond stars representing the planets pavé-set into the palm.

OPPOSITE TOP A 'white on white' diamond cuff with fringe and a diamond ring by New York jeweler Paul Flato, created for socialite Mrs Jay O'Brien in 1937.

OPPOSITE CENTER Hobé-style, unsigned, hinged bracelet with aquamarines and rubies, circa 1940, decorated with tiny gold filigree leaves and flowers.

OPPOSITE BOTTOM Two brooches by Hobé: a purple cabochon and clear rhinestone wirework brooch and a large oval dress clip set in gold-tone filigree with chartreuse unfoiled rhinestones and clear quartz cabochons.

ABOVE CLOCKWISE Red, clear and blue unfoiled rhinestone bracelet; hinged bracelet and earrings with gold overlay leaves and pink rhinestone roses; floral bouquet brooch accented with a huge pink rhinestone; two-part pendant brooch with pink and purple rhinestones; sterling and moonstone floral bouquet brooch; sterling with gold wash floral brooch with aqua rhinestones; sterling brooch with a faux star sapphire cabochon center. All by Hobé.

Fulco di Verdura

Born to an aristocratic Sicilian family and brought up in his grandmother's country house, the Villa Nescemi just outside of Palermo, Fulco Santostefano della Cerda, the Duke of Verdura (1898–1978), began his career as head of textiles at the House of Chanel. The couturier was quick to notice that his talents clearly lay elsewhere, in jewelry, and she commissioned him to create pieces for the boutique but also to re-set her own fabulous collection that had been gifted by a selection of rich and generous admirers. Jewels from the Grand Duke Dmitri of Russia were crafted into a cuff bracelet incorporating a huge Maltese cross, which became a recurring motif in both Chanel and Verdura's work (see also page 58).

After moving to New York in 1934 his impeccable aristocratic and couture connections made a meeting with *Vogue* editor Diana Vreeland inevitable, and in turn he was introduced to Paul Flato, established jeweler to the stars. The subsequent line, 'Verdura for Flato' was such a success that 'the Duke,' as he was now being known, opened his own boutique specializing in beautiful bespoke jewelry on Fifth Avenue in 1939, with the backing of composer Cole Porter, whom he had met while holidaying in Venice.

Noted for his incredible technical proficiency in handling mixtures of both precious and semiprecious stones, signature pieces included knotted bows, pomegranates, seashells and winged hearts. Verdura had a preference for 18-karat gold—he said it reminded him of the sunshine of Sicily—and his use of the metal paved the way for change. The platinum-and-diamond combination that had dominated for decades was superseded by an aesthetic of traditional opulence, as can be seen in his sea-horse brooches studded with sparkling stones.

In 1937 after a client from Palm Beach commissioned Verdana to create a special Valentine's Day gift that would symbolize his eternal love for his wife, Verdura designed an exquisite cabochon ruby-and-diamond brooch in the shape of a gold-wrapped heart, and his trademark design was born. Customers included movie legends Joan Crawford and Katharine Hepburn, for whom he designed all the jewelry she wore in the film *The Philadelphia Story* (1940), and Tyrone Power, who commissioned a heart made entirely of rubies and tied with a ribbon of diamonds. Shells were also incorporated into his work, caught up in twining tendrils of shimmering diamonds.

BELOW LEFT A spectacular gold, sapphire and diamond brooch in the form of a lion's-paw scallop shell by Fulco di Verdura, circa 1940.

BELOW RIGHT The large ruby and diamond 'wrapped heart' brooch of 1941 by Fulco di Verdura in 18-karat gold and platinum, set with 62 cabochon rubies and 232 round diamonds. Originally commissioned by a wealthy Palm Beach client as a Valentine's Day present for his wife, this became a trademark piece of the jeweler's.

RIGHT Coco Chanel and Fulco di Verdura in the late 1930s inspect a Maltese Cross hinged cuff. Chanel commissioned the jeweler to create pieces for her boutiques before he opened his own establishment selling bespoke jewelry in New York City.

BELOW RIGHT A pair of Chanel's original Maltese Cross cuffs from 1930 by Fulco di Verdura, key heritage pieces from the back catalogue that are regularly reinterpreted by the House of Chanel. These silver and ivory, colored enamel hinged cuffs are set with multicolored cabochon and faceted gemstones.

Diamonds: The Birth of a Tagline

The power of the motion picture was such that it could do more than just market a jeweler's name in the 1930s, it could entirely change the image of a gem. The Great Depression caused consternation among diamond merchants, including the De Beers Company, who realized that many of the traditional customers of expensive estate jewelry had a bit of a problem with funds. The image of the diamond as the preserve of the rich and stunningly successful had to be changed in order to appeal to a different market.

One of the first moves came from an association of powerful stakeholders in the diamond industry, the International Diamond Merchants, who commissioned Coco Chanel to apply her talents to real gems instead of fake in 1934. By changing tack and deciding that real jewels were better than her witty trinkets, it was thought that Chanel could make sumptuous jewelry fashionable once more and she was duly employed to update the image of the diamond. Chanel, together with her coterie that included interior decorator and socialite Lady Sibyl Colefax and interior designer Elise de Wolfe, created a ravishing collection that was quite literally cosmic. Earrings took the shape of stars and comets that left their trails in sparkling diamonds around the throat and, in a nod to hard times, she made many pieces convertible. Earrings could be used as brooches; tiaras, following the Edwardian model, could be taken apart and re-used as bracelets and pendants. The most spectacular of the pieces was the Comète necklace of 1932, a star with a cascading trail of 649 diamonds which was to be worn cured around the shoulder and neck with the tail nestling against the throat. The collection was an immediate press success but was clearly more than most people, even the very rich ones, could afford. The Baroque Revival style of such planetary pieces was to resurface though in the 1940s and appeared in the work of Chanel's great rivals, Elsa Schiaparelli, as well as Boucher and Juliana.

What next for the diamond? De Beers began to realize that the high fashion was not the right route to rebranding the gem—it paled in significance in the public's imagination when placed next to any style tips emanating from Hollywood. People were far more influenced by the living and breathing characters on the silver screen than by what was coming out of a snooty Parisian atelier. Accordingly De Beers and other jewelers turned their attention to Warner Brothers rather than the world of haute couture—surely here was a way of branding diamonds with more mass-market appeal?

The next step was to recruit American advertising agency N W Ayer to research into the prime reason why people bought diamonds. The result was clear: the glittering gems were a symbol of love. Consequently a marketing strategy was devised that would take the generic symbol of the 'diamond' rather than the name 'De Beers' and target the maker of dreams—Hollywood. Movie magazines would feature celebrities bedecked in dazzling diamond jewelry, screenwriters should be persuaded to inject scenes into the movie narrative where diamonds would be given as tokens of romance, suitors would be persuaded that a diamond ring signified his emotional as well as financial investment, and hopefully the idea would catch on. The campaign was a resounding success and more and more prospective couples fell for De Beers' famous line, 'A Diamond is Forever.' By 1941 sales of diamonds had gone up by 55 percent and 80 percent of all American engagements were celebrated with a diamond ring.

A company who capitalized on this vogue were Helzberg, known as the 'Middle West's Largest Jewelers,' who pioneered expansion into the American suburbs after the end of the war. They specialized in diamond jewelry, sold from their new air-conditioned stores.

OPPOSITE Chanel used the popular motif of the ribbon bow, lending a casual insouciance to a luxurious diamond necklace. The piece was commissioned by the International Diamond Merchants, who hoped her high profile would lend fashionable cachet to the rock.

BELOW Chanel's exquisite Comète necklace comprises a huge diamond star with a cascading trail of 649 diamonds curling around the shoulder and neck.

Harry Winston

A name immortalized by Marilyn Monroe in the song, 'Diamonds are a Girl's Best Friend,' Harry Winston (1896–1978) opened his doors in 1932 and became the destination of choice for both Hollywood and high society. The son of poor Ukrainian immigrants, Winston was a man who had a true love affair with diamonds and, as the story goes, swung from feeling incredible power when acquiring a particularly fine example to a deep sense of loss when letting one go. Collaborating with De Beers, the business went on to acquire the world's most flawless gems, including the most famous diamond in the world, the Hope, in 1949, 45.52 carats of shimmering blue with a list of former owners that included Louis XIV.

Harry Winston jewelry starts with the acquisition of the gem, which is then cut, polished, designed and set in the company's Fifth Avenue building in New York City. The journey ends when the diamond adorns the body of an iconic (and wealthy) woman, such as film star Mae West who was dressed in Winston diamonds for her stage version of *Diamond Lil* in 1949. She wore, according to the program, a 'seven-part waist decoration, $500,000; necklace, $100,000; three bracelets, $200,000; 46-carat emerald-cut diamond ring, $300,000; and a 30-carat oval-cut diamond ring, $75,000.' The 'ice' was ferried by couriers each night to the vault and then brought back under guard to the Coronet Theater in time for each performance. Other devotees of Harry's wares included Jean Harlow, Elizabeth Taylor, Paris Hilton and Jennifer Garner, who was given a 6.1-carat Harry Winston ring by actor and husband Ben Affleck.

What marked Harry Winston out from his competitors was that he understood the nature of celebrity power and made his name known by loaning his creations to every major star at every major event. His own face was out of bounds though, and throughout his career he refused to be photographed, shielding himself at every opportunity for 'security reasons.' This canny operator knew how to add to his mystique.

BELOW As the Depression lifted, the diamond began to stage a spectacular comeback. Here a model with a hairstyle by Antoine de Paris wears nautilus-shaped diamond ear clips by René Boivin.

RIGHT In 1939 socialite Brenda Frazier wears the spectacular million-dollar Jonker Diamond owned by Harry Winston at a New York fashion show. The huge ice-white diamond was found by Johannes Jonker in South Africa in 1934 and weighed 726 carats, at the time the fourth largest diamond ever unearthed.

▶ Diamonds

Due to the advertising efforts of the diamond merchants, diamond sales increased 55 percent. This diamond and ruby bow brooch, part of the Duchess of Windsor's personal collection, was sold in 1987. Many of her 1930s pieces were designed by Suzanne Belperron, Van Cleef & Arpels, Cartier and Harry Winston.

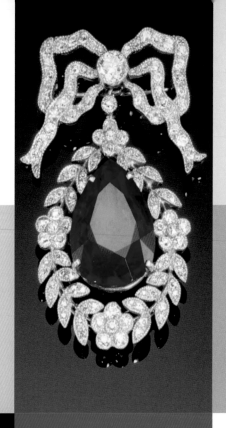

Stepped motifs and circles

The geometric forms of Modernism remained popular in the 1930s and found their way into jewelry of every price range —stepped motifs, chevrons and circles are typical of this decade's mainstream production.

Key looks of the decade
1930s

▼ Floral motifs

Flower motifs came back into fashion, but this time was streamlined and stylized rather than overtly figurative. This fashion illustration from 1931 depicts a platinum necklace and matching brooch by Mauboussin in the form of exotic orchids in enamel set with diamonds.

▲ Filigree settings

Gold- and silver-plated sterling, often combined with crystal gems, formed filigree settings for showy pieces, the best known of which were by Hobé. Here a 1930s French gold-colored filigree brooch features blue rhinestone glass jewels.

▶ Dime-store Deco

This term is used to define the kind of jewelry that would have been bought in the five-and-ten stores that were a major sector of American retailing by the 1930s, the best known being Woolworth's. The motifs of the prevailing fashion were provided in cheap and cheerful examples, such as this Deco-inspired buckle and button set.

◀ White on white

American actress Irene Dunne shows off a diamond bracelet in the 'white on white' style, circa 1935. This glossy luxe look was a popular trend in both jewelry and Hollywood set design, where white fur mixed with diamonds and marabou perfectly fit the monochromatic demands of black-and-white film.

Flashy fakes

Whether real or faux, jewelry in every price range became distinctly flashy in the 1930s. Fine stones were brilliantly cut to give as much fire as possible and costume jewelry followed the same sparkling aesthetic.

▲ Dress clips

Popular from the late 1920s to the 1950s, dress clips are a good starting point for any budding collector. Most manufacturers of costume jewelry in the 1930s made them as their price suited Depression incomes and their versatility meant they could add interest to any outfit. Some were mounted in frames so as to be worn together as a single brooch.

1940s:
F for Fake

In a world of war, costume jewelry was an important boost for feminine morale when fashion was under ration and austerity held sway. As clothes were forced to become increasingly utilitarian to fit the austere mood of the times, costume jewelry stepped in as the perfect antidote —it could 'jolly up' any amount of tweed. Jewelry production slowed right down in Europe and widespread bombing decimated important manufacturing centers such as Birmingham in England and Pforzheim in Germany. Paris, although occupied, had a wealthy audience and its prestigious firms kept going despite a lack of materials. During this period many pieces of unwanted jewelry were broken up and reset, and the market for antique jewelry expanded.

Patriotic jewelry boosted the spirit both at home and abroad with red, white and blue being a symbolic and emotional color combination, the colors of both the American Stars and Stripes and the Union Jack. As Austrian Swarovski crystals became harder to source, companies found ingenious ways to give showy effects to their jewelry lines such as using polished Lucite instead of gemstones.

Platinum was an impossibility as it was essential for the production of armaments, so gold became the principal precious metal, although lighter, thinner sheets were used. Large brooches were popular but many were hollow inside and the snake or gas-pipe chain, a sinuously ribbed flexible gold tube, became the height of fashion. For those who could not afford pure gold, vast quantities of sterling silver were plated with gold to create vermeil, which was easily mistaken for the real thing. This idea of plating silver with gold was not new; in fact, it dates back to the eighteenth century when jewelers applied mercury and gold to silver and then exposed it to extreme heat. As the mercury vaporized, the gold adhered to the silver, although the toxic fumes caused artisans to lose their sight—the technique was banned by the nineteenth century. Gold vermeil in the 1940s was produced using the electrolytic process.

Taking a lead from Chanel, the whole nature of fake changed; instead of imitating the real, it glorified in the artificial—no real gem could assume such gigantic proportions. Plastic became completely acceptable as a malleable material that could assume any form a confident woman was prepared to wear; it was molded into Scottie dogs, cowboys with lassos, huge necklaces of bright berries or dancing harlequins.

Fantastic Plastic

The ultimate in modern materials, plastic could be speedily molded using industrial processes that could keep up with fashion. Its cheapness made pieces ephemeral—if they didn't cost much, they could easily be discarded in favor of next season's latest look. Celluloid and galalith had been used before, most notably in the work of Art Deco designer Auguste Bonaz, but Bakelite, a mixture of phenol and formaldehyde, reigned supreme in this decade after having been invented by Dr Leo Baekeland in 1907 (see also pages 67 and 213). This synthetic material was incredibly hard, heat-resistant (which is why it was used for the casings of so many electrical devices, such as light switches and hairdryers) and it could also be dyed a variety of colors. It was well suited to Art Deco geometry and early pieces combined red, black and cream with shiny machine-age chrome.

By the end of the 1930s Bakelite was ubiquitous—it could be seen almost everywhere, from the kitchen and bathroom to a woman's lapel. It was also used to produce the most beautiful and colorful costume jewelry and was worked by lathe to create figurative brooches of flowers, fruit and animals or deeply carved hinged cuffs. The most sought-after Bakelite is 'apple juice,' a translucent golden-yellow color, and the so-called Philadelphia style, where up to five brightly colored pieces including butterscotch, green and red are glued together to create striking geometric effects. When one was sold at a Philadelphia auction in 1988, a bidding war broke out which ended at $17,000 and the name subsequently stuck.

Sleeper gave Bakelite a handcrafted touch: Bakelite piggybank pin with penny, a witty reference to jewelry worn in a time of austerity; flowerpots pin with chain attachment; Bakelite pig pin with Sleeper's trademark flash painting; Bakelite birdhouse pin; carved and flash-painted Bakelite carousel horse pin.

Martha Sleeper

Aka the *Gadget Girl* (1910–83), Martha Sleeper was a former film star and comedienne who had been signed to the Hal Roach Studios in 1925 when she was a mere 17 years old. After retiring from show business in the 1930s she began a new career as a jewelry designer and was noted for her charming Bakelite jewelry, which distracted her buyers' attention from the bleak days of the Depression. Sleeper managed to take an industrial material and make it look amusingly handcrafted with designs that included carved Bakelite elephants with little gold leather ears, Dutch girls in clogs with hand-painted shawls and a collection of charm bracelets hung with motifs that symbolized good luck (the black cat being one of her favorites). A school-themed bracelet, complete with pen, inkpot, globe, open atlas and pencil charms, was one of her most popular designs.

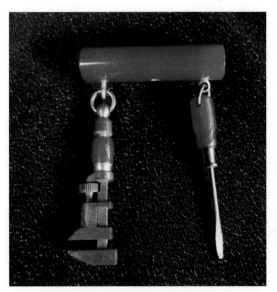

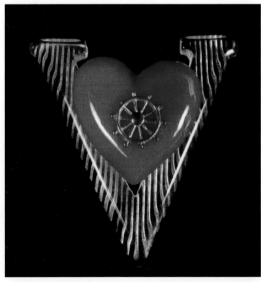

FAR LEFT A Martha Sleeper Tool Pin brooch features miniature implements in metal and Bakelite. Her humorous touches were a refreshing change from the dominance of floral motifs.

LEFT A Bakelite 'V' for Victory Pin worn in the 1940s to show support for the war and the American soldiers serving overseas.

Cocktail Hour

As European jewelry manufacturers turned over their factories to the war effort, American firms began to dominate the market. Eisenberg, a Chicago-based concern, produced large white-on-white pieces using hand-set Swarovski crystals—some of its extravagant creations cost an average woman up to one week's wages. Eisenberg's work was symptomatic of a decadent, fantasy-inspired style that could be seen in the global vogue for huge Baroque bijoux in the manner of Joseff of Hollywood (see pages 72–3) and was seen onscreen in scheming *film noir* heroines such as Joan Crawford and Barbara Stanwyck. Joan summed up this excessive style with, 'If you want to see the girl next door, go next door.'

Many skilled refugees fled Europe to work for firms such as Trifari, Monet, Pennino and Napier, and Rhode Island consolidated its position as the center of the jewelry-making industry in the US. A distinctly American look was evolving with home-grown fashion designers Clare McCardell and Travis Banton creating a way of dressing that was understated yet exclusive, a look that combined deluxe materials with simple, classic shapes—the 'cashmere and diamonds' approach that can be seen today in the work of Donna Karan and Calvin Klein. At home on a Long Island beach or in a Lexington Avenue boutique, the casual ease and cosmopolitan chic of this great American fashion provided an elegant backdrop for jewelry—and the more individual and exuberant, the better.

RIGHT American costume jewelry in the 1940s was exuberant and glamorous. Cocktail jewelry was designed to turn heads and discretion was definitely not the order of the day. This jewelry ensemble dates from 1941.

BELOW An Eisenberg Original fur clip by designer Ruth Kamke, who designed for the company for over 30 years from 1940. This bejeweled cupid also came in an enameled version to simulate porcelain.

THIS PAGE A rhinestone set from 1946. Costume jewelry was big, bold and sparkling in the 1940s, taking its cue from the theatrical excess of Hollywood's silver screen. Matching sets were at their height of popularity.

Alfred Philippe at Trifari created a whole range of insects, dogs, cats, penguins and other whimsical animals called Jelly Bellies (after their colored Lucite middles), set in sterling silver or gold plate. Philippe's attention to detail was such that Trifari's costume pieces could be favorably compared with fine jewelry, and by 1953 Mamie Eisenhower broke with tradition and wore Trifari to the inaugural ball of the new presidency. Philippe designed a pearl choker, a three-strand bracelet and earrings to complement the First Lady's pink silk *peau de soie* gown by Nettie Rosenstein of New York. Despite the fashion designer's much quoted motto, 'It's what you leave off a dress that makes it smart,' the dress was studded with two thousand rhinestones.

ABOVE A 1940s brooch in a design of shell scrolls and two long composite feathers by Trifari from Providence, Rhode Island.

RIGHT, FROM TOP A gold-tone and rhinestone double-pronged fur clip by Trifari, 1948, designed by Alfred Philippe in a yin-yang pattern. A 1941 pearl and silver leaf brooch with a faceted surface to emulate rhinestones, which were in short supply during the war years. A striking, paisley-shaped, gold-tone and rhinestone brooch by Trifari. In 1937, when the name Trifari was trademarked, every single piece made by the company was marked to make them easy to identify and hard to copy.

Cocktail jewelry was deliberately showy, glitzy and glamorous; vigorous combinations of volute or stepped shapes in yellow gilt and mesh metal were inset with foil-backed paste stones. Coro's design director Adolph Katz produced a range of styles that suited every budget including their *tremblant* brooches mounted on a spring, so as to subtly shiver when the wearer walked, particularly effective when the motif was a rhinestone butterfly. In the work of Alice Caviness, a former fashion model, silver filigree bows, lovebirds and flower baskets harked back to a nostalgic femininity in the midst of a harrowing war. Coro's popular range of Duette dress clips in enameled pot metal or silver set with crystal baguettes were mounted on a frame so that they could be worn individually or together as a single pin. Higher-end pieces were produced under the name Corocraft. For cocktail hour, bags and jewelry combined, most significantly in the minaudiére, a combination of purse and powder compact invented by Van Cleef & Arpels that took the form of a sleek metal box. Many of the finest had several articulated and hidden compartments that could hold cigarettes, money and cosmetics and were made of engine-turned gold, silver or layers of glossy Japanese lacquer. Cartier created a stunning example in gold-and-black enamel that held a tiny tube of lipstick, which had to be sent back to the jewelers every time it needed to be refilled.

LEFT A Hobé brooch, top, from 1942 is in a stylized, naturalistic style that is typical of the period. A silver rooster pin, circa 1940, is stamped 'Sterling by Corocraft.' Corocraft was a subsidiary of the brand Coro, which was in business from 1901–79.

ABOVE A model in the outdoorsy American look that revolutionized fashion in the 1940s and acted as a counterpoint to stuffy French couture. This grass green shantung dress of 1945 is accessorized with a gold Coro pin.

PPOSITE FAR LEFT A Victorian Revival hand pin by Coro in brass, holding white flowers with pink rhinestone centers and accented with a large aqua rhinestone. By the 1940s, the nineteenth-century hand motif also hinted at fashionable Surrealism.

Marcel Boucher

Boucher (1898–1965) produced some of the most extravagant work in the 1940s. A French jeweler, who had trained at Cartier in Paris before moving to their branch in New York in the 1920s, he set up his own business, Marcel Boucher et Cie, in 1937. Business partner Arthur Halberstadt worked in the front of the shop while Boucher designed in the back. The influence of Cartier can be seen in the firm's output of Rococo swags and bows but the classic French style has been exaggerated to a achieve a more flamboyant effect. The firm also produced large naturalistic brooches in the shape of feathers, flower and fruit plus Boucher's trademark and highly collectable exotic birds-of-paradise, which anticipated the luxury of 1950s couture. The birds were the best of the cocktail genre, superbly worked with every feather engraved in gold-tone metal, breast and tail feathers pavé-set with diamanté and perched on branches bedecked with leaves and flowers. Boucher also designed mechanical jewelry that moved, such as a brooch of a pelican whose mouth opened to receive a fish and the Night-and-Day flower series whose petals furled and unfurled as if moving their heads to the sun. After Boucher died in 1965 his wife Sandra, a talented designer in her own right, led the company until 1972 as well as designing for Harry Winston and Tiffany.

LEFT A flamboyant rhinestone flower brooch by Marcel Boucher in a 'white-on-white' style that displays his training at Cartier, who popularized the style in the early twentieth century.

LEFT TOP A Marcel Boucher pin of enameled cherries, 1941. The cherry, with its bestowing of sweetness onto the wearer, is a long-standing motif in jewelry and was at its most popular in the 1940s and 1970s.

LEFT BELOW A pair of goldstone cupids holding a rhinestone ribbon with dangling faceted red crystal hearts—a modern take on French Rococo by Marcel Boucher.

BELOW A 1942 patriotic fur clip in the form of a goldstone hand holding the torch of liberty, the flame is depicted in pink faceted glass crystal. Attributed to Marcel Boucher.

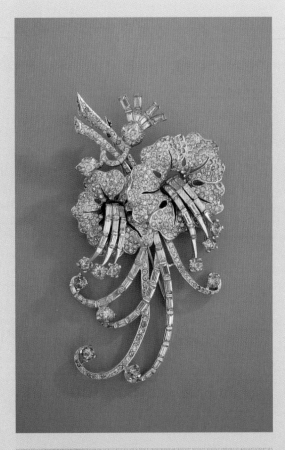

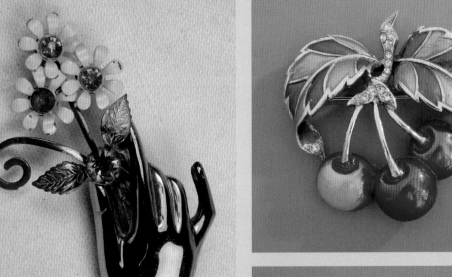

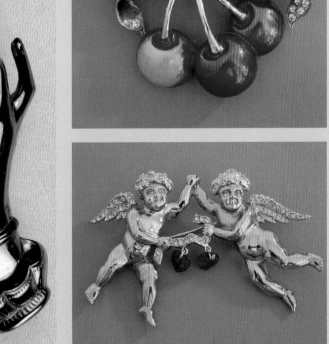

Miriam Haskell

American costume jeweler Miriam Haskell (1899–1981), whose firm still exists today, was born in Albany, Indiana, in 1899, one of four children. She began designing and producing jewelry in 1924 and opened her first boutique, Le Bijou de l'Heure, in 1926 in the McAlpin Hotel, New York City. Here she showed collections that owed more to the legacy of Art Nouveau than Art Deco; their motifs derived from nature rather than the machine, and asymmetry over geometry is the key design feature.

Haskell *bijouterie* was bought by some of the leading lights of New York's fashionable scene. Customers included film stars Joan Crawford, who was reputed to have several pieces from every Haskell season; Lucille Ball, who regularly flew out from Los Angeles for a private showing of the latest looks; and the coolly elegant Duchess of Windsor, through whom she was introduced to Coco Chanel. The French couturier and the American designer were both independent, free-spirited women of means in the competitive world of fashion and they struck up a firm friendship, gossiping over coffee as they sourced fabulous blown-glass Murano beads at their favourite Maison Gripoix.

Together with head designer Frank Hess, with whom she worked until his retirement in 1960, Haskell created costume jewelry of understated beauty and meticulous detail. Every Venetian bead, Bohemian crystal and faux baroque pearl was handwired to intricate brass filigree and then backed to a second filigree to conceal any trace of its construction. Beads were then worked up into three dimensions to create textural layers, held together with soft honey-toned metal filigree wiring. As a result one piece may have taken as long as three days to create, a lifetime in the world of costume jewelry and reflected in the occasionally prohibitive cost of each piece.

The advent of the Second World War forced Haskell to use alternative materials including plastics beads, shell and crystals—all sourced a little closer to home. Later, in the early 1950s, Haskell designs became increasingly elaborate and showy as women wanted a more obvious glamour in their lives after the deprivations of war. Trinkets from this period include a pair of flamboyant Gauguin-inspired hibiscus earrings in painted porcelain and gold, and flashing stickpins of a style that can only be described as Hollywood Baroque. Huge necklaces had strands of multiple crystal beads separated by Japanese pearls, coral or huge gold-tone leaves, and brooches were set with a multitude of stones, pearls and tiny glass seed-beads in shades of aqua, robin's egg blue and pastel pink.

BELOW A Miriam Haskell and Frank Hess grand parure, with accompanying original artwork (bottom center) by Larry Austin. The pink set comprises a three-strand bracelet, three dress clips and a necklace.

BELOW LEFT AND RIGHT Original watercolor artworks by Larry Austin promoting the Haskell parures pictured opposite, top left and bottom.

COLLECTING MIRIAM HASKELL

* Because all pieces are handmade, they are quite fragile and difficult to restore.
* Unmarked until 1947, work was stamped with her name on a horseshoe cartouche, an oval stamp, and on the hook or clasp.
* Early unsigned necklaces tend to have elaborate box clasps; later signed pieces use a distinctive adjustable hook and tail.
* A good way to identify an authentic Haskell is by vintage ads, such as those opposite.
* Nearly all have a pierced metal (pre-1943), plastic (during war years) or filigree plate (postwar) onto which the decorative details were attached. Mesh was never used.

TOP LEFT A Haskell and Hess parure, including a bracelet, brooch and three clips of goldstone nasturtium leaves.

TOP RIGHT An unsigned 1940 parure attributed to Miriam Haskell featuring poured glass pink and lavender petals.

FAR LEFT A 1940 parure by Haskell and Hess, including a lariat wrap necklace of aqua glass beads with silver-tone leaves decorated with rhinestone pavé, a necklace of aqua glass bead balls and clear rhinestone leaves and a four-strand bracelet.

The Bizarre Influence of Surrealism

In the 1930s, an alternative to Modernism appeared with a flourish in the morphing form of Surrealism, an art movement that was to have its full effects on jewelry in the 1940s. Surrealism reveled in the bizarre and hallucinogenic, at its most compelling in the work of Salvador Dalí, Leonora Carrington and René Magritte. Artists and designers took inspiration from a rich source of imagery that had been missing in the move toward pure abstraction. Inspired by the work of the Viennese psychoanalyst Sigmund Freud and following his seminal work *The Interpretation of Dreams* (1899), in which he had revealed that understanding dreams was the route to understanding the unconscious, artists sought recourse in their inner self, trying to give visual form to the unexpected juxtaposition of objects. Described by the poet Comte de Lautréamont, the macabre description of 'the chance encounter of a sewing machine and an umbrella on a dissecting table' was the epitome of Surrealist chic.

Women artists who were members of the Surrealist circle applied these ideas to their own fashionable identity; Meret Oppenheim's fetishistic Fur-lined Teacup, Saucer and Spoon of 1936 is one of the most well-known examples of the group's work. In a photograph taken by Man Ray in the late 1940s she wears a pair of champagne corks for earrings and artist Mina Loy was also captured by the same photographer with a thermometer hanging from each ear.

Elsa Schiaparelli

As Paris was the center of both Surrealist activity and haute couture from 1924, the two were eventually bound to collide, as they did to glamorous effect in the work of Roman-born Elsa Schiaparelli (1890–1973) and the mysterious artist Salvador Dalí. Schiaparelli was a feisty single parent from an intellectual Roman background who had moved to Paris to create fashion with shock-chic appeal. She designed hats shaped like high-heeled shoes, lamb chops and exposed brains; buttons in the shape of circus clowns and acrobats and glass birdcage bags.

In the shop window of Schiaparelli's boutique on the Place Vendôme, Dalí created bizarre window displays that included a shocking-pink teddy bear with drawers in its torso, perched on a sofa inspired by film star Mae West's lips. Women such as socialite Daisy Fellowes wore Schiaparelli's suede Shoe hat accessorized with a necklace shaped like a row of aspirins—the everyday transformed into treasured *objets de la couture*. Many early Schiaparelli designs were produced in collaboration with her artist friends including Dalí, Christian Bérard and Jean Cocteau and their designs had a macabre quality that had much in common with the feel of Art Nouveau

practitioners like Wolfers (see page 15). Peapods and insects hung from necklaces, brooches took the form of hands, eyes and bagpipes. As Schiaparelli summed up, 'In difficult times fashion is always outrageous.'

In 1940 Elsa Schiaparelli left Paris for New York in order to expand her fashion operation and opened a boutique in New York selling prêt-a-porter, perfume, lingerie and jewelry. She also saw that the company's revenue could be used if she licensed her name, something many canny fashion designers like Dior only recognized in the 1950s, and accordingly the David Lisner Company produced Schiaparelli-branded jewelry. Designs are spectacular and showy and include the well-known, prong-set, molded iridescent-glass stones, which are usually described as 'watermelon,' and big aurora borealis rhinestones that were developed by Swarovski in 1955. Elsa retired in 1954 and the Schiaparelli jewelry line discontinued around 1955. She sold the rights to her name and business in 1973 and American manufacturers continued producing her designs up to 1974.

Salvador Dalí

At the outbreak of the Second World War the artist Salvador Dalí (1904–89) left Spain for America and in 1948 branched out into jewelry. The first Dalí designs were made in collaboration with Fulco di Verdura, who had been introduced to the artist by American heiress Caresse Crosby at a meeting stage-managed by the maverick artist in a derelict house. The artist was found posed in a room full of books and cobwebs, an appropriately Surrealist *mise en scène*, and suggested to Verdura that they should visit the cemetery together to go bone picking and use the 'lovely little shiny bones' for jewelry. Dalí described their working relationship and philosophy in an article he wrote for American *Vogue* in July, 1941, 'Fulco and I have tried to discover whether it was the Jewel that was born for Painting or Painting for the Jewel; we are sure, however, they were born for each other. It's a love marriage.'

The first works were Dalí miniatures in miniature, painstakingly painted on ivory and gold and set with semiprecious stones that took the form of beetles and bones. A bizarre gold cigarette holder, based on an animal's shinbone with rubies set to resemble dripping blood, was exhibited at Dalí's one-man show held at the Museum of Modern Art, New York, in 1941. By 1949 Dalí had signed a contract with Argentinean goldsmith Carlos Alemany and his Finnish business partner Eric Ertman to provide designs on paper that would then be translated into fine jewelry by a team of craftsmen. The most Dalí-esque motifs were used: telephones sculpted in 18-karat gold and set with rubies and emeralds; Mae West's red lips transformed into a brooch of rubies and little pearl teeth in 1949; a diamond-encrusted eye within which an iris takes the form of a tiny clock with working hands. The Persistence of Memory brooch (1948–49) was taken from the 1931 painting of the same name with the iconic melting watches rendered in three dimensions in gold and black enamel and studded with diamonds.

Heiress Rebecca Harkness commissioned Dalí's most infamous design—an Etoile de Mer (a diamond-and-ruby starfish) brooch with a pearl at its center, growing from a cluster emerald-studded leaves. The arms of the starfish were engineered so they could be maneuvered into different positions and when worn on the hand could give the impression that the fabulous creature was desperately clinging on. Harkness, a little more provocatively, wore it over her left breast.

Paris-born Raymond Georges Yves Tanguy (1900–55) was another Surrealist artist who took motifs from his paintings when he created a series of rosewood rings, circa 1937, that evoked the rock formations from his well-known abstract 'submarine' dreamscapes (the rings were recast in gold in the early 1960s). In 1938 patron of the arts Peggy Guggenheim commissioned a pair of miniature paintings from Yves Tanguy that were then set in gold and worn as earrings. As she recalls in her memoirs:

I was so excited I couldn't wait for them to dry and ruined one by wearing it too soon. I then made him paint me a second one. The first two were pink, but he now made one blue. They were beautiful little miniature paintings and [art critic] Herbert Read said they were the best Tanguys he had ever seen.

However, one of the most impressive of Surrealist jewels was not, in fact, created by Dalí but by a long-established Parisian firm, the Maison Boivan. In 1938 an eccentric Texan multimillionaire walked into the establishment with the skull of a longhorn ox, which had come from her ranch, and asked for it to be copied as a brooch. Germaine Boivan, founder René Boivan's daughter, made a 4-inch (10 cm) high, stunning object of desire covered in pavé diamonds with a wreath of emerald leaves spilling from one eye socket, a purple sapphire sash and polished gold horns.

Bijoux Beatnik

There had to be a reaction to all this extravagance in a troubled world. Retrospective styles seemed to be part of a culture that had ignored the horrors of war by taking refuge in the nostalgia of the past and Surrealism was infused with a deadly decadence that ignored the political nature of conflict. Young people turned on by the existentialism of Jean-Paul Sartre or Jack Kerouac's Beatnik prose sought a new form of expression.

In 1940 a revolutionary Modernism began to appear in American jewelry, which anticipated the hippie movement in its disavowal of crass commercialism. In San Francisco and New York artists such as Alexander Calder, Harry Bertoia, Sam Kramer, Rolph Scarlett and Margaret de Patta began to turn their attention to handcrafted jewelry, making the same aesthetic decisions with small-scale design as they had with their art. This one-off wearable art was worn by a discerning bohemian consumer who wanted to display humanist rather than capitalist values. One customer in a counter-cultural Greenwich Village jeweler's remembers,

> About 1947 I went to Ed Wiener's shop and
> bought one of his silver square-spiral pins
> because it looked great, I could afford it and
> it identified me with the group of my choice—
> aesthetically aware, intellectually inclined
> and politically progressive. That pin was our
> badge and we wore it proudly. It celebrated
> the hand of the artist rather than the market
> value of the material. Diamonds were the badge
> of the philistine.

In 1948 a touring exhibition opened at the Walker Art Center in Minneapolis entitled 'Modern Jewelry Under Fifty Dollars' and displayed the work of many of the new Modernist artist-jewelers including New York's Paul Lobel and Art Smith and San Francisco's Margaret de Patta and Bob Winston. Reviewers realized there was now a modern alternative to the status jewelry that was so popular. Deluxe materials were vulgar; brass and copper could take the place of gold and mini-sculptures made figurative flourishes look desperately suburban.

ABOVE A pared down style in both fashion and jewelry appeared in America after the war. Here, two models wear costume jewelry designed by Van Cleef & Arpels—a simpler style that anticipates the abstraction of the 1950s.

RIGHT American beatnik and jeweler Sam Kramer, at work on a new design in Greenwich Village, circa 1955. He was a pioneer of the American Modernist movement that dominated studio jewelry in the 1950s.

ABOVE An uncompromisingly abstract metal choker and brooch designed by Sam Kramer in a biomorphic style inspired by Surrealist artist Tanguy, circa 1955.

Sam Kramer

The work of Sam Kramer (1914–64) straddles both the American Modernist movement and Surrealism, providing an important aesthetic link between the two. Originally training as a journalist at the University of Pittsburgh, it was while working as a Hollywood reporter in the late 1930s that he began making jewelry to de-stress from his work. After learning techniques from a craftsman in Pittsburgh, Kramer opened his own studio and shop in New York's Greenwich Village in 1939 and began to produce silver jewelry with a strong Surrealist influence, incorporating precious metals with found objects such as reef coral, cowrie shells and glass taxidermy eyes. Brooches and earrings in the form of strange distorted animals with a Cyclops' eye standing for the head were bought by intellectuals connected with the Beatnik vibe of the Village and as word spread, his fame and fortune grew.

With a doorknob in the shape of a bronze hand, which in the depths of winter was given a pigskin glove, the shop itself was a draw for customers. Kramer's advertising ran 'Fantastic Jewelry for People Who Are Slightly Mad' and one journalist wrote in 1942 that 'His slogan is a psychological trick, successful because people are put into a buying mood by the suggestion that they are not quite Humdrum types and come into his place, wave one of his pamphlets, and say "I'm slightly crazy," and buy heavily. A card he distributes reads in part, "We have things to titillate the damnedest ego—utter weirdities conceived in moments of semi-madness." The writer then revealed that Kramer had 'incorporated a number of molars in pieces of custom-made jewelry, and the other day embodied a piece of meteorite in a brooch for a customer who claimed to have taken it from the Museum of Natural History.'

Surrealism had proselytized over allowing the subconscious free play and advocated automatism in work, a form of creative spontaneity that yielded creative effects almost by accident. Artists like Max Ernst created images using automatic drawing where the pen was allowed to doodle randomly across the paper allowing forms to emerge with no conscious thought, and Sam Kramer found a similar source of inspiration when he accidentally spilled metal when trying to formulate a new casting technique. He began to imagine how 'silver and gold could be blasted by flame until it ran almost fluid then controlled, built-upon and fused again until it resulted in small sculptures with the texture and all the flame-like movement of this kind of primal ordeal by fire.' He said: 'Personally, I am preoccupied with the emotional context of art. Jewelry, I feel, should express these same emotional conditions, sometimes subtly and sometimes with powerful impact and often in ways that are difficult to say. Pieces should make the observer feel and think.'

Alexander Calder

American-born artist Alexander Calder (1898–1976) is known for his abstract mobiles and stabiles in black-and-red painted steel, a form of kinetic sculpture that is regarded as one of the high points of American Modernism. He was also an accomplished jeweler and his designs play with the same formal qualities. Each Calder piece is handcrafted, hammered on an anvil out of metals such as brass, silver and gold—copper had been a favorite since 1906 when he fashioned necklaces for his sister's dolls out of copper telephone wire that he had found discarded in the streets. He incorporated found objects such as driftwood, beach glass and pieces of broken pottery into his work, linking him with Surrealist experimentation. The spiral was one of Calder's favorite forms—for him it was a symbol of fertility well suited to the production of the gold spiral wedding ring, which he gave to his wife Louisa.

LEFT Simone de Beauvoir, French writer and pioneer of feminism, wearing a brooch designed by the artist Alexander Calder. Women with such intellectual credentials ignored flash jewelry in favor of that with arty appeal.

BELOW A tribal-inspired bracelet by Alexander Calder hammered out of silver in the shape of a spiral, an elemental symbol that recurs in his work.

Margaret de Patta

Metalsmith Margaret De Patta (1903–64) was trained by European émigré and Bauhaus visionary László Moholy-Nagy at the School of Art and Design in Chicago in the early 1940s. A pioneer of abstraction in fine art and design, Moholy-Nagy's Constructivist influence can be seen in Patta's Modernist shapes made up of interlocking planes and dynamic angles. In her best work the stone and the structure work as one, helped by her working relationship with cutter Francis J Sperisen, a self-taught faceter. Patta and Sperison understood the dynamic light effects that could be achieved when a stone was cut or 'opti-cut' in a certain way and Patta made balsa-wood models of the settings for the gems so both could work out the optical potential. A transparency or distortion of tone was sought, rather than a brilliant sparkle, and stones such as amethyst, tourmaline and smoky quartz were chosen to create diffused effects, working in tandem with the chased surface of the metal setting beneath. As Patta put it:

I find work problems as set for myself fall into these main directions: space articulation, movement to a purpose, visual explorations with transparencies, reflective surfaces, negative positive relationships, structures and new materials. A single piece may incorporate one or many of these ideas. Problems common to sculpture and architecture are inherent in jewelry design, i.e. space, form, tension, organic structure, scale, texture, interpenetration, superimposition and economy of means— each necessary element playing its role in a unified entity.

CLOCKWISE FROM RIGHT A simple silver incised ring from 1946; a ring from 1947 is an exercise in geometry, with the transparency of the tourmaline in quartz highlighting the simplicity of it setting; a 1939 bio-morphic brooch in silver; a brooch in sterling silver, moss agate, quartz crystal and black onyx showing the influence of Russian Constructivism in its combination of dynamic geometric elements; a yellow gold, topaz and peridot pin from 1960, playing with simple balancing elements.

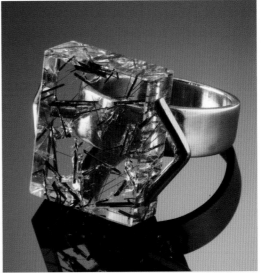

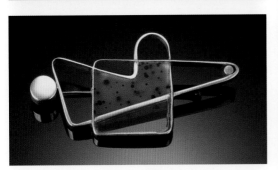

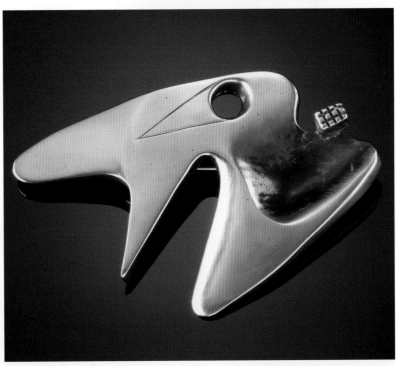

▼ Metal and wood

The war led to shortages of precious materials, so designers looked elsewhere for inspiration. This Italian necklace and brooch have been fashioned from a combination of metal and wood, 1942–5. Italian designers, such as Salvatore Ferragamo, led the way in this type of fashion experimentation.

Surrealism

One of the key Surrealist themes, natural forms were explored because of their symbolism and structural beauty. Along with Dalí, Verdura and Schiaparelli, there were biomorphic shapes from Calder, Kramer and de Patta.

▲ Jelly Belly

A design for a swan pin with a baroque pearl by Fulco di Verdura circa 1940. This is a deluxe example of the popular Jelly Belly style that is associated with Alfred Philippe at Trifari. Jelly Bellies were manufactured in myriad of figurative forms with Lucite 'bellies' set into silver- or gold-plated settings.

▼ Rhinestones

Rhinestones, a faceted stone made of glass to imitate diamonds, featured heavily in 1940s jewelry, particularly those made in Providence, Rhode Island—the center of American costume jewelry production. The cheapness of this artificial gem meant that women could copy the razzle-dazzle they saw in the cinema.

Key looks
of the decade
1940s

Patriotic pins

Flags, stars, military motifs, souvenir and sweetheart themes in the popular red, white and blue all found their way into 1940s jewelry, especially those crafted with Bakelite, metalwork or enameling.

▶ Sterling silver

As a result of the lack of precious materials during the war, sterling silver increased in popularity as it was one of the few precious materials allowed for use in costume jewelry. A high-grade alloy, sterling silver contains a minimum of 92.5 percent silver and 7.5 percent of another metal, usually copper.

▲ Floral motifs

The geometry of Art Deco, which had dominated jewelry production in the inter-war years, was taken over by stylized floral motifs in the 1940s. A neo-Victorian nostalgia was unleashed by the threat of war, and women who were operating under rigorous conditions sought a dreamy romance in their jewelry with added rhinestone glitz.

▲ Vermeil

Derived from the French word for 'veneer,' vermeil is also known as silver gilt. The process involves coating sterling silver with a thin gold plating by electrolysis to give it the impression of being solid gold. This clip brooch is vermeil with semiprecious stones fretwork and snake-link hangings.

▲ Fine jewelry

Fine jewelry was as elaborate as costume jewelry; sometimes the two were difficult to tell apart. Firms like Hobé even used real gems among artificial ones in their work. Here, actress Meg Mundy Is wearing a set of cabochon emeralds and diamonds.

1950s:
Mid-Century Sparkle

After years of war, the doors of Paris were open at last; couture houses were in full swing again and women, hungering after new looks, waited with breathless anticipation to see where style would go next. They didn't have to wait too long—in 1947 the world woke up to a fashion revolution. In couturier Christian Dior's Paris atelier an enraptured audience was introduced to a new grown-up glamour: Dior's Corolle line, so-called because he wanted women to appear like the corolla (petals) of a flower. Dior gave his clients clothes that made their bodies emerge as if from a sea of silk and satin petals; tailoring was tight, waists waspie and the look was decadently deluxe. After years of scrimping and saving, making do and mending, women welcomed the retrospective romanticism of Dior's New Look, as it was dubbed by fashion magazine *Harper's Bazaar*, with open arms.

Yellow gold was still popular, this time with a textured surface and set with gems in color combinations of turquoise and coral or amethyst and pearl that deliberately quoted the seasonal palettes of the inventive French couturiers—although diamonds were still women's stone of choice. In fact, pearls enjoyed something of a renaissance, their ladylike appeal, when worn by the patrician Grace Kelly, given a modern kick in new shades of champagne, coffee and mink.

Modernism kept running alongside all this frippery; this time the influence was from Scandinavia, whose designers introduced a soft, organic version, seen to its best expression in the designs of silversmith Georg Jensen. Abstract forms associated with what was known as the 'Atomic Age' ran rampant in textile design, interiors and jewelry, providing a fresh source of inspiration in the post-war world. Starbursts, biomorphic shapes and molecular structures were rendered in diamonds by the most prestigious firms, or in copper and ceramics on the high street.

French Figurative Jewelry

The frivolous and whimsical figurative designs studded with sparkling diamanté and vibrantly colored cabochons that had been popular during the war years remained so in this decade, but with a French twist. La couture had led to the resurgence of interest in all things Parisian and, for many, France was the home of good taste. Any symbol of French-ness was popular, however much a cultural cliché, and Eiffel Towers abounded with primped and beribboned poodles cast in pot metal and twinkling with diamanté. Women's fashion was cut to show off such amusing jewels: bracelet or three-quarter sleeves displayed the wrists to full effect and called for a bracelet full of charms; at night a plunging décolleté was a perfect backdrop for an extravagant bib necklace. The French jewelry firm Cartier introduced the first of their 'great cat' jewels at this time, designed by Jeanne Toussaint and Peter Lemarchand. Their gold, sapphire and diamond panthers were a huge success and many of the original designs are still being produced today.

The Cocktail Ring

In America Hollywood still reigned, and its flamboyant inhabitants not only wore the astonishing cocktail creations of American costume jewelers, such as Stanley Hagler, but also starred in their lucrative advertising campaigns. Joan Crawford was more than happy to pose for Miriam Haskell and Lana Turner advertised Napier's wares. Doris Day was one of a hundred stars who gave ardent fans style tips. In 1953 she said, 'For an after-dark date, a pair of pearl stud earrings and matching choker is the perfect combination. A set of diamond earrings will make you feel like a million dollars—fake or not!' and she told her audience: 'You don't have to be rich to be chic!'

The vocabulary of cocktail jewelry was extended with the cocktail ring, which reached huge proportions in this decade—veritable knuckledusters in heavy gold-tone metal were set with a myriad of dazzling faux gems. The glove was an important accessory; in fact, no respectable woman would consider leaving home without wearing a pair and the elbow-length evening glove discretely drew the eyes up to a pair of creamy shoulders and swan-like neck. It became *de rigueur* to wear a flashy ring on the finger over, as opposed to under, the glove, as memorably demonstrated by Marilyn Monroe in the sassy musical number 'Diamonds are a Girl's Best Friend' in the film *Gentlemen Prefer Blondes* (1953).

Flowering Jewels, Glittering Shoe

- First, a gold brooch; an open flower, its dark centre a cabochon sapphire; Cartier.
- The stem of the flowerpiece, a serpentine gold chain. This is from Cartier, too.
- The brooch is a shining rose in bud, gold glowing with rubies. From Benson.
- Next, a brooch like a vase of flowers: gold sparked with precious stones; Boucheron.
- The bracelet is gold mesh, blazing with topaz; Garrard, Crown Jewellers.
- Gold and coral flower brooch with diamonds winking at the cefitre; Cartier.
- A diamond, gold and ruby spray; Garrard.
- The shoe: flower-printed gold leather with a new aluminium heel, spiky but not brittle. Bally of Switzerland; 7 gns., at Saxone, 297 Oxford St.
- On the toe, a dangling chain mail bracelet with diamond collets; Cartier. And a rose brooch in two colours of gold, yellow and red; Benson.
- Pendent over the heel, a gold and diamond brooch clustered with coral; Cartier.
- On the thumb: carnelian and diamond flower brooch, and a white crystal pansy with sapphire heart, gold leaves, diamond and platinum stem. Both Garrard, Crown Jewellers.
- First finger: gold flower ring set with diamonds, rubies, sapphires; Benson.
- Middle finger: gold, ruby and diamond ring; Garrard.
- Third finger: matt polished signet ring aflame with a glittering band of rubies; Cartier.
- Little finger: a gold trellis ring brilliantly spangled with diamonds; Cartier.
- The bracelets: gold laced with diamonds and pink tourmalines; Boucheron. The glistening handcuff, two shades of gold banded with rubies, from Garrard. The plaited gold bracelet with rubies and sapphires in the interstices, from Benson.
- The colour on the jewel-bright finger tips: Rose d'Alger Nail Varnish by Lancôme.

PHOTOGRAPHS BY JOHN ADRIAAN

RIGHT Pearls made a comeback in the 1950s, thanks in part to its appearance of the necks of sophisticated fashionistas Grace Kelly, Audrey Hepburn and Jackie Kennedy. This seven-strand pearl necklace of 1959 is the height of luxury, an opulence intensified by the diamond and turquoise earrings and ring.

Jean Schlumberger and Tiffany's

Alsace-born Schlumberger (1907–87) worked with Elsa Schiaparelli in the 1930s designing whimsical buttons and Rococo-themed jewelry, including the popular cupid-and-pearl motif, before joining Tiffany & Co. in 1956. Here the designer had his own salon on the mezzanine, reached by a private elevator, where he created the most fantastical designs that breathed life into the Dalí-esque motifs of Surrealism. His naturalistic designs of complex jewel-encrusted leaves, shells, tropical plants and marine life were modeled with incredible dexterity and worn by the Duchess of Windsor, Elizabeth Taylor and Jackie Kennedy. Millicent Rogers, the Standard Oil heiress, sported a Schlumberger brooch designed for her in 1951 that took the form of a string bean plant, complete with jade beans and leaves studded with demantoid garnets.

As the designer said, 'I saw nature and I saw verve' and Schlumberger's flowers are caught just at the moment of blossoming, their movement seeming just momentarily arrested, an otherworldly quality that can be seen in the best work of Dalí. Butterflies and bees with wings of diamonds, bodies segmented and studded with the most precious of stones, were caught mid-flight or casually alighting to crawl along the side of a ring or necklace.' As he put it, 'I try to make everything look as if it were growing, uneven, at random, organic, in motion.' Business partner Nicholas Bongard described how Schlumberger's ideas were pulled quite literally from the sea when they holidayed in Mexico, 'We were out in a boat and he reached out in shallow water and pulled out a shell with algae attached to it—and by the next morning I saw the drawing he had done in the studio.' The resulting bracelet took the form of a diamond-encrusted shell amid emerald algae in a sapphire sea. Another marine creature, a jellyfish, had a body set with a domed cluster of cabochon moonstones, accents of circular-cut diamonds and long flexible polished gold tentacles set with baguette-cut sapphires. In 1957 Schlumberger set the fabled Tiffany diamond, the largest and finest canary diamond in the world, in a necklace that surrounded the gem with swirling diamond-studded ribbons.

TOP A 1950s sapphire, diamond and 18-karat gold flowerhead clip brooch by Jean Schlumberger, mounted in platinum and gold. The cinquefoil design is made up of petals with pavé-set diamonds, oval-cut sapphires and raised, stylized pinecone finials.

BOTTOM A necklace by Schlumberger for Tiffany, circa 1950, in the form of an intricately worked gold rope fringe set with rubies and brilliant-cut diamonds. This was spectacular jewelry for the fabulously rich.

RIGHT In 1952 Schlumberger created this fantasy floral pin, displaying his love of all things naturalistic. Nature is made the height of luxury in much of his 1950s work. With curved clip earrings by Trifari.

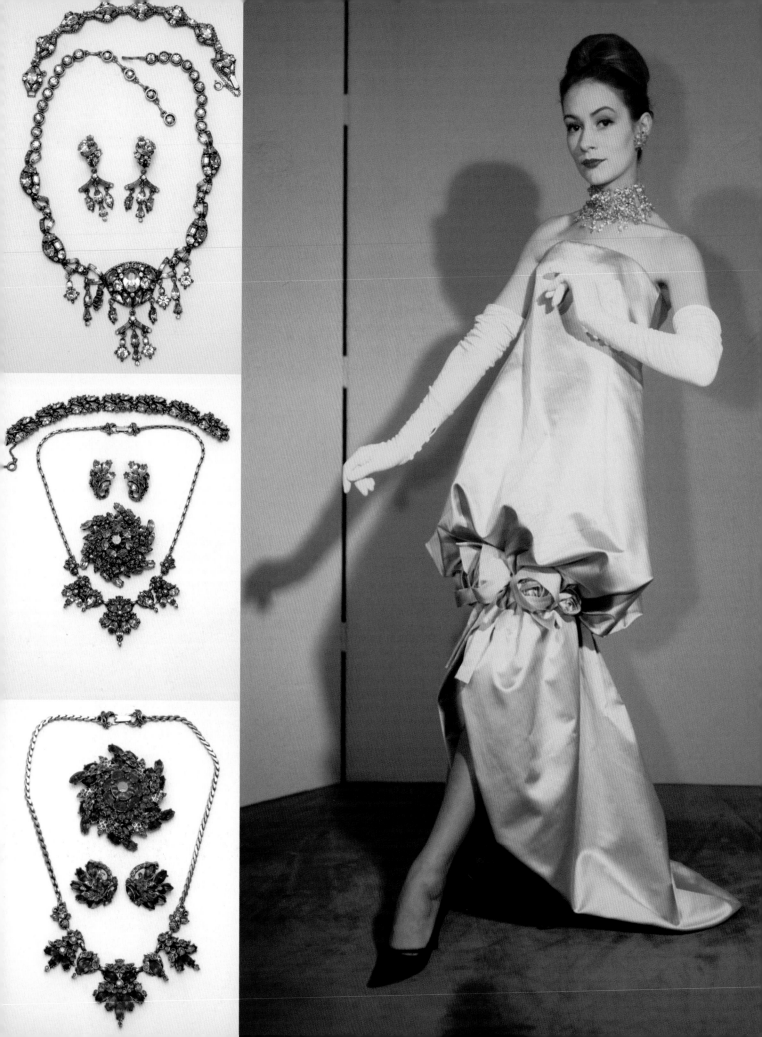

Opulent Nostalgia: The Influence of Christian Dior

Christian Dior's New Look emphasized glamour, grooming and coordinated accessorizing. His head-to-toe outfits changed every season and needed Dior jewelry to match. Canny costume jewelers, realizing that a seasonal change in jewelry as well as gowns meant increased revenue, followed his example —some even sending designers to the Paris shows to get inspiration from the couturier's latest looks. The most prestigious Dior pieces were commissioned from leading lights of the day, including Henry Schreiner, Mitchell Maer, Coppola e Toppo, Sam Kramer, Robert Goosens and Josette Gripoix, and were worn by the world's wealthiest women. Dior jewelry was opulent, nostalgic and Neo-Victorian in tone, like his New Look clothes—Dior had reintroduced the huge crinoline, for example, in both day- and eveningwear, and when the full skirts were first shown they were so voluminous they brushed the audience's cheeks.

The floral motifs of nineteenth-century jewelry were made modern by rendering them on a larger scale with obviously faux stones. The couturier's jewelry, over which he kept strict quality control, managed to successfully tread the tightrope between sophisticated glamour and high-powered glitz with the use of large petal-shaped rhinestones, prong-set into hand-soldered settings in regal combinations of red, black and gold. Mitchell Maer was licensed to produce jewelry for the House of Dior from 1952 until 1956 and created the much sought-after unicorn brooches that continued this monarchic feel. Soon it was impossible to keep up with the demand for Dior jewels in-house, so the atelier licensed others to produce jewelry using the Dior name, such as the German company Henkel & Grosse, who manufactured jewelry for Dior from 1955.

Dior's Neo-Victorian look was such a hit that 1950s firms such as Florenza, Art (aka Mode Art) and Judy Lee began producing their own variations of the couturier's themes. Hollycraft, a subsidiary of the New York company Hollywood Jewelry that was founded in 1938 by Joseph Chorbajian, is a case in point. The Hollycraft range started production in 1948, reacting rapidly to Dior's New Look collection that had launched the year before. Their range of Victorian Revival jewelry used many nineteenth-century motifs such as floral clusters, garlands and swags made of gold and silver-tone pot metal, which was then set with a rainbow of rhinestones. The pastel-colored parures struck a chord with the public and were a huge success.

BELOW LEFT In the 1950s Dior commissioned manufacturers of high quality costume jewelry to produce ranges for his prestigious atelier. Kramer was one such company, this beautiful rhinestone brooch with safety chain was created by the firm in the mid 1950s.

BELOW RIGHT A Kramer brooch designed for Dior in the 1950s. The rounded triangular shape is formed by half circles of dark plum colored, prong-set chatons, joined with ruby red baguette circles to form an internal triangle.

OPPOSITE FAR LEFT Three Victorian Revival parures from New York firm Hollycraft, a subsidiary of Hollywood Jewelry. Their Dior-inspired pieces of the 1950s were an instant hit and are highly collectable today.

OPPOSITE LEFT An outfit from the autumn/winter 1959–60 Dior show by head designer at the time Yves Saint Laurent, who had taken over after the death of Christian Dior. The Edwardian-inspired hobbled skirts featured in the collection caused both furor and wild applause, but were never popular. This example in lustrous satin is accessorized with matching jewelry in peridot green and white rhinestones.

The Triple Row of Pearls

Dior's regality chimed with reality in the 1950s as the popular young Princess Elizabeth was crowned Queen of England following the untimely death of her father in 1953. In the lead-up to the ceremony, newspapers regularly printed Elizabeth's first introduction to the world: the famous photograph of Queen Elizabeth the Queen Mother holding her firstborn child, the future Queen, while wearing a triple row of pearls.

Her necklace was significant; royalty and pearls have almost always been inextricably linked, acting as a visual indicator of authority for any prominent member of a dynastic family since the reigns of Henry VIII and his daughter Elizabeth I, and who can forget Lady Diana Spencer in a piecrust-collared blouse and a single strand of pearls trying to dodge photographers before the royal engagement was announced in 1981? The iconic Armada Portrait of Elizabeth I, displaying the monarch as a figure of splendor and power covered in pearls, literally from her head to her knees, reinforced the pearl's regal status as the epitome of style and taste.

In 1969 Richard Burton bought one of the world's largest black pearls, La Peregrina, which originally belonged to King Philip II of Spain, for the most infamous member of Hollywood's 'royal family,' his wife Elizabeth Taylor. Soon after he presented it to her, she lost it. She resonantly describes her panic in her book, *My Love Affair with Diamonds*:

> *I went out and sort of started humming 'lalala,' and I was walking back and forth in my bare feet, seeing if I would find anything in the carpet. I was trying to be composed and look as if I had a purpose because inside I was practically heaving I was so upset. I looked over and saw the white Pekingese…and I saw one chewing on a bone. And I did the longest, slowest double-take in my head. I just casually opened the puppy's mouth and inside his mouth was the most perfect pearl in the world. It was—thank God—not scratched. I did finally tell Richard. But I had to wait at least a week!*

The pure white lustre and flawless quality of the pearl embodied class—as contrasted to the vulgarity of the rather more showy diamond—and any fashion icon who wanted to inject a little regal status into her image chose a pearl necklace. America's First Lady and twentieth-century fashion icon Jackie Kennedy wore the classic triple row of pearls on many state visits, including those to Japan, Greece and most famously, an official trip to India in 1962. The iconic photograph of Jackie in Udaipur, India, published in *Life* magazine shows her in a fitted, bow-fronted apricot silk dress by Oleg Cassini, white gloves and the ubiquitous pearl necklace. Another well-known image from the White House shows her son John on her knee, playfully pulling the necklace over his mother's face.

Jackie made pearls fashionable again, and so compelling is her continuing allure that at the sale of her jewels after her death in 1996, the pearls were sold for $211,500. This was an incredible figure considering they were fake, purchased in the 1950s from department store Bergdorf Goodman for around $35. The winning bidder was the company Franklin Mint, who analyzed the 139 European faux-glass pearls and molded exact reproductions, giving them 17 coats of lacquer like the originals. The company sold over 130,000 copies of the pearls, grossing $26 million.

BELOW LEFT Jackie Kennedy wearing a classic triple row of pearls to accessorize her apricot silk dress, by Oleg Cassini, on an official trip to India in 1962.

BELOW Elizabeth Taylor's La Peregrina pearl, weighing in at a hefty 203.84 grams, was originally discovered in 1513 in the Gulf of Panama by a slave who was set free after bringing it to the Spanish court.

OPPOSITE A Christian Dior ensemble in 1956, accessorized by the ubiquitous pearls. Their regal quality perfectly suited the sophisticated glamour of French couture, where fashionable styles were designed for soignée women of undisputed elegance.

Swarovski Crystals

In 1955, Manfred Swarovski and Christian Dior worked in collaboration to create a new version of the popular rhinestone—the iridescent aurora borealis stone. This breakthrough gem had a polychrome metal coating that gave a high shine and a kaleidoscopic visual effect, which can be compared to the action of petrol on water. It was just the push the Tyrolean company needed after being unable to supply jewelers with their high-quality crystal during the long years of the war.

Swarovski, a name now known globally as a manufacturer of crystal products, grew out of a small family business, a Bohemian glass foundry that was first established in the early nineteenth century. Bohemia was the center of the European glass industry with a reputation for creating glass that was both high quality and inexpensive, compared to Murano glass in Italy.

The original founder's son, Daniel Swarovski (1862–1956), was a born innovator, fascinated with glass in all its forms, and he introduced many techniques still used today to give the requisite sparkle. Swarovski's real breakthrough came in 1892 when he developed a way of precisely cutting and multifaceting glass crystals by machine, producing a prismatic chaton that sparkled with the intensity of a diamond. He patented his prototype machine before setting up his own company in 1895 in Wattens in the Austrian Alps, helped by financiers Frank Weis and Armand Kosman. The choice of location was key: the new glass-cutting process depended on huge amounts of power and the factory was adjacent to a hydro-electricity plant that provided an efficient source of cheap electricity.

By the early twentieth century, Daniel's sons, Alfred, Friedrich and Wilhelm, streamlined the glass-production process so that by 1913 it was practically fault-free and their crystals gained the reputation of being the finest in the world. In the 1920s, couturiers Coco Chanel and Elsa Schiaparelli used their glass gems, but it was Christian Dior who really understood the fashion potential of the Swarovski stone by inventing and marketing the aurora borealis. Schiaparelli was one of many jewelry designers who fell in love with this fantasy stone and used it over and over after she moved to America, in both abstract and floral designs that achieved their effect through flashing borealis stones in dramatic color combinations such as teal green and dark aubergine or iridescent navy blue matched with a dark ruby red.

In the 1970s, Swarovski brought out the mouse, the first of their popular line of crystal and reputedly created after one employee was abstractedly playing around with the individual parts that made up their crystal chandeliers. It was also in this decade that the company created their most fabulously convincing fake diamond, the cubic zirconia, which still dominates today's costume jewelry production. The company also expanded and started production of their own line of costume jewelry in Providence, Rhode Island, rather than producing crystals for others to set. Glass gems that created incredible light effects were used, such as the Alexandrite back-faceted crystal stone and the blue Pagoda crystal, which had three different shades of blue that shimmered when the wearer moved.

LEFT TOP A gold-tone Napier floral cuff from 1955, set with the new Swarovski aurora borealis stone with a polychrome metal coating to give it both a high shine and prismatic color effects.

LEFT CENTER A demi-parure of brooch and earrings by Miriam Haskell from the 1950s. The brooch uses transparent Lucite to give a 'light as air' feel to the piece, which is surmounted with glass and roses montees (crystal beads).

LEFT BOTTOM A stunning, angel-shaped brooch and matching earrings from Canadian designer Gustave Sherman. They date from the mid 1950s and use round and marquise-cut Swarovski aurora borealis crystals. Sherman manufactured costume jewelry from 1947 to 1981.

RIGHT Model Suzy Parker wearing a faux moonstone necklace and earrings by Miriam Haskell, whose trademark delicate floral style has been put to one side in favor of a couture-inspired, 1950s opulence.

The Etiquette of Jewelry

Good grooming was a prerequisite of post-war women, who were exhorted to 'hold their beauty' for their man and provide him with a vision of loveliness when he returned from work. In this brave new world women were compelled through popular culture to look fabulous for every occasion, both inside the home and out. Rules governed every aspect of their fashionable appearance and books abounded with hints and tips on how to look well turned-out. Anxious to avoid any sartorial *faux pas*, the housewife learned the rules of accessorizing with jewelry through tomes such as George Henschel's *The Well-Dressed Woman*, published in 1951, a popular manual that taught women how to dress 'correctly.' The author wrote, 'There are two kinds of jewelry: artificial, or 'costume' jewelry, which can be made with anything that is decorative; and real, which consists of precious or semiprecious stones set in gold, silver, platinum or, if we are very rich and very modern, palladian. Both kinds can be lovely, but should not be worn together.' His rules ran:

- Do not over-bedeck yourself when wearing ordinary, country or casual clothes.
- Rings draw attention to the hands and fingers; when you wear them, hands and nails must be well-groomed.
- You should never wear more than one ring on any finger except your wedding-ring one.
- Long pendant or drop earrings are only for evening or very formal wear; for everyday, small clip or stud ones are best.
- It is always more effective to wear one good or striking piece of jewelry than to decorate oneself like a Christmas tree.

RIGHT A woman of the 1950s was supposed to look at her absolute best from day to night, with an emphasis on good grooming practices. Jewelry had etiquette all of its own—the correct earring for daywear was the clip, dangling earrings by day would have constituted a sartorial faux pas.

The Chandelier Earring

The dangling chandelier earring was a case in point—one false move and they could make you look really quite cheap. With shorter hair fashions in the 1950s, the focus was on the earlobe and for daywear, clip and screwback earrings sat close to the ear. By night it was a different story—dangle, dangle all the way as the chandelier earring trickled down from Hollywood to the rest of the world. The chandelier style was derived from India and the Middle East where large tiered earrings in gold had for centuries been a mark of wealth and status. It crossed over into Western fashion in the eighteenth century with the fad for the pendeloque earring. The 1950s version was far more flashy and called 'chandelier' because the outsize stones used in the long drop of the earring resembled those hanging in the tiers of a chandelier. The longer the drop, and some literally brushed the shoulders, the heavier the earring, so the style called for faux gems and lighter metal settings.

By the end of the decade, the chandelier earring was being worn by movie stars who had a reputation for being rather risqué, charismatic, knowing women, famed as much for their tempestuous affairs in real life as on screen. Marilyn Monroe, Ava Gardner, Jayne Mansfield and Elizabeth Taylor transgressed the codes of respectable domestic femininity and by holding themselves up for inspection on the silver screen, they made it plain to many women that glamour was not necessarily to be found in playing at being domestic. This was a new identity for women: loud, sexy and the feminine embodiment of va-va-voom.

LEFT The chandelier earring became a focal point of fashion, with the universally adopted short hairstyles of the 1950s. It had been a mark of social status, imported from India and the Middle East in the eighteenth century, but in this decade chandelier danglers were produced by most costume jewelry manufacturers in a range to suit all pockets.

The Charm Bracelet

The concept of a magical amulet or charm attached to a bracelet is an ancient one; in Polynesian culture bracelets were hung with cowrie shells and Egyptians —the symbols were attached to ward off malevolent spirits and give the gods of the underworld clues to understanding the owner's status. In more modern times, the pieces on the Monopoly board were reputedly inspired by the charms that had been on the inventor Charles Darrow's wife's bracelet, including a top hat, flat iron and battleship.

The charm bracelet, as we know it, was first worn in the late nineteenth century by Queen Victoria who, after the death of her beloved Prince Albert, began wearing a gold chain with miniature lockets that opened to display portraits of her family. Victoria's charm bracelet was an intensely personal item of jewelry, with each charm having some emotional significance rather than being a more general folkloric talisman of good luck.

In the late 1940s and early 1950s soldiers returning from the war in Europe brought trinkets for their sweethearts, such as old coins and other small souvenirs that were drilled and attached to a chain, thus starting a vogue for this ancient jewelry form. Jewelers recognized a new trend and began especially creating charms such as ballet shoes and horses to appeal to little girls who, it was hoped, would embark on creating their own history for a wrist. Teenage bobby-soxers loved charm bracelets and there were thousands to choose from—platinum or high-karat gold for the rich, pot metal for those with less income—and they were churned out in response to the latest fads: a Liberace charm bracelet complete with piano and candelabra for his many fans; the New York World's Fair; the first Sputnik; an Elvis bracelet first produced in 1956 which had charms of a guitar, a broken heart signifying his hit record 'Heartbreak Hotel' and a locket containing his photograph. Older women soon got in on the act, following charm-enthusiast Lucille Ball who wore one on her popular TV show *I Love Lucy*, and celebrity milliner Lilly Daché. One of the most prominent wearers was Mamie Eisenhower, who had a collection including one with 21 charms that depicted important milestones in her husband's career, which was specially made by a Fifth Avenue jeweler.

By the 1950s charm bracelets had become a ritual of American girlhood with the gold or silver chain commemorating her entry into the teenage years and charms added at significant moments throughout her life, such as the sixteenth birthday, high-school graduation, her wedding and the birth of any children. Honeymoon destinations were there—even sand from a romantic encounter on a beach could be trapped in a vial and hung from the chain. Perhaps because of the domesticated femininity displayed in such gendered

charms the bracelets fell from favor as women began questioning stereotypes at the start of the feminist movement. The charm bracelet also seemed out of place with the countercultural hippie movement. With the changing times, many were hidden away at the bottom of a drawer or even melted down, relics of a traditional femininity that lots of women were trying to overthrow.

More recently this genre of jewelry has enjoyed a renaissance, thanks to the obsession with all things retro. Chat-show host Oprah Winfrey is a collector of charms, Paris Hilton designs bracelets and Jennifer Aniston wears them on her wrist. Actress Keira Knightley has one for its original talismanic function, saying: 'I am a great believer in luck. I have a lucky charm bracelet. It is my grandfather's watch chain with my grandmother's charms, plus various additions. My agent added a sword and a boat at the start of *Pirates of the Carribean*, for example.' Fashion genius Miuccia Prada has even created an entirely new type—the handbag charm to be clipped onto a status, logoed bag, its metallic jangling drawing attention to the very latest *sac du jour*.

Scandinavian Modernism

The 1950s was not only the decade of glitz; it had a polar opposite in a cool Scandinavian aesthetic that mounted a veritable Viking invasion into all areas of design, including jewelry. Silver was the metal of choice as Norway, Finland, Sweden and Denmark had a centuries-old tradition of silversmithing, plus silver was malleable and thus easily fashioned into the striking angles and abstracted molecular shapes that seemed wholly suited to the post-nuclear age. There were political principles involved too; in a humanitarian environment, silver was demonstrably cheaper and more democratic than other precious metals.

The Scandinavian Modern design aesthetic was the legacy of the German Bauhaus School but with a brand-new spin. Designers such as Hans Hansen, Nanna Ditzel and Bent Gabrielsen ignored the machine-age excesses and overt glamour of Art Deco that Bauhaus had inadvertently spawned in jewelry design in favor of a more pure, quieter style of absolute simplicity. Many shapes were amoebic, boomerang or palette and had much in common with the 'Contemporary' style wowing Britain at the Festival of Britain (a huge exhibition on the South Bank in London) in 1951. This aesthetic was seen to its most convincing effect in the furniture and textiles of Robin and Lucienne Day.

But there were deeper principles at work in Scandinavian jewelry too, in particular the cultural idea that good design provided comfort in countries that suffered long, dark winters before the first shoots of summer. Any object had to be *bruskunst*, meaning 'useful art'—to provide some kind of emotional and visual enrichment for daily life. The most humble of domestic objects were to be treated in the same way as the noblest, existing as more than just a mere symbol of wealth and social status. The way to creating *bruskunst* was, in principle, the same as the Bauhaus philosophy of good design—form should follow function and there must be honesty and simplicity in any object of design. The key difference was in the mode of production. Bauhaus designers believed in industrial production for the masses, Scandinavian designers thought design should emanate from smaller-scale specialist workshops where man had mastery over machine. In particular, Georg Jensen's remarkable work influenced a new generation of young jewelry designers in the 1950s and Norse-mania led to rival firms from outside Oslo or Helskinki producing their own faux Scandinavian lines, such as Danecraft of Rhode Island, Viking Craft of New York and William Spratling's work for Taxco in Mexico.

Georg Jensen

A long-running and globally successful Danish firm, Jensen was originally Arts and Crafts in character under the auspices of silversmith and founder Georg Jensen (1866–1935), who was renowned for his high-quality handcrafted silver jewelry in which an expert understanding of high-relief modeling belied his original training as a sculptor. Silver was given unexpected warmth with the inclusion of unusual semiprecious stones such as opal, coral and malachite, which became a signature stone in Scandinavian Modern jewelry of the 1950s.

Henning Koppel (1918–81) was another sculptor-turned-jeweler who trained at the Royal Danish Academy of Arts and later at the Academie Ranson in Paris. Koppel began work for the Jensen company in 1945 and in the same year created his first range of silver jewelry. The designs are a perfect manifestation of Scandinavian Modern style, with silver necklaces and bracelets comprized of linked amoebic or vertebrae–like shapes. The pieces were modeled first in clay to achieve soft, organic lines that were inspired by the biomorphic art of Surrealist Jean Arp and the attenuated sculptures of Constantin Brâncusi.

ABOVE Arno Malinowski (1899–1976) was a silver designer and sculptor who worked for Jensen from 1936–44 and 1949–65, creating jewelry in the Scandinavian Modern style, including this 1940s bracelet.

LEFT TOP Henning Koppel designed many of Jensen's most abstract, and most collectible, jewelry designs in the 1950s and 1960s. The Splash necklace in sterling silver was designed in 1947 and has remained in production ever since.

LEFT BOTTOM Sterling silver necklace designed by Malinowski for Jensen from the 1940s. Many of his designs had figurative elements, as well as being examples of pure abstraction like this.

David-Andersen

Gold- and silversmith David Andersen (1843–1901) founded his company in 1876 in Oslo, Norway. After his death in 1901, his son Arthur took over the running of the firm and employed many leading Scandinavian silversmiths to design jewelry. In the 1950s, Harry Sørby and Bjørn Sigurd Østern were designing both biomorphic and figurative work for the company, including silver bird pendants and brooches that took the form of runes and Nordic hammers. The company's work became elegantly minimalist with simple, natural themes, such as leaves fashioned from silver and *basse-taille* enamel. Hallmarks were rarely used on the Andersen jewelry until the 1960s when a D-A designer mark was used with the abbreviation 'inv.,' for inventor, and the initials of the designer.

Torun Bülow-Hübe

Swedish designer Torun Bülow-Hübe (1927–2004), the first woman silversmith to gain an international reputation, came from an artistic family; her mother was a sculptor and her siblings all went on to pursue careers in the arts. Torun studied at the School of Arts, Crafts and Design in Stockholm in 1945 and then traveled to Paris in 1948, where she met the great French masters Pablo Picasso, Georges Braque and Henri Matisse. From 1954, she began showing silver jewelry at the Galerie Saint Germain-des-Prés in a city that was beginning to bloom as a fashionable center once again after years of occupation. Her asymmetric silver-and-agate neck rings and flowing silver-and-quartz pendants were widely copied.

After meeting and marrying Walter Coleman, an established African-American artist, Torun began to immerse herself in underground culture. At the Left Bank jazz clubs they frequented, she met stars such as Billie Holiday, for whom she created special body pieces designed to show off the singer's curves when she performed. In a 1958 exhibition of Torun jewelry, held at the Picasso Museum in Antibes, France, the silversmith showed work that incorporated pebbles from the beach and gained herself another celebrity client: the legendary French film star Brigitte Bardot.

LEFT TOP A sterling silver collar and double pendant with crystal, designed by Torun Bülow-Hübe and stamped with the Swedish hallmark of 1955.

LEFT BOTTOM Torun Bülow-Hübe's uncompromising designs were a clear break with tradition, like this minimalist silver Zeta collar designed in the 1950s.

BELOW In the mid 1950s, Torun Bülow-Hübe began a long working relationship with Georg Jensen, using rock crystal, moonstone and quartz rather than more traditional and valuable stones. This pendant necklace combines silver and quartz.

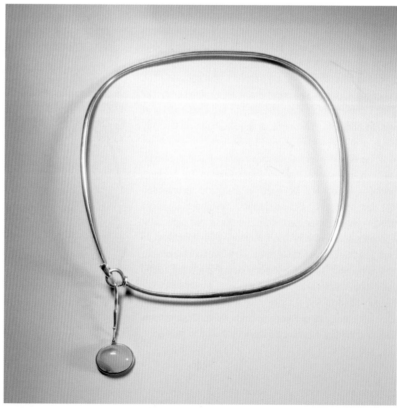

RIGHT Torun Bülow-Hübe was the most internationally celebrated Swedish silversmith of the post war period. The beaches of the Cotes d'Azur inspired this sterling silver, crystal and beach pebble necklace from the 1950s.

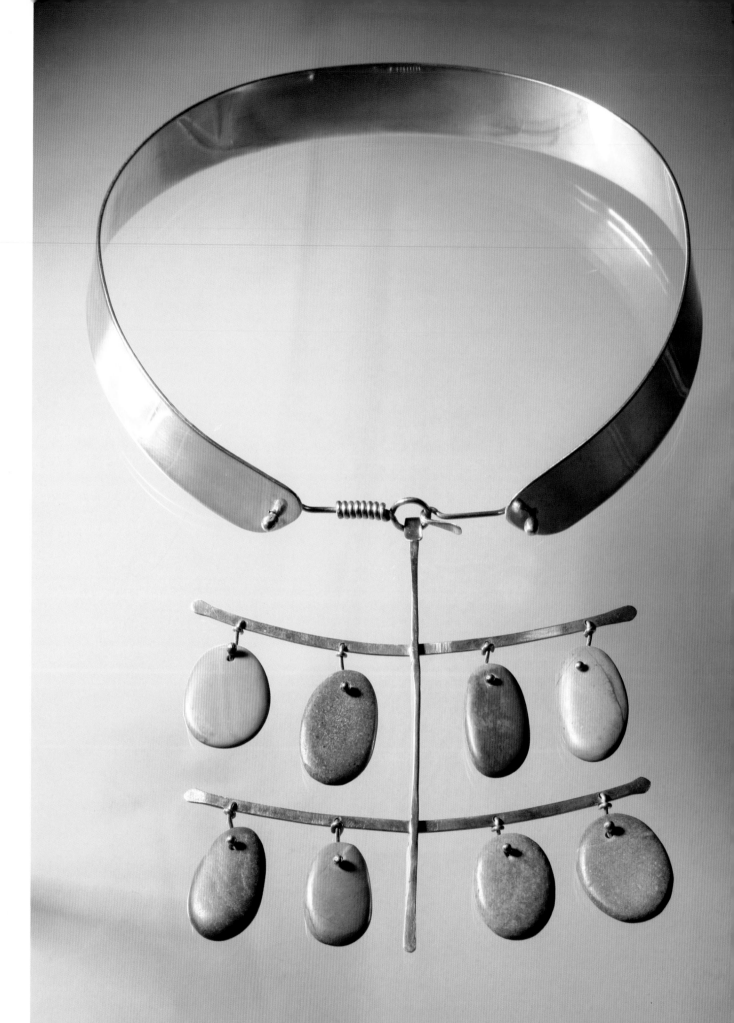

Torun's designs began to be produced by the Georg Jensen company in the mid 1950s. Silver provided sinuous settings for nontraditional semiprecious stones such as moonstone, quartz and rock crystal, pieces that anticipated the bold, futuristic body jewelry of the 1960s. Her workshop in Biot became a mecca for young silversmiths such as Urban Bohlin and Bengt Liljedahl, as well as her favorite jazz musicians until she moved to Indonesia, where she lived until her death.

Torun is perhaps best known for her creation of 1962 —the first stainless-steel bangle watch. Now a design classic, it was made for an exhibition in the Louvre, Paris that had the brief 'An Object You Dislike.' She described the idea behind her contribution:

The relentlessness of time is what I abhor, so I designed a watch with no numbers; it was intended to be an ornament, not a chronometer. At first it only had a seconds hand, but when Georg Jensen began producing the watch in 1967, we added both the hour and minute hands. The bracelet did not completely encircle the wrist, but was left open at the outside so as not to feel oneself a prisoner of time.

Torun also produced a series of innovative rings inspired by African, Egyptian and Oceanic culture, which included designs such as the figure-of-eight, symbolizing 'infinite love,' and the silver spiral that, for her, summed up 'the intense vibration of life.' Designs such as Torun's Button ring and Moebius silver bangle are in still production by Jensen today.

OPPOSITE Torun Bülow-Hübe's most experimental pieces, such as this huge collar of silver strung with beach pebbles, were created in her own workshop in Biot, France.

LEFT Torun Bülow-Hübe's minimalism anticipated developments in jewelry design and her work remained popular in the 1960s. This simple silver and mother-of-pearl ring fitted perfectly with the pared down silhouettes of 1960s fashion.

ABOVE Sterling silver and beach glass collar with matching earrings. Torun Bülow-Hübe's jewelry was worn by bohemian women in the 1950s to mark themselves out from the mainstream with their artsy fashion and Scandinavian-style jewelry.

▼ Florals and natural themes

Nature remained a popular theme for both fine and costume jewelry, but the Scandinavian designers understood the spiritual and elemental qualities of the natural world and presented it in a more abstract way. This Hattie Carnegie leaf and berry brooch is typical of the mainstream floral look of the period.

Chandelier earrings

The decade's shorter hair fashions changed the focus to the earlobe, with long drop earrings becoming fashionable. Oversized shoulder-skimming styles were possible due to lighter settings and faux gemstones.

▲ Beads

The 1950s was a decade of color, after the drab khakis of wartime uniform. Palettes were strong and vibrant, and fashion followed suit. This Miriam Haskell necklace of banana yellow shows how the work of this company adapted to the 1950s zeitgeist.

▶ Textured gold

Yellow gold remained popular, but was given a contemporary twist with the application of a textured surface. This wide, basket-weave, hinged bracelet, 1955, is by Hattie Carnegie, a New York fashion entrepreneur who created her own lines of ready-to-wear and costume jewelry.

▲ Scandinavian Modern

Scandinavian Modern, with its emphasis on natural materials, was a breath of fresh air. Kalevala Koru, the largest manufacturer in Finland, was founded in 1937 and, like other Scandinavian firms, based its design aesthetic on vernacular culture and nature, like this ring from 1959.

Key looks of the decade
1950s

▶ Figurative brooches

The whimsical jewelry that cheered up the drab fashions of the 1940s remained popular and the increase in foreign travel meant that global culture was plundered for motifs. Countries were rendered in clichés—the Eiffel Tower stood for France and a diamanté-encrusted sombrero for Mexico.

▼ Parures

A parure is the name for a suite of jewelry designed to be worn all at the same time such as a necklace, bracelet and earrings. This early 1950s parure by Weiss features sparkling navette and chaton stones. The company was known for floral and figurative designs featuring carefully color-coordinated, Austrian rhinestones.

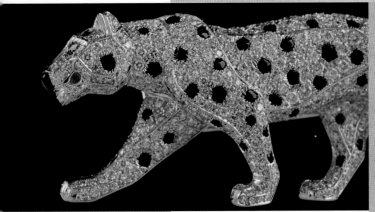

▲ Luxury jewelry

After the impasse of war the prestigious jewelry houses returned to producing incredible work that fitted in with the deluxe couture look, such as this iconic panthère brooch in platinum by Cartier, encrusted with 511 diamonds, 72 onyx spots, and emerald eyes.

▲ Copper jewelry

Renoir of California, founded in 1946 by Jerry Fels, produced copper jewelry until the mid 1960s and the Matisse mark was used on a series of enameled pieces that were produced from the early 1950s. These 1950s Renoir Matisse pieces take the form of autumn leaves accented with red enamel.

◀ Pearls

The 1950s was the era of pearls; natural, cultured or faux, and they appeared on every type of jewelry throughout the decade. Gold-tone pieces accented with huge faux pearls, like this Trifari pin and clip earrings with pearl, were used to accent simple tailored suits by day.

Charm bracelets

By the 1950s, the charm bracelet was a must-have accessory, with a new link to record each rite of passage and interest, from birthdays and anniversaries to hobbies and travel. Today some of these vintage bracelets sell for remarkably high prices at auction.

1960s:
POP Goes the Future

The 1960s was a decade that looked to the future with optimism; culture was harnessing the 'white heat of new technology,' stated the British Prime Minister Harold Wilson, whose prophetic words went on to define the key characteristics of the era. The structured silhouette of 1950s couture and the voluptuous curves of the Hollywood bombshell disappeared in the early part of the decade to be replaced with a new fashionable ideal—the androgynous, pre-adolescent figure, as exemplified by London model Twiggy. Her sporty, futuristic, even anti-maternal image and pared-down geometric clothes made 1950s fashion look too prim, too grown-up—just too plain old.

Fashion was no longer aimed at the privileged elite. Parisian designers lost their hold on the market with the death of Christian Dior in 1957, as the fashionable silhouette took its influence from London and the emerging Mod scene. Excessive grooming and ladylike primness were cast aside in the rush for liberation by postwar baby-boomers who were newly defined as 'teenagers.' Adolescence was infinitely extendable, it seemed, as the young became more financially independent and rejected parental control—it was everything to be young.

Italian style emerged as France's successor, with names such as Gucci, Pucci and Ferragamo signifying youthful cool. In London, the designs of Mary Quant sparked a sartorial revolution and were positioned as the fashion equivalent of the Beatles. Any intimation of adulthood in dress was rejected; hats, gloves and handbags were incongruous in a decade of miniskirts, Sassoon bobs and knee-length boots. Precious jewelry was still being bought, but worn in a more insouciant way and many women bought into the idea that wearing too much high-end jewelry could be ageing.

The bangle became a perfect medium to convey the futuristic motifs of the 1960s. Oversize accessories in saturated color or Space-Age metallic referenced the work of artists such as Frank Stella and Bridget Riley, who provided a fertile seam of inspiration. Images of the Op and Pop artists—stripes, targets and optically challenging black and white —were incorporated into an array of high-street and high-end jewelry. Scandinavian jewelry retained its 'arty' reputation in this decade and designers such as Finnish duo Timo and Pentti Sarpaneva and Björn Weckström sought inspiration from their native landscape using textured bronze, indigenous stones such as quartz and gold nuggets from Lapland. David-Anderson settled back into the Norwegian company's trademark aesthetic of restrained simplicity and stated, 'We view with a measure of scepticism those aspects of design which are considered high fashion and which rely for their effect on the sensational.'

Costume and Crystal

The traditional 'trickle down' effect of ideas moving from haute couture to the street was reversed; youth movements influenced both high fashion and fine jewelry design. Established jewelry houses had to consider the new simplicity and democracy of fashion and Swarovski crystal and plastic beads took over from pearls and diamonds, as seen in the work of brother-and-sister team Lyda Toppo and Bruno Coppola, who were based in Milan. Their huge crystal clustered bibs, collars and bracelets were commissioned by fashion designers such as Valentino and Pucci. Lyda Coppola retired in 1972 and the company discontinued their trademark in 1986.

Brash, bright costume jewelry was, if anything, larger and even more elaborate than in the 1950s. Roger Jean-Pierre at Maison Francis Winter in Paris designed elaborate paste pieces using prong-set crystals and Juliana created their celebrated Easter Egg pins.

The public interest in the Pop, Op and psychedelic art movements was reflected in the popularity of dynamic-colored gems in black metal settings, rather than the more traditional silver or gold, and stones such as turquoise and tourmaline began to be chosen for their beauty rather than their intrinsic worth. Enamelwork enjoyed a huge renaissance because of the clear hues that could be achieved with this technique—Marcel Boucher created a range of jewelry aping Pucci prints and Van Cleef & Arpels' Disney-influenced Winking Cat brooches, first introduced in the 1950s, made cartoon animals a must-have accessory on any self-respecting jet-setter's lapel.

MORE ITALIAN NEWS

CAPUCCI
Romantic revival for hot summer evenings is Capucci's long, young chiffon dress with a look of the teagown.
This one is dark red, caped, wrapped over in front, ruffled all round, and sashed with a butterfly bow.
Models who showed this series of dresses wore evening wigs, Japanese-style, by Filippo of Rome.
The red crystal necklace is from Coppola e Toppo.

DRAWING BY CROSTHWAIT

PAGE 128 In a new decade of optimism, bright saturated color entered design inspired by Pop Art and American abstract painters such as Frank Stella. A model in 1966 wears a tomato-colored linen dress with geometric neckline by B H Wragge and huge clip-on abstract earrings.

TOP A crystal bead collar by Milanese designers Coppola e Toppo accessorizes a chiffon gown by Capucci in 1960. The duo's work first appeared in *Vogue* in 1948 and they worked for many Italian fashion houses.

LEFT A striking multi-strand, red, faceted crystal and baroque pearl necklace by Coppola e Toppo, 1960s. Their intricate beadwork was hand-wired and is among the most elaborate of designer costume jewelry of this decade.

ABOVE A Coppola e Toppo blue crystal bracelet from the 1960s. The solid metal S-shaped base is typical of the duo's work, and provided the foundation for subtly graduated colored beadwork that moves through dark to light blue.

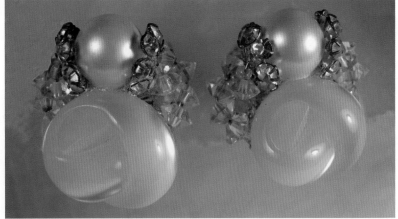

ABOVE The oversized chandelier earring is typical of 1960s jewelry design. This stunning example from 1967 was created by Robert Originals, located in New York, who were renowned for their use of filigree and beaded design. The company had set up in 1942 under the name of Fashioncraft and changed their name in 1960.

RIGHT A pair of Vendome beaded earrings from the 1960s. Vendome costume jewelry enjoyed huge popularity in the this decade, in some ways due to the work of head designer Helen Marion, who used the highest quality rhinestones and faceted crystal beads.

RIGHT An extravagant 1961 parure by Schreiner shows the popular bib necklace shape of the decade in a regal red and glittering rhinestone color combination. Schreiner jewelry was in production from 1939 until the early 1970s and one trademark is the reverse setting of its rhinestones. Never manufactured in vast quantity, its relative scarcity makes it very collectable.

TOP A prototype crystal bib necklace designed by Alice Caviness' head designer Millie Petronzio in the 1960s. This extravagant piece never went into production due to the high cost of materials required for manufacture. The bib has three rows of large blue and purple faceted crystals accented with dangling purple aurora borealis in a gold-tone setting.

ABOVE A Juliana crystal parure comprises a necklace, clamper bracelet, pin and earrings. The glass stones are molded to imitate geode quartz and are set in gold-tone with prong-set chatons circling the edge.

BELOW A Juliana parure of brooch, clip earrings and bracelet in silver-tone with grey chatons and ruby red rhinestones with central cat's-eye cabochon stones. Juliana was made by William DeLizza and Harold Elster of New York and sold to other jewelry companies and was marked by a paper tag. It is recognizable by incredibly colorful art-glass stones.

RIGHT TOP A vivid 1960s Juliana-style red and lavender aurora borealis rhinestone brooch.

RIGHT CENTER Juliana demi-parure of interchangeable brooch/pendant with matching clip earrings. The brooch has a large oval watermelon faceted stone in the center surrounded by sparkling pink and aurora borealis rhinestone accents.

RIGHT BOTTOM This prototype parure by Millie Petronzio for Alice Caviness in clamshell and glass featured in *Women's Wear Daily* in 1960. The central decoration of both bracelet and necklace uses a combination of gold-tone leaves, mother-of pearl discs, clam shells, pearlized navettes and beads coated with aurora borealis.

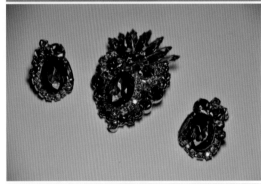

Countess 'Cis' Zoltowska

The diminutive 4 foot 10 inch (1 meter 47 centimeter) Countess Cis Zoltowska, though small of stature, bestrode costume jewelry like a Colossus in the swinging 1960s. She cut a glamorous figure; her blue-black hair adorned with an exotic orchid, her clothes amazing in their vibrant color clashes. Said to wear 'more than her bodyweight in jewelry,' the Countess produced huge, sparkling collars of glass that are much sought-after by collectors today.

Cis Zoltowska was born Maria Assunta Frankl-Fonesca in Vienna. During the Second World War she sought refuge in the neutrality of Switzerland, where she met and married the impoverished Count Zoltowska in 1951. That same year she moved to Paris, where she began crafting handpainted buttons for the seasonal collections of Cristóbal Balenciaga, Jacques Fath and Pierre Balmain, among others. Zoltowska's compelling personal style and striking designs eventually caught the eye of Balenciaga, for whom she worked for 14 years designing the jewelry for all of his couture collections. As word spread, she began to export her work out of Paris to the department store Bonwit Teller of New York and she appeared on the covers of *Vogue*, *Paris Match* and *Harper's Bazaar*. In 1967 she relocated permanently to New York.

For four months of the year the Countess resided in Thailand, a country that had an unmistakable influence on her jewelry design, especially her trademark collars made up of huge tiers of semiprecious stones and oversize crackle-glass cabochons. Her color palette displayed a keen artist's eye, as atypical colors were set against each other: bruised purples nestled next to olive green; lime green met apple; and a zingy lemon yellow on stones that were sometimes marbled and accented with handpainted gold. Many of her necklaces included clear settings within the color so that the groovy Pucci print of a modish outfit, for example, was allowed to show through. One of her most popular designs, the Dandelion brooch, came in many different colorways, including deep pink, lavender and pale blue. The glass stones are set with their points upward on the end of metal tendrils to give the illusion of a dandelion clock that might disappear in a puff of wind. Few of her pieces are signed but the style is immediately recognizable. Occasionally one can find a signature 'CIS' stamped under a crown.

LEFT A model in 1960 wears jewelry designed by Countess 'Cis' Zoltowska, comprising a headpiece, necklace and bracelets of multicolored semiprecious and imitation stones.

ABOVE A 1960s demi-parure of necklace with matching clip earrings by Cis. The necklace is constructed of a row of prong-set crackled glass cabochons in lilac, olivine and purple and another of aurora borealis stones in a gold-tone setting.

LEFT CENTER A pair of Cis clip dangle earrings with prong-set faux turquoise cabochons and aquamarine-colored crystals accented with fox-chain braided tassels, circa 1960s.

LEFT BOTTOM A Cis brooch with stunning sapphire and clustered emerald colored rhinestones from the 1960s. The cup mounts are typical of Cis and similar in construction to her popular Dandelion brooch.

Kenneth Jay Lane

'I only make unimportant jewelry,' says the self-proclaimed 'costume jeweler to the beautiful people,' Kenneth Jay Lane (1930–), whose clients have included Audrey Hepburn, Elizabeth Taylor, the Duchess of Windsor (who is reputedly buried in one of his belt designs) and Diana Vreeland, an early champion after his stint as an art director at American *Vogue*. Born in Detroit and educated at the Rhode Island School of Design, Lane moved to New York in 1954. After *Vogue*, he worked as a shoe designer for Roger Vivier at Dior, moving between Paris and New York.

Vivier, dubbed the 'Fabergé of Footwear,' created *haute couture* stiletto-heeled shoes that were jewelry for the feet. Fantastically beaded and bejeweled, some were studded with the most precious of stones. Lane was entranced by the trimmings but began to experiment with jewelry rather that shoe design, buying plastic bangles wholesale and smothering them with embellishment. At first these showy pieces were gifted to friends, who were persuaded to wear several at once in the manner of a rather more light-hearted Nancy Cunard, but after photographs appeared in the press, retailers took note. This was jewelry for a bourgeois audience that didn't look bourgeois—it was modern, fresh and fun, perfectly suited to the zeitgeist.

Lane's jewelry literally 'swung' like the decade itself: huge plastic earrings swept the shoulder; gilt metal belts hung in diamanté loops; glinting gilt and glossy black enamel panther, leopard and snake brooches screamed sex appeal. No era was sacrosanct as inspiration and history was an image-bank to be raided for source material as Lane paid homage to ancient Egypt, Art Deco, the Indian Maharajahs and high Victorian style in his exuberant designs. Jewel-encrusted Maltese crosses on wide bangles quoted Coco Chanel, glittering Swarovski crystal aped Cartier's upmarket wares. As Lane later said, 'If I haven't copied you, then you're not worth copying.' His Headlight necklaces were set with huge crystal stones, Cleopatra lotus-shaped pendants covered in turquoise and tigers-eye and huge eighteenth-century necklaces were inlaid with marcasite crystals in bold formations of flowers, teardrops and bows.

BELOW LEFT Goldplated Kenneth Jay Lane chandelier clip earrings with a pear-shaped mount suspending a bell pendant with alternating dangles of crystal and faux turquoise.

BELOW RIGHT Kenneth Jay Lane chandelier clip earrings in a pendant style with faux turquoise cabochon encircled by prong-set rhinestone crystals, 1960s.

OPPOSITE TOP Snail brooch with enamel and pavé-set crystal. Lane took the sumptuous style of fine French jewelers such as Jean Schlumberger and rendered it fun and fabulous in his costume jewelry pieces of the 1960s.

OPPOSITE BOTTOM A Kenneth Jay Lane belt from the 1960s in goldplated, rope mesh brass, inset with faceted crystals and colored cabochon to resemble turquoise, coral and jade. The filigree buckle mount is accented with prong-set crystals and cabochons.

LEFT BOTTOM Kenneth Jay Lane goldplated hinged bracelet with alternating colored resin squares divided by a ridge of pavé-set faceted foiled-back crystals, 1960s.

KENNETH JAY LANE TALKS JEWELRY

* Wear brooches high up or pin one onto a strand of pearls.
* Wear fake jewelry for worry-free traveling.
* Don't be afraid of costume. Six strands of real pearls is showing off, but simulated jewelry—it's fashion!

RIGHT Model Marisa Berenson wears serpentine armlets and rings in gold with a thin gold belly chain in 1968. Designers looked to global culture for inspiration in the later part of the decade and a multicultural wanderlust influenced fashion.

Pop Plastic

The influence of Pop Art was paramount in the 1960s. The movement had its origins in the previous decade when artists Eduardo Paolozzi and Peter Blake found inspiration in the brightly colored visual language of popular culture rather than the introspective musings of Abstract Expressionism. In New York, Andy Warhol was painting large-scale versions of supermarket products such as the Campbell's Soup Can series and Roy Lichtenstein copied the style of the comic strip. These paintings glorified the bright gaudy aesthetic of advertising and product design, and a new primary palette entered the world of design.

Richard Hamilton was one of the founders of the Pop Art movement in Britain and his collage work such as *Just What Is It That Makes Today's Homes So Different, So Appealing* reflects the postwar boom years when domestic products were freely available and imbued with glamour. Hamilton had a set of rules for the new art that ran: '[It should be] Popular (designed for a mass audience); transient (short-term solution); expendable (easily forgotten); low cost; mass-produced; young (aimed at youth); witty; sexy; gimmicky; glamorous; and last but not least, Big Business.' These same principles were applied to the decade's jewelry design; much of it was cheap and cheerful, was produced in huge quantities and with a built-in obsolescence—it was not meant to last. Materials such as plastics, particularly Perspex and vinyl, were molded into chunky geometric shapes and colored with primary hues by designers such as Raymond Exton. Partners David Watkins and Wendy Ramshaw took the notion of expendability to the extreme in their paper jewelry, which could be bought in kit form at Mary Quant's Bazaar and the Way In boutique on the top floor of Harrods, Knightsbridge, in the 1960s. Watkins said recently:

When we first designed paper jewelry back in the 1960s, we were motivated by our desire to use processes outside the mainstream of jewelry production. The idea of printing jewelry really appealed to us. We wanted to create things that were fast and simple and fun and inexpensive. And throwaway—the throwaway concept was intriguing at the time.

RIGHT A bright primary palette is one of the hallmarks of 1960s jewelry, reflecting the optimism of the post-war 'baby boomer' generation. Plastics, seen as innovative and futuristic, were molded into huge pieces of gaudy jewelry as in this huge neckpiece of 1967.

RIGHT Twiggy was a top model and style leader in this decade and together with the Beatles was responsible for importing the so-called 'Swinging London' style into America. In 1965, she wears yellow plastic earrings with the daisy motif, which had been popularized by British designer Mary Quant.

BELOW A selection of 1960s enamel flower brooches. These huge colorful flower pins were one of the most popular jewelry forms of the decade, as they were a visual symbol of 'flower power,' a slogan used by the American hippie movement.

The Black and White of Color

'Op Art' was first coined by *Time* magazine in 1964, which went on to describe the new art movement as 'an attack on the eye.' Artists such as Bridget Riley, Richard Anuszkiewicz and Victor Vasarely used perceptual research to create geometric patterns that produced dizzying visual effects in the viewer. Black-and-white canvases shimmered, shifted and flowed at the Responsive Eye exhibition held at the Museum of Modern Art in New York in 1965 and although proclaimed 'optical hysteria' by one critic, their influence quickly filtered through to fashion. American dress manufacturers like Larry Aldrich saw the potential of this bold monochromatic look and commissioned fabrics inspired by his own collection of Op Art paintings; in London Ossie Clark and John Bates created Op Art clothes for their hip clientele.

Op Art jewelry was a short-lived fad, designed quickly and cheaply to match the black-and-white clothes. Plastic could create stark checkerboard effects and was molded into bangles, dangle earrings and bold bead necklaces. Target designs were popular in red and white, as well as in black, and became a motif of the burgeoning Mod movement that was to revive Carnaby Street as a fashionable destination and pinpoint London across the world as a new 'swinging' capital of style. Mary Quant's black-and-white daisy motif appeared on acrylic jewelry, although it was less Op and more personal in its significance. Quant relates how as a teenager she had fallen for an older man and wished his girlfriend dead. To the designer's absolute horror she expired of appendicitis; her name, Daisy. The Op Art style may have been short-lived in its purest form but its effects lasted longer. Public taste began to swing to abstract rather than figurative forms in jewelry design and an innovative vocabulary of asymmetrical, splintered and minimalist shapes began to appear.

RIGHT A selection of Op Art-inspired acrylic and metal jewelry by Wendy Ramshaw, originally a textile designer, and David Watkins, a sculptor and jazz musician. The couple made this range of Optik Art Jewelry from 1963 and it was sold through boutiques such as Mary Quant's Bazaar. Ramshaw used the technique of screen-printing onto sheets of acrylic, instead of the more usual spray-painting; the acrylic was then cut up into small sections for the jewelry.

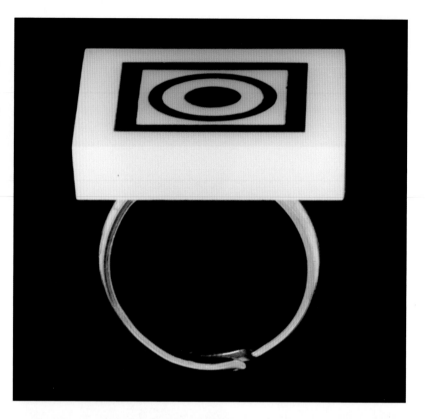

BELOW Actress Jill Haworth wears enamel earrings and bracelet by Giorgio di Sant'Angelo for Vendome in primary-colored plastic, 1967. Sant'Angelo had a studio apprenticeship with Picasso, who urged him to experiment with new materials. He combined plastics such as Lucite in vibrant jewelry that was spotted by Diana Vreeland, who employed him as a stylist on American *Vogue*. He went on to become one of America's most important fashion designers.

Future Shock

The yé-yé designs of mid 1960s designers André Courrèges, Rudi Gernreich, Paco Rabanne, Emanuelle Khanh and Pierre Cardin were the shot in the arm that French couture needed to re-establish Paris as a fashion center. Couture was in desperate need of rebranding; many houses were stuck in 1950s mode, rigidly organized by the Chambre Syndicale de la Couture Parisienne with a rapidly ageing clientele. Residual products such as bags, perfume and jewelry were seen as the way forward, real money-spinners that could save ailing fashion houses from closure. However, to gain youth appeal, a big shake-up was necessary. Fashion had to be fresh and futuristic and Pierre Cardin was the first out of the block in 1964 with his Space Age collection of white knitted catsuits and tubular shift dresses. In 1965 Emanuel Ungaro showed what one journalist described as 'a silver binge: silver wigs; silver-soled boots; silver buttons, collars and mesh stockings. Aluminum necklaces doubling up as bras were juxtaposed with see-through, flower-appliquéd trousers.'

This science-fiction trend influenced jewelry. Paco Rabanne, originally a jewelry designer who had worked with Hubert Givenchy, was the first to blaze the trail. Believing that the only new frontier left in fashion was the discovery and utilization of new materials rather than the old couture method of changing lines from season to season, Rabanne totally broke with tradition, experimenting with plastic and aluminum, to create some of the most eccentric yet influential garments and accompanying jewelry of the 1960s.

In 1966, he presented a collection of 12 experimental dresses in plastic and metal, assembled with a pair of pliers and a blowlamp instead of needle and thread. His sixties jewelry followed the same chainmail aesthetic in plastic and aluminum. That year the designer calculated he was using up to 100,000 feet (30,500 m) of Rhodoid plastic per month. One extraordinary artifact was a bib necklace made of phosphorescent plastic discs strung together with fine wire and matching huge hooped earrings reminiscent of Alexander Calder mobiles. When Rabanne had exhausted the possibilities of plastic, he created another version of chainmail using tiny triangles of aluminum and leather held together with flexible wire rings or chrome strung with acrylic. Rabanne called it anti-jewelry saying, 'I make jewelry for the alternative side of a woman's personality, for her madness.' In the high street the Space-Age look led to a burst of shooting stars, planets and rocketships, all in lightweight plastic. Hooped earrings could be huge white circles and gigantic tiered triangles of transparent acrylic.

OPPOSITE A silver-sequined sleeveless dress by Joan Arkin,1966, employs a chainmail technique similar to that used by French couturier Paco Rabanne, and is accessorized with huge metal chandelier earrings. Clip earrings took over from pierced in the 1960s as the weight of such large pieces could only be accommodated with a large clip over the lobe.

LEFT TOP AND BOTTOM Body jewelry from the 1967 'Sculpture to Wear' exhibition in London by Dutch husband-and-wife team, Gijs Bakker and Emmy van Leersum. Blue anodized aluminum, plastic, silver and gold were hammered into huge Space-Age shapes. This revolutionary jewelry related to the shape of the wearer's body, but also maintained its own clear forms. The couple's radical approach to body adornment made them leaders in avant-garde jewelry design in Europe, following Bakker's avowal 'to seize control of the material and to force it into almost impossible forms.'

Sigurd Persson

Born in Helsingborg to a silversmith father, Swedish jewelry designer Persson (1914–2003) opened his own workshop, specializing in silver, in 1945. He achieved global recognition in 1965 when he produced a range of futuristic jewelry for an exhibition at the Nordiska Kompaniet department store. Persson created earrings that secured by being looped over the ear and sculptural bracelets that held jutting sprays of chalcedony and rose quartz. Rings were huge and architectonic, cleverly conceived to be both extravagant and sophisticated or gem-studded Space-Age starbursts. Yet Persson also created subtler rings of geometric severity; silver cubes set into silver bands, one side gilded to give a hint of modern luxury were a perfect accompaniment to the simple silhouettes of the decade. In the early 1970s Persson infused his work with a Pop Art sensibility —his Soap Bubble earrings of 1974 could have been mistaken for the real thing. Persson uses the maker's mark SIGP, which is stamped alongside the Swedish triple crown hallmark, 'S' for silver and the date letter.

BELOW LEFT Silver ring with gilded geometric sawed top by Sigurd Persson, designed in 1960. A proponent of the architectonic style of jewelry-making, along with others such as Margaret de Patta and Danish Bent Exner, Persson's work is linear, geometric and three-dimensional.

BELOW RIGHT Persson's designs took motifs from machinery and architecture, though sometimes also from nature, as in this gem-studded starburst bracelet of 1962. The clean lines of this piece are a clear manifestation of Swedish Modernism, for which he was renowned.

The Artist-Jeweler

The new pop and rock aristocracy wanted a different kind of fine jewelry on which to spend their self-made wealth. Instead of the stuffy wares of the great jewelry houses, clients were keen for a dose of informality with their diamonds. The market responded very quickly; in 1961, for instance, the Worshipful Company of Goldsmiths and the Victoria and Albert Museum in London held a landmark exhibition of modern jewelry by international designers, such as Gilbert Albert for Patek Philippe, Harry Winston, Gerda Flöckinger and Andrew Grima, set against art by Picasso and sculptures by Elizabeth Frink. The aim of the exhibition was to boost Britain's jewelry trade and to show the young London in-crowd that it could be used for individual self-expression as well as monetary status.

Andrew Grima

One of the most creative jewelers of the decade, Andrew Grima's (1921–2007) work was worn by Jackie Kennedy, film star Ursula Andress and Princess Margaret, among other members of the British Royal Family. His training began after serving in the Second World War when, after demobilization, he began working on the accounts of a small-scale jewelry workshop, the H J Company, owned by his father-in-law. Salesmen would visit regularly, hawking stones which did little to spark Grima's interest until one case was opened to reveal an array of Brazilian aquamarines, amethysts and citrine. Grima described the change:

> [Our] jewelry was beautifully made but in the traditional style of the period; flower pins set in platinum. In 1948, two stone-dealer brothers arrived at our office with a suitcase of large stones in quantities I had never seen before. I persuaded my father-in-law to buy the entire collection and I set to work designing. This was the beginning of my career as a modern jewelry designer.

Grima used these rough-hewn rocks set in gold in a first collection that relied on the effects of natural texture rather than glitz. He went on to make direct casts from nature: leaves, moss, even volcanic lava cast in gold. In 1966 the British Royal Family awarded Grima a warrant to supply them with jewelry and in the same year he opened his first premises in Jermyn Street, London. The shop was a bold experiment in such an old-school setting—a fortified exterior of steel latticework and slabs of slate had small showcases punched through to catch the light. To enter, one stepped on the doormat and the door automatically opened to a James Bond-style interior with two floors linked by a Perspex spiral staircase.

Throughout the 1960s and 1970s Grima launched a series of stunning collections, including: Rock Revival, which used oversized uncut stones and carried the texture of the stone through to the gold mounting; Supershells; and Sticks and Stones, which used long uncut tourmalines. After his business partner was declared bankrupt, Grima resigned his royal warrant and in 1986 emigrated with his wife to Switzerland. In 2008 fashion designer Marc Jacobs was spotted at an opening at the Serpentine Gallery in London, hosted by Louis Vuitton, in an emerald-and-gold crystalline necklace by Grima. When asked about his choice, Jacobs said, 'I went shopping for a swimsuit today and came back with this. It's a woman's piece. I wondered, "Can I wear it?" Then I thought, "Why not? I can wear what I like!"'

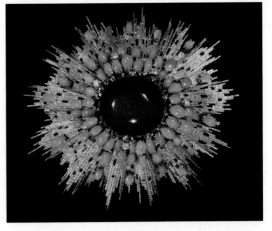

BELOW Designer Andrew Grima with a model wearing a selection of his jewelry in 1966. Grima designed fine jewelry for the new rock aristocracy of the 1960s who wanted symbols of status that were removed from the traditional work of the prestigious French jewelry houses.

LEFT Andrew Grima brooch, 1967–8 in his signature textured gold, studded with turquoise. His work was organic and abstract in form and used large semiprecious stones.

Hippie-Chic

Non-western cultures were rifled for inspiration, particularly those that had suffered as a result of colonialism—wearers could then score an important political point at the height of the Vietnam War. Northern American Indian beading was popular, as were the more obvious hallmarks of the peace and love espoused by hippie adherents—love beads, peace slogans and flower-power daisies became high-street fashion statements when worn by teenagers outside of America. The stylized flower symbolized the hippie rejection of authority in favor of a back-to-nature lifestyle and became a potent symbol of free love, even when rendered as a white plastic brooch.

A multicultural wanderlust influenced high fashion too, with Zandra Rhodes creating chiffon kaftans in prints inspired by Native American culture. Fine-jewelry designers were quick to react to this ethnic trend. New York jeweler David Webb had a high-profile list of clients that included Elizabeth Taylor and Diana Vreeland, for whom he created an exotic zebra-print bangle. In 1969 he designed a dramatic Indian-inspired ruby and cultured pearl necklace for Doris Duke that consisted of a multi-strand fringe of 1,136 ruby beads interspersed with pearls and hung from a polished gold chain. In costume jewelry, Trifari launched their jadeite-set Jewels of India collection in 1966 and Kenneth Jay Lane made paisley-print brooches and peacock-feather earrings.

RIGHT TOP Established costume jewelry firms like Trifari responded to the new hippie aesthetic by creating jewels that made vague ethnic references, such as in this fringed peacock pendant in gold-tone.

RIGHT BOTTOM A fashion editorial of 1968 displays jewelry incorporating the hippie aesthetic conflating rosaries, Native American beading and ropes of coral into one multicultural melting pot.

OPPOSITE Model in Afro wig reclines on Thea Porter cushions wearing body jewelry by Adrien Mann in a 1969 issue of *Harper's Bazaar*. Family firm and wholesale jewelers Adrien Mann, founded in 1945, specialized in fashion jewelry in the lower price ranges and quickly responded to contemporary trends.

Remembrance of Things Past

As the decade neared its end, retrospection was in the air. Female fashions had moved as if in a whirlwind through the contrasting styles of Mod, Space Age and hippie chic, and such a catalogue of innovation was a shock to some sensibilities. It was time for retrenchment and designers began to look backward to what appeared to be a less transient age, re-examining the past with nostalgia. Biba took refuge in the 1920s and 1930s, creating what one fashion journalist described as, 'slithery gowns in glowing satins, hats with black veils [and] shoes stacked for sirens.' The whiplash lines of Art Nouveau reappeared in the psychedelic jewelry sold in high-street boutiques, its natural colors replaced by Day-Glo clashing pink and green and Art Deco underwent a reappraisal spearheaded by Bernard Nevill, professor of textiles at the Royal College of Art and head of print at Liberty of London. The films *Bonnie and Clyde* (1967) and Ken Russell's *The Boyfriend* (1971), which starred Twiggy as a tap-dancing 1920s flapper, helped filter the nostalgia trend to a mainstream audience.

Lea Stein

Paris-born Lea Stein (1931–) began designing jewelry after her chemist husband, Fernand Steinberger, discovered a process of laminating celluloid using wafer-thin acetate sheets, achieving intricate multilayered patterns in a variety of bright colors. The sheets were baked and then hand-carved into a template then used to create simple, yet very stylish, Art Deco-inspired caricatures in the shape of cats, hats and female heads, some with a lace-effect, snakeskin or glitter top layer. The technique was first put to use when Stein began designing buttons for the fashion industry, including Chanel. In 1969 a jewelry range was launched that included brooches, necklaces, bracelets and earrings, which was sold through retailers until 1981. Stein's most popular brooch, the Fox, was designed in 1975; the tail a stylish flash and outstretched paws of curling plastic. It was available in many different colorways and patterns.

The company reopened in 1991 and now creates a small collection of new designs each year, which are snapped up by eager collectors. Unusually, some of the more modern pieces are worth more than those produced in the first phase of the designer's career, as the number in each range is so much smaller today than in their glory years of the 1970s. The distinctive patterns make Lea Stein instantly recognizable, as do the 1920s-inspired shapes and decorative effects. Brooches also have a distinctive V-shaped clasp and are always signed 'Lea Stein Paris' on the back, unless they date from the very early 1960s.

ABOVE Interior and fashion from Biba, 1969. Biba was instrumental in the creation of the late 1960s vogue for nostalgia. Biba jewelry was a contemporary take on Art Deco—here a model wears an oversized bead necklace and silver rings.

RIGHT Selection of jewelry by Lea Stein from the late 1960s and 1970s. From left clockwise: A laminated celluloid rainbow-striped cuff and earrings; her instantly recognizable Fox brooch showing back pin and stamps and front with outstretched paws; back of a bird pin and a Vintage Banger pin; bird pin from front; musical note pin; monochrome pin, front of a Vintage Banger brooch.

▶ Black is Beautiful

The Black is Beautiful movement of the late 1960s led to the vogue among young black people for fashion that expressed their cultural and historical identity. Natural hair was grown into an Afro rather than pressed straight and a more Afro-centric style included huge beaded collars and bib necklaces.

Revival jewelry

Victorian Revival style came back for a short time, with jewelry that took the form of plastic and resin cameos, such as the collectable Gerry's and Juliana cameos, as well as engraved and antiqued metalwork buckles and bangles.

Key looks of the decade
1960s

▼ Space Age

A Paco Rabanne dress made up of linked plastic squares from April 1967. Rabanne made his name in the 1960s with a series of futuristic garments. When viewed on the catwalk they appeared to be Space-Age prototypes rather than high fashion.

▲ Op and Pop

Geometric effects were a simple way of making jewelry modern and were influenced by the Op Art paintings of Bridget Riley and Victor Vasarely. A model wears a navy and orange cotton wrap by Gayle Kirkpatrick for Atelier with oversized drop earrings with the ever-popular daisy motif from Tree House in 1966.

Zingy colors

The 1960s were the decade of bright primary color, as seen in this enamel butterfly pin by Trifari. The work of Pop artists such as Andy Warhol and Roy Lichtenstein used the visual language of popular rather than high culture and bright hard-edged graphics found their way into all areas of art and design including jewelry.

▶ Hippie motifs

'Flower power' was a term originally coined by Beat poet Allen Ginsberg in the late 1960s as a call to peaceful anti-Vietnam demonstrations and passive rather than violent resistance. Hippies adopted the flower as decorative motif, and it entered mainstream fashion jewelry.

◀ Pendants

Huge pendants became fashionable and continued to be so in the 1970s. Most costume jewelry manufacturers like Sarah Coventry and Goldette through to upmarket silversmiths like David-Andersen, produced them. Shapes included articulated animals such as owls, ethnic motifs and the ubiquitous Maltese cross.

Ethnic trends

Interpretations of East Indian, Egyptian and Asian looks worked their way into jewelry design, often with combinations of one or more ethnic elements. These styles, which carried on into the 1970s, often used bold colorful jewels such as in the creations of Kenneth Jay Lane, Accessocraft, Trifari and Goldette.

▲ Plastic

After the Space-Age experiments of designers such as Pierre Cardin, Courrèges, and Rudi Gernreich, plastic became a popular material, as seen in the plastic furniture of Joe Columbo and bright plastic jewelry such as these Perspex rings from the mid 1960s.

1970s:
The Body, Bold and Beautiful

Recession and protest dogged the early years of the 1970s as disillusionment set in on global culture—the hippie philosophy of 'Make Love, Not War' was increasingly untenable in a post-nuclear world. Jewelry began to display spirituality rather than obvious wealth, for many believed that there was no room for vulgarity in such sober global circumstances. Fashion reflected the same understated trend—the hippie look turned mainstream and clothes continued to make reference to 'ethnic' origins in the form of kaftans, patchwork peasant skirts and cheesecloth shirts. In the heady world of international style, Yves Saint Laurent, Bill Gibb and Zandra Rhodes converted the countercultural garb of the hippie movement into the high-status fashion of 'poverty deluxe'—or 'radical chic' as writer Tom Wolfe dubbed the look in America. A similar strategy was taken in the design of high-end jewelry, with established houses adapting to ethnic influences and street style.

The rise of radical feminism underscored the fact that the demonstration and protest of the previous decade were to continue as Germaine Greer's compelling book *The Female Eunuch* (1970) would attest. In her heady polemic, the fashion system was systematically trashed in print as an example of women's oppression in a patriarchal culture. Greer saw the bounties of nature being plundered to decorate the 'Eternal Feminine' to insidious effect: 'the depths of the sea are ransacked for pearl and coral to deck her; the bowels of the earth are laid open that she might wear gold, sapphires, diamonds and rubies.' Jewelry took a serious turn and became an art form, embodying earnest polemic about its very status in the world more akin to conceptual art rather than luxury and status, as seen in the work of Dutch jeweler Robert Smit and Czechoslovakian goldsmith Hubertus von Skal.

Trends and Influences

Jewelry had to tread a tightrope between reserve and opulence. Van Cleef & Arpels led the way using gold set with rubies, emeralds and diamonds in works that maintained a sense of Western luxury with reassuring references to Indian culture. Bulgari, an Italian house that rose to fame in this decade, similarly created expensive jewels that combined cachet with the casual—pieces were deliberately designed to be worn from day to night in polished gold set with baguette and step-cut diamonds. Bulgari's first international outlet opened in New York City's Pierre Hotel on Fifth Avenue and by the end of the decade the company had stormed the ramparts of the rich in Paris, Geneva and Monte Carlo. Influences were refreshingly exotic, including the Treasures of Tutankhamen Exhibition that toured from 1972–79 and led to a host of ancient Egyptian-inspired designs worn by stars such as Sophia Loren and Audrey Hepburn.

The client most associated with the firm was the diamond-obsessed Elizabeth Taylor. Taylor's love affair with the stone was chronicled throughout the decade especially in reference to the huge rock bought for her by her husband Richard Burton in 1970, which became known as the Burton-Taylor Diamond. It was flawless and pear-shaped, weighing in at 69.42 carats and cut from a stone that had been bought by Harry Winston in 1968, set into a dazzling necklace by Cartier. Taylor wore it for the first time at Princess Grace of Monaco's fortieth birthday party.

Coral, the skeletal remains of the marine animal *polyp corallicum*, enjoyed a renaissance that crossed all

LEFT A Sarah Coventry strawberry pin from the early 1970s, an alternative to hippie-inspired jewelry. The company ran from 1950 until it was taken over in 1984, and manufactured pieces that were sold to customers through parties hosted by 'fashion directors.'

PAGE 152 A model wears a printed, georgette Japanese-inspired kimono over mauve pajamas by Rafael and a large, leaf-emblazoned necklace.

LEFT An Eisenberg rhinestone pin with a faux baroque pearl dangle. The well-known Eisenberg company produced costume jewelry until 1977. From 1970 ornate pieces, such as this pin, had 'Eisenberg Ice' written on the reverse.

OPPOSITE An ornate coral, onyx, diamond and mother-of-pearl pendant necklace by Bulgari. Bulgari has always been quick to respond to cultural influences, such as the craze for Egyptian-styled pieces after the success of the Treasures of the Tutankhamen exhibition in the mid 1970s.

ABOVE A selection of 1970s diamond jewelry by Bulgari. The hippie sensibility was overtaken in the 1970s by a darker and more decadent aesthetic, as can be seen in this shoot for French *Vogue*. Prestigious firms created pieces that were unapologetically luxurious for the new rock aristocracy.

consumer barriers in much the same way as it had done in the 1920s (see the Cartier powder compact on page 49). Those with cash to flash could buy an eye-wateringly expensive Piaget *peau d'ange* parure, those with a little less money could order a plastic coral pendant and drop earrings by firms such as Avon or Sarah Coventry. Unfortunately so much coral was imported in this decade, from Hawaii and Taiwan in particular, that the sea's stock was overharvested and coral suitable for jewelry became increasingly difficult to find.

Disco

It would take disco to sex up jewelry again and by the light of a glitter ball, the dissolute, decadent 1970s emerged. In 1975 music journalist Mark Jacobson wrote, 'the new scene was all kinky 8-inch platforms, luminous make-up and outrageous sexuality. It soon became clear that these discos were for, as the Jackson 5 say, "Dancing, dancing, dancing machines." And madness ensued.'

Studio 54 was launched in 1977 and before closing two years later became the place to be seen with guests including Andy Warhol, Cher and Liza Minnelli. The high-octane glamour of metal, shimmering under the strobe lights, led to a vogue for mesh fashioned into collars and faux bandanas that were worn on glistening bodies clad in spandex, body glitter and lip gloss. Hoop-in-hoop earrings were a popular fad and were worn as clips on the ears as the size and weight were impossible for a pierced ear to accommodate. Large pendants began to be worn by men as well as women.

OPPOSITE A Khaki utility shirt by Katharine Hamnett is accessorized with coral jewelry from Liberty of London. From the moment its doors opened in 1875, Liberty has had a tradition of showing design from all over the world. Jewelry was imported from Africa, Tibet and India, among other countries, in the 1970s.

LEFT A carved *pelle d'angelo*, coral and diamond bangle and cocktail ring by Cartier. Bracelets with animal-head terminals, in this case the fire-breathing Chinese chimera, are one of the oldest forms of jewelry and date back to the eighth century BC. Cartier has been using this design since the early twentieth century; from 1954 artistic director Jeanne Toussaint gave it fashion cachet by using coral.

BELOW Imports from Liberty in the 1970s: the silver and coral collar and earrings are Moroccan and the wide silver bracelet is from India.

COLLECTING VINTAGE CORAL

* Coral, from the species *Corallium,* can be found in a variety of colors ranging from a pinky white to an oxblood red; the most prized are oxblood and angel-skin pink.
* Coral used in jewelry is compact and features no visible indentations.
* Beware of imitations. In vintage pieces Bakelite is often mistaken for red coral. To test, place the coral in a glass of milk—it should turn the milk pink.
* Many Victorian brooches and earrings were made using natural or branch coral.
* Coral, like jet, is relatively soft so it can be carved easily. Cameos, rings, brooches, bracelets and beads were all made in abundance.

Ethnic Jewelry

Mainstream jewelry fashion continued to display ethnic credentials. Chunky pieces of Mexican silver were popular, as were symbols such as the Egyptian ankh and the Italian horn. Huge Navajo silver beaded necklaces were worn by stars such as Cher and incorporated large turquoise stones mined in Arizona, accented with coral and bear claws. David Webb's naturalistic aesthetic retained its popularity and his use of rock crystal and other semiprecious hard stones such as jasper and crocidolite, also known as tiger's-eye, influenced most of the prestigious houses, who incorporated them into their work alongside the use of textured metal. Fashion designer Diane von Furstenberg, inventor of the eponymous wrapdress that became a uniform of choice for fashionistas in this decade, graced the cover of American *Vogue* wearing a huge Webb necklace offsetting her lion's mane of glossy hair.

RIGHT Navajo silver bracelets with turquoise stones from Arizona, 1970. For the Native American Navajo, turquoise was a gift from the sky and had the power to heal. The Navajo learned silver-smithing from Mexican artisans and incorporated it into their own motifs.

ABOVE LEFT This plastic bracelet from the 1970s shows the more naturalistic autumnal colorways that took over from the bright primaries of the 1960s.

ABOVE RIGHT A Lea Stein bangle from the 1970s that shows how the designer's vibrant color palette became more subdued to match the style of the times.

RIGHT Yves Saint Laurent's muse and collaborator Loulou de la Falaise photographed by Bert Stern in 1970. She wears 'poverty deluxe' hippie-inspired fashion with suitably 'ethnic' jewelry.

ABOVE A massive tassel and beaded earring by Giorgio di Sant'Angelo, 1970. This fantastic piece was not intended to be functional, but to create a fantasy, hippie deluxe editorial. The positioning of the clip is to support the earring's weight.

Body Jewelry

The legacy of the 1960s preoccupation with sexual liberation, the increased availability of contraception and the skimpiness of female fashion led to a focus on the body in both fine art and popular culture in the early 1970s. On March 9, 1960, the artist Yves Klein performed his *Anthropométries de l'Epoque Bleue* (Anthropometries of the Blue Period) at the International Gallery of Contemporary Art in Paris. A formally dressed audience looked on with admirable aplomb as naked models left the imprint of their bodies on huge sheets of white paper that had been laid out on the gallery walls and floor to the strains of Klein's 'The Monotone Symphony.' This literal 'body' painting began to be linked to fashion when model Veruschka posed for photographs with her body painted in trompe l'oeil designs and when Yves Saint Laurent commissioned sculptor Claude Lalanne to cast her breasts in metal. Avant-garde jewelry designers such as Giorgio di Sant'Angelo channeled the new body-consciousness by creating huge pieces such as breastplates and gem-studded bras that worked with the body's physicality and interacted erotically with its curves.

Robert Lee Morris

One of the pioneers of the idea of jewelry as wearable body art, Robert Lee Morris (1947–) is now known for his catwalk collaborations with designers Calvin Klein, Karl Lagerfeld and Donna Karan, with whom he has worked on and off for more than 20 years. Morris was born in Nuremberg, Germany, in 1947 where his American air force father was stationed after the Second World War. As his father moved from post to post, Morris was exposed to different cultures (at least 25 he now estimates) including Brazil and Japan, where the family lived in a paper house in the country for five years. This world view informed the jeweler's oeuvre, which takes inspiration from global culture and the amulets and talismans of ancient history.

After graduating with a degree in art and archaeology from Wisconsin's Beloit College in 1969, Morris joined an artist's commune and started designing simple jewelry forms using brass and steel wire from the local hardware store. When the commune was destroyed by fire in 1970 he moved to Vermont and began to refine his skills, forging sculptural pieces out of brass, silver and gold that relied on the use of undulating organic shape rather than precious stones. Here he experimented with new techniques that gave an ancient feel to modern forms, in keeping with the retrospective spirituality of his counter-cultural companions, such as the muted Etruscan finish he gave to overtly shiny gold by layering 24-karat gold over brass. He also experimented with patinas that evoked the weathering of stone and forms that recalled the feel of medieval armor, always placing the value of design above that of materials.

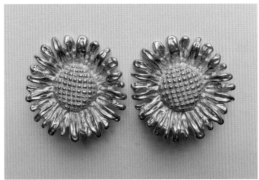

LEFT TOP Robert Lee Morris's famous Cannoli Belt of 1977. Cannoli is a pastry dessert from Sicily that takes the form of tubes of fried dough filled with ricotta cheese. Here, Morris takes the traditional Italian shape and renders it in brass, copper and leather.

LEFT CENTER Goldplated brass sunflower earrings by Robert Lee Morris, late 1970s. The designer has experimented with a variety of finishes and patinas throughout his long career.

BELOW Sculptural herring-bone collar in verdigris patinated brass from Robert Lee Morris, 1978. During the 1970s, Morris's work relied on the use of metal, rather than the inclusion of semiprecious stones, to create visual interest from simple shapes and experimental patinas.

His work debuted in the early 1970s at the avant-garde New York gallery, Sculpture to Wear. Run by Joan Sonnebend and held in the Plaza Hotel, the gallery sold one-off pieces by artists such as Alexander Calder, Picasso and the Surrealist photographer Man Ray. Morris' work outsold all of them, so he went solo and opened his own gallery, Artwear, in Manhattan in 1977. At this time his monumental jewelry was inspired by Aboriginal art, Bronze Age artifacts and African tribal ironwork. His overtly sculptural pieces, such as primitive crosses, gladiator cuffs, collars and belts, and knuckleduster rings, were created out of huge discs, hearts or sculptural Xs and plated in nickel or gold. The work was displayed to stunning effect on plaster casts of torsos in Artwear's windows and worn by Candice Bergen, Cher, Bianca Jagger and Grace Jones.

In 1985 Morris began his long collaboration with designer Donna Karan, designing simple yet sensually organic pieces for her first catwalk show, which launched her elegantly wearable version of power dressing and included the ubiquitous 'body.' Later he incorporated silver elements into the actual structure of Karan's garments. By the 1990s Morris had worked with all the New York big-hitters including Calvin Klein, Michael Kors and Geoffrey Beene and more recently designed jewelry for the TV celebrity twins, Mary-Kate and Ashley Olsen. As he put it:

… mass fashion jewelry, in my mind, is purely decorative, employing a cacophony of glittery values to achieve a dazzling effect. This is as much a part of human culture as the bright plumage of birds, and will remain with us, as it should. But it has always been against this world that I design my work placing value on classicism and heirloom status over the thrill of contemporary trends. My concepts are generally anthropological and my attitude is 'less is more.'

Tone Vigelund

Norwegian jewelry designer Tone Vigelund (1938–) was born in Oslo and trained at the National College of Arts, Crafts and Design. After a silversmith apprenticeship, she was accredited as a master-jeweler and set up her own studio in 1962. Her 1950s designs use the popular atomic shape and were produced by Norway Silver Designs at Plus Applied Arts Center in Frederickstad. By the 1970s she was creating jewelry that was bold and beautiful, designed with the whole body in mind rather than the simple adornment of a finger or wrist, and with an emphasis on flexibility so that the designs would always be comfortable to wear. Combinations of steel, feathered silver, mother-of-pearl and simple hand-forged iron nails were fashioned into huge collars and oxidized silver was woven into a mesh of flexible chainmail that undulated with the body.

OPPOSITE TOP By the latter half of the 1970s the traditional mix of glittering gems set in precious metal was out of fashion. Jewelry was wrought out of simple metal shapes that adorned far larger areas of the body than in any other decade. Here, in 1977, model and singer Grace Jones wears matching metal armlets.

OPPOSITE BOTTOM Tone Vigelund's bold and beautiful designs are among some of the most creative of the 1970s. They were fabricated with a high degree of flexibility to give wearability to the most avant-garde of designs.

RIGHT In the 1970s, body jewelry relied on sculptural effects rather than expensive gems. This Pierre Cardin collar and huge dangling pendant has taken the minimalist shapes of Scandinavian Modernism and exaggerated them for dramatic effect.

Jewelry Explored

Pioneering artist and jeweler Gerda Flöckinger brought jewelry closer to the boundaries of fine art than it had ever been before, playing a pivotal role in the development of modern jewelry in the UK, which had been very slow to accept the Modernist aesthetic. She also became an accomplished teacher who influenced generations of students after creating her Experimental Jewelry course at Hornsey College of Art in 1962 under principal Harold Shelton. Due to the efforts of a group of talented and dedicated jewelers, including Flöckinger, London and its environs became an important center of the new craft movement, progressing the idea of studio jewelry from simply the use of natural materials and an implicit functionality into one that could also incorporate the synthetic, as can be seen in the later work of David Watkins and Wendy Ramshaw. Flöckinger, with her fused abstract and textured pieces in gold and silver, implicitly refused to retreat into historical or archaic forms; according to Watkins, 'she works her chosen material dangerously close to the point of disintegration in pursuit of its enrichment, scattering precious stones as if in metallic lava.' Pioneer jewelers, such as Flöckinger, had a new and very important outlet for their work when Barbara Cartlidge opened her Electrum Gallery in South Molton Street in 1971, championing avant-garde jewelry. Flöckinger's solo show, conceived in 1969, also opened at the Victoria and Albert Museum in London in 1971—she was the first living woman artist to achieve such an accolade.

In 1976 an important traveling exhibition organized by the Scottish Arts Council and the Crafts Advisory Committee opened in the UK. Entitled 'Jewelry in Europe: An Exhibition of Progressive Work,' it was devoted to transforming the idea of what jewelry could be and showed a cross-section of the most vital European designs. The jeweler was viewed as an explorer and, as organizer Ralph Turner wrote in the accompanying catalogue, 'this exploration may result in work not intending to adorn. Indeed the jeweler may react defiantly against this principle and we may be witnessing a transition from the realm of jewelry to that of sculpture, or to a new area which combines the qualities of both fields.'

Exhibitors included German goldsmith Ulrike Bahrs, who created brooches in the form of miniature paintings. Evoking scenes from the Jungian subconscious rendered in lapis lazuli and unpolished ebony, precious metals were combined with cast-iron, acrylic, mother-of-pearl and found objects from nature, including crystals, pebbles and flower petals, and fashioned into ancient symbols such as pyramids, magic circles and archaic squares. In the work of Gijs Bakker, a strong link could be seen to the prevailing vogue for conceptual and performance art that dominated fine-art production in this decade, itself a direct descendent of the hippie 'happenings' of the 1960s. The Dutch jeweler, born in 1942, took the relationship of jewelry and the body

to extremes; in 1973 he made a 'bracelet' from thin gold wire that was then bound on the arm as tightly as possible until the wire disappeared into the flesh. As Bakker explained, 'Only an indication (marking) is visible. The attention is placed more on the body than on the object. In the next step I don't use a wire, I only show the imprint from the wire which has been there before. The imprint has the function of a piece of jewelry.'

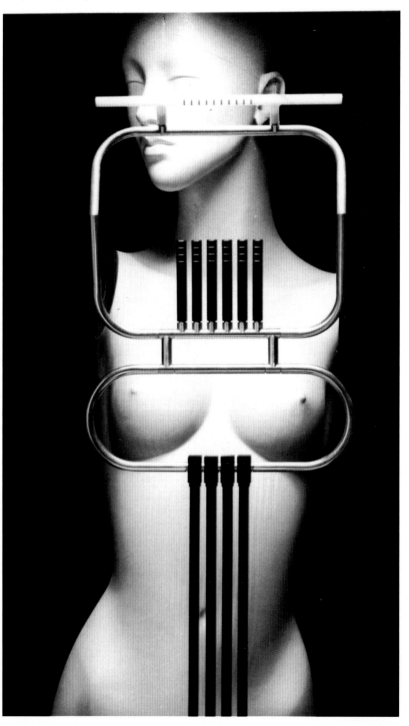

David Watkins

Watkins (1940–) explored the futuristic forms that had been kickstarted by his work as a model-maker when he worked on the special effects for the film *2001: A Space Odyssey* (1968) directed by Stanley Kubrick. He created miniature spacecraft that were used in many of the sci-fi scenes and which required a precise eye for detail, and his early jewelry work shows evidence of this formative influence; the shapes of space stations and lunar probes inspired necklaces and brooches in silver and white enamel and his trademark neckpieces were flagrantly futuristic. In the 1970s Watkins' minimalist pieces played with the interpenetration of simple shapes on the body in sparse yet elegant shapes, continuing the legacy of Bauhaus Modernism. Color added a new dimension to his work in the 1980s, enhancing Watkins' exploratory use of materials that included paper and both precious and industrial metals. Science, rather than historicism, continues to provide inspiration; recent pieces include a monumental neckpiece of white acrylic with two interlocking computer-generated patterns cut out by water jet.

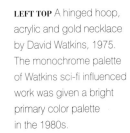

LEFT TOP A hinged hoop, acrylic and gold necklace by David Watkins, 1975. The monochrome palette of Watkins sci-fi influenced work was given a bright primary color palette in the 1980s.

LEFT CENTER A forged steel and blue steel bangle by David Watkins, circa 1970, with 18-karat gold lines, relies on simple geometry for its visual intensity.

LEFT BOTTOM A minimalist, sci-fi-inspired bangle by David Watkins that takes the form of a series of concentric circles in machined aluminum, 1977.

BELOW This steel and acrylic bracelet from 1970, by Gerd Rothmann, is in the form of a bagatelle game. Rothmann was one of a small group of pioneering artist-craftsmen who, inspired by Pop Art in the early 1970s, promoted the use of acrylic in jewelry.

OPPOSITE A large pendant body piece created by David Watkins in 1975 in acrylic, gold and aluminum. Watkins' early jewelry shows the influence of his employment as a model-maker on Stanley Kubrick's sci-fi masterpiece *2001: A Space Odyssey* (1968) in its futuristic minimalism.

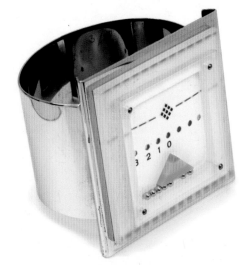

Wendy Ramshaw

First represented at the 'Jewelry in Europe' exhibition in 1976, Ramshaw (1939–) went on to an illustrious career, basing her work on the manipulation of a series of simple abstract shapes such as the circle, square, ring and band, which were repeated in changes of scale. Born in Sunderland, County Durham, Ramshaw studied illustration and fabric design in Newcastle from 1956–60 and was made a Freeman of the Worshipful Company of Goldsmiths in 1973. Her anodized silver and gold rings, inlaid with colored enamel and glass, were to be worn in multiples and contained moveable parts that interacted with one another. Lathe-turned stands were created to display them as small sculptures when not being worn. Ramshaw's early 1970s pieces were inspired by machinery and Space-Age technology while later collections referenced sources as diverse as aboriginal art (after a residency in Australia), Picasso and lace collars in seventeenth-century portraiture. One pin, called Petrified Lace, was 'tempted by the idea that lace, so soft and delicate, a magical material, might become reinvented in a harder and stiffer state to be worn in a different way.' As she puts it, 'All I ever wanted to do was to make things. It's about imagining them and working towards their existence in the world.'

ABOVE In the 1960s, husband-and-wife team David Watkins and Wendy Ramshaw formed a company called Something Special that produced affordable, self-assembly paper jewelry in bright, Day-Glo colors, selling through outlets in London and Japan. Here is a selection of their paper earrings suspended from wire, circa 1968.

ABOVE LEFT AND RIGHT
Two 1968 paper brooches by Something Special—a psychedelic, printed-paper butterfly brooch with wire and bead antennae and a silver and gold brooch.

ABOVE Wendy Ramshaw
rings on her trademark acrylic
stacks, 1978. Ramshaw's
rings are designed to be
joined together and worn in
multiples. When they are not
in use they form miniature
sculptures when placed on
acrylic or metal columns.

The Canadian Brutalists

A small group of studio jewelers from Canada rose to international prominence in the 1970s and moved from crafting one-off pieces to large-scale production. Brutalism, an aesthetic more commonly associated with post-war architecture and which can be described as a more stringent form of Modernism, flourished. The movement, called attention to the structure and materials of buildings—as theorist Reyner Banham described it, 'to make the whole conception of the building plain and comprehensible. No mystery, no romanticism, no obscurities about function and circulation.'

This 'truth to materials' approach can be seen in the work of Rafael Alfandary, Robert Larin and Gilles Vidal, who created a range of ultra-modern abstract jewelry that expanded women's range of choices. Eschewing any standard notions of glitz or glamour, Alfandary specialized in kinetic designs in hammered copper and brass, set with vividly colored Murano glass cabochons or more diffused tones of natural stone. Montreal-born Robert Larin had a factory on the Rue Papineau between 1968 and 1972 where he and his team made Brutalist abstract forms out of pewter, cast using the 'lost wax' process (see glossary, pages 217–9). The pewter pendants, brooches and bracelets were then filed down by hand to retain a pitted surface texture that echoed the surface of the moon and either left plain or plated with silver or gold. Like Larin, Gilles Vidal, also based in Montreal, worked primarily in pewter but in finer, more elegant, abstract shapes. As Brutalist architecture is now considered as a pivotal moment in the history of architecture, so it is only a matter of time before these Canadian names enjoy a much-owed renaissance.

CENTER LEFT Robert Larin's spiderweb brooch with a faux pearl in the center.

CENTER RIGHT Earrings by Montreal-based designer Gilles (aka Guy) Vidal in his custom mix of pewter and silver alloy.

TOP LEFT AND RIGHT Robert Larin's alien-inspired brooch, circa 1970, in silverplated pewter. Larin was one of a number of avant-garde jewelers working in Montreal during the 1970s that can be recognized by their hand-wrought, Brutalist style. His hallmark detail on the reverse is seen right.

BOTTOM The bracelet, left, matches Vidal's abstract pendant, far right, carrying the same central ball motif. The pendant shows the hand-wrought feel given to Modernist geometry. Vidal's maker's mark is shown inset center.

TOP LEFT A huge, gold plated, pewter pendant with faux amber insert: attributed to Robert Larin, circa 1970.

TOP RIGHT Two sides of a reversible, square-shaped pewter pendant by Gilles Vidal. It shows his trademark textured surface, a design detail that appears in lots of Canadian avant-garde jewelry of the 1970s, with abstract lunar relief work.

CENTER This elegant, signed pin by Gilles Vidal is an exercise in geometry.

BOTTOM LEFT A silver ring with a faux pearl and abstract relief sculpture in the center.

BOTTOM RIGHT A brooch displaying Larin's use of a highly textured surface, often referred to by collectors as 'lava bubble.'

Punk: The Deconstruction of Jewelry

In 1977, fashion anthropologist Ted Polhemus documented a new street style that seemed to be rather perturbing to the public. Describing a lone punk girl on a London street for British *Vogue*, he wrote:

…a red light shines on a girl with fluorescent orange hair. Her face is chalk white and her eye sockets blackened. She is wearing a black leather dog collar and studded wristbands. Her T-shirt is adorned with metal chains and zips and her skin has been replaced with black PVC, terminating in ice-pink stilettos.

Punk was shock-chic at its most aggressive; teenagers paraded the streets with brightly dyed, spiked hair and tribal make-up, wearing a bricolage-inspired style where found objects of the lowliest kind were converted into countercultural street fashion. The humble safety pin became an emblem of the movement; a mixture of the domestically forgettable and thrillingly sadomasochistic, it was at its most iconic when pierced through the lip of Queen Elizabeth II in the work of graphic designer Jamie Reid. On the streets or at clubs like the Roxy in London or CBGBs in New York, the safety pin was simply used to pierce the flesh of an earlobe or upper-lip for instant shock value, but it soon found its way into jewelry-making such as in the construction of huge collars worn Nefertiti-style by the New Romantics at the end of the decade or bejeweled and pinned onto punk couture designs by Zandra Rhodes, herself condemned by many for injecting notions of taste and craftsmanship into punk—a street style that celebrated the cheap and tacky. It was through figures such as Poly Styrene and Fay Fife of the Rezillos that kitsch jewelry in neon plastic made its way back into fashion, having lain dormant since the previous decade. Thrift shops were scoured for mod earrings, lurid psychedelic beads and 1950s poodle brooches and plastic fruit salad parures, which were combined with leopard-skin print and lashings of studded leather.

The punk movement had far-reaching effects, most notably as a breeding ground for a whole host of young designers who were to dominate avant-garde jewelry-making in the early 1980s. The most daring was Judy Blame, who remains a London-based stylist and accessories designer today. His bricolaged work with legendary stylist Ray Petrie included the imaginative use of paper clips to adorn collars, cuffs and lapels, which graced the pages of style magazines *ID* and *The Face* in the early 1980s. More recently he has worked as a creative consultant for many prestigious fashion houses, including John Galliano at Dior. Blame, formerly Chris Barnes, changed his name, and as he says, 'I wanted a lady name because everyone changed their name to one of the same sex, so I thought I'd confuse people. Judy was a nickname given to me by a friend, and Blame just sprang to mind one day. It sounds like a trashy B-movie actress from the '50s—a bleached blonde tart who only made one film and never got anywhere—I like that.'

BELOW Long-term collaborators and friends, Zandra Rhodes and Andrew Logan. The glamorous baroque of Logan's jewelry had a visual equivalent in the colorful textile designs of Rhodes, one of Britain's foremost fashion designers.

OPPOSITE LEFT Artist-jeweler Andrew Logan wears a collection of his shimmering, mosaic mirror jewelry. Each piece is handmade by the artist and inspired by a bricolage of memories, emotions and events, including travels to India, neon lights and Pop Art.

OPPOSITE RIGHT A model in Zandra Rhodes Punk Couture collection of 1977. Rhodes took the raw power of punk and converted it into couture using beaded gold safety pins and silver ball-link chains on dresses of knitted rayon jersey. Gemondo produces a range of her safety-pin Punk Chic jewelry today, studded with pink Swarovski crystal.

Blame's subversive style incorporated the punk ideology of *detournement*, which in turn had been appropriated from the Situationists of late 1960s Paris. To *detourne* was to convert objects of low culture into art and thus bring about a change in their meaning. To this end Vivienne Westwood changed fetish into fashion with her Bondage collection of 1977 and razor blades and safety pins became talismanic jewelry rather than objects of insignificance. Blame continued this approach by constructing pieces that had the barbarous, tribal anarchy of punk with a theatricality that fitted the New Romantic excess of London's club culture. His huge necklaces and bracelets of linked chain, from which dangle pearls, feathers, beer caps, plastic soldiers, seashells, African fabric and vintage buttons, were worn at clubs where gendered stereotypes of appearance were in flux. Any object had the potential to be jewelry—for one show by Yoshiki Hishinuma, Blame decked out the models in accessories made out of balls of wool and blue dustbin bags.

Andrew Logan

Born in Oxford and originally having trained as an architect, Andrew Logan (1945–) entered the field of jewelry design after an encounter with fashion designer Thea Porter in 1970, with whom he worked before beginning a long-term collaboration with Zandra Rhodes. A key figure on the London art scene—he had a studio in Butler's Wharf, the same warehouse as film director

Derek Jarman and artist Howard Hodgkin—he believed 'art can be discovered anywhere.' The trashy Pop Art exuberance of his aesthetic can be seen in the founding of the high camp Alternative Miss World, which has been running since 1972, and his oversized mosaic jewelry designs, which incorporate bright shards of mirrored glass in a searing neon color palette. Huge cuff bracelets, tiaras and bejeweled butterfly brooches continue to accompany Zandra Rhodes' designs whenever they are shown on the catwalk, their chunkiness offsetting her diaphanous chiffon prints.

▶ Stickpins

As flashy costume jewelry went out of fashion in the 1970s, more discreet pieces became mainstream. Stickpins enjoyed a vogue. Originally worn by men to hold a necktie or cravat in place, they were adopted by women and worn on the lapel of the jacket. This Givenchy version is typical of the period.

▶ Textured metal

Metal in all its forms dominated 1970s jewelry design. The absence of glittering stones forced designers to concentrate on textured surface effects and forms that were carved or molded in relief. This Gilles Vidal pendant is typical of the influential work produced in Canada during this period.

Key looks of the decade
1970s

▲ Rope rings

As the fashion for sparkling gems declined, simpler rings in earth colors and natural materials, such as rosewood, ivory and ebony, took over and were worn in stacks on each hand. Here, the popular gold rope ring is mixed with others of cornelian, plain gold and chyrophase, a green-colored chalcedony or quartz.

▶ Fashion jewelry

Costume jewelry relied more on the effects of metal than colorfully coordinated stones. This lariat tie necklace and earrings in gold-tone by Monet anticipates developments in the 1980s, when faux gold was the metal of choice. Monet, formerly Monocraft of 1928, was bought by Liz Claiborne in 2000.

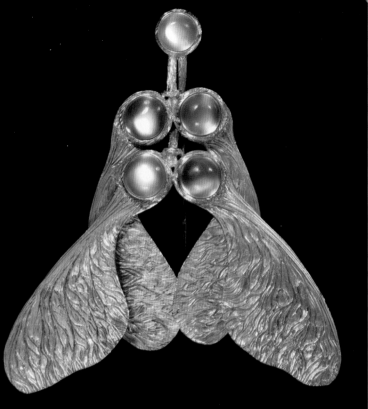

◀ **Art Nouveau Revival**
The continued influence of the hippie movement stimulated a craft revival and a re-awakening of interest in Art Nouveau. Malcolm Appleby—who continues to produce exquisite jewelry today—created this engraved gold brooch, taking the form of two sycamore wings with the seeds fashioned from moonstones, in 1975.

▲ **Body jewelry**
The sexual permissiveness of late 1960s hippie culture continued into the 1970s with an increasing pre-occupation with the body. Jewelry began to take over from clothes as a way of fashioning the body, and designers from every level in the market produced their own versions. This Pierre Cardin collar dates from the early 1970s.

Bronze
In the 1970s, many designers, following the lead from Finnish jewelers such as Jorma Laine, began producing jewelry in bronze. A cheap alternative to gold, it was easy to cast and had a folksy feel. Tino and Pentti Sarpeneva used bronze in combination with amethyst and rose or smokey quartz.

▲ **Turquoise**
Silver and turquoise jewelry from Mexico and Arizona was especially fashionable in the early part of the 1970s. It's relationship with down-trodden cultures struck a chord with the Vietnam War generation. Cher, seen here in 1974, is part Cherokee and was regularly photographed in Native American jewelry.

1980s:
The Power and the Glory

The fashion experimentation of the late 1970s continued into the early years of the 1980s. Designers such as Vivienne Westwood, Jean-Paul Gaultier and Franco Moschino worked with gender play and a plethora of historical references. Moschino, in particular, picked up where Elsa Schiaparelli had left off with Surrealist-inspired designs such as a quilted black denim mini with plastic fried eggs decorating the hemline, a jacket embellished with bottle tops, bodices made out of safety pins and earrings fashioned out of plug sockets.

The love of costume jewelry in all its forms reawakened interest in pieces from the past, which became immensely collectable. Original baubles, bangles and beads by earlier designers such as Hattie Carnegie, Joseff and Hobé began to increase in value and interest peaked when the first exhibition entirely devoted to costume jewelry, entitled 'Jewels of Fantasy: Fashion Jewelry of the Twentieth Century,' opened at the Museo Teatrale alla Scala in Milan in 1991. Visitors gawped at over 600 pieces by René Lalique, Elsa Schiaparelli, Miriam Haskell, Trifari and Christian Dior, among others, and the traveling show legitimized nonprecious jewelry as an art form worthy of worldwide recognition. American designer Robert Sorrell worked with the same spirit when he created handcrafted large-scale pieces in the manner of the Hollywood master-jewelers of the 1930s and 1940s in flashing Austrian crystal, pieces used by Thierry Mugler for his extravagant catwalk shows.

Moschino and Post-Modernism

As capitalism triumphed, wages boomed and credit became easily accessible, designer labels became a prime indicator of success in the workplace. Moschino parodied such conspicuous consumers of fashion with visual gags like a triple pearl choker with an attached croissant, thereby creating jewelry out of a power breakfast, and a necklace made out of Rolex watches. His jokes at the expense of the fashion victim continued throughout the decade with the use of sarky logos on a series of garments such as cashmere jackets with the words 'expensive jacket' embroidered in gold thread across the back or 'Bull Chic' on a matador-inspired outfit. This catwalk clobber was supposed to make the wearer feel duped into spending vast amounts of money on designer clothing but ironically, after achieving considerable publicity, caused flocks of fashionistas to buy his clothes. The iconoclasm of Moschino was destined to be the chicest thing on the catwalk.

Moschino was using the language of fashion to comment upon itself, creating a two-way theoretical dialogue that was given the name Post-Modernism in the 1980s. This aesthetic, first detected in late 1970s architecture, was to dominate the decade and, as a global style, proclaimed the death of moribund Modernism by calling for a return to historical forms. The past was rediscovered and formed a catalogue of motifs that were plundered with wit and irreverence, rather than with the eye of an archaeologist. Decorative detail made a resounding return and the rather serious minimalism of 1970s jewelry was overtaken by a mad exuberance where Rococo swags in shiny gold met cupids, bejeweled bows, Venetian masks and primary-colored Perspex in the gaudiest of mixes.

PAGE 174 Status jewelry was back with a vengeance in the 1980s, and exaggeration was a key aesthetic. These models are wearing jewelry by Stephen Dweck in 1985. The designer is known for his use of huge stones, such as Brazilian tourmalines, Australian boulder opals and South Sea pearls, for one-off pieces called OAK (One of a Kind).

RIGHT Madonna made her mainstream film debut in *Desperately Seeking Susan* (1985) wearing rubber bangles and multi-strand necklaces by Maripol. Maripol also styled Madonna for her *Like a Virgin* album cover, shot by photographer Steven Meisel.

Tom Binns and Vivienne Westwood

Vivienne Westwood was a Post-Modernist designer par excellence, plundering sources as varied as eighteenth-century pirates, Peruvian folk costume and New York's emerging hip-hop culture. She collaborated on the catwalk with jewelry designer Tom Binns, who began his nonconformist career in 1981 after graduating with a degree in jewelry design. Inspired by the anarchic and confrontational Dada art movement of the early twentieth century—a movement that changed the vocabulary of fine art with its use of found objects to create sculpture—Binns collected shards of sea glass, bent forks and shells, combining them with reconstructed vintage costume jewelry to create work that had a tough, punkish appeal. Binns' alchemical eye turned junk into jewelry. His huge layered and charmed necklaces, thick studded silver cuffs and Gothic skull stud earrings were dubbed the 'sunken treasure' look—a perfect fit for Westwood's 1981 Pirate collection. Binn's first collection in his own name

was in the same year and was created entirely in rubber, a material much used in punk styling and in the Italian label Fiorucci's first jewelry collection, designed by Maripol in 1978. Flash forward four years and in the film *Desperately Seeking Susan* (1985) Madonna can be seen with an armful of Maripol rubber bangles, multi-strand pearl-and-diamanté necklaces and her omnipresent crucifixes.

In 1987 Binns showed copper jewelry in the form of hands that encircled the wrists or bizarre brooches that appeared to clutch the chest; in 2009 he etched huge silver collars with the words 'statement piece' and painted crystal collars with neon graffiti. His Get Real collection of 2010 was made from photographs of rings, earrings and necklaces, laminated in plastic with safety pin closures. In the same year Binns collaborated with film director Tim Burton on huge chain charm necklaces and heart earrings for the film *Alice in Wonderland*, saying, '…jewelry is always a treasure, and though it may not be made of gold and diamonds, it should still have that sentiment.'

BELOW By the early 1980s the shock-chic of punk had moved from the street to high fashion, as designers began to incorporate tough tribal and fetish elements into their work. In this 1983 shot, the model wears a black lace dress by Norma Kamali, black feather earrings by Pauletta Brooks and black rubber bracelets by Sherry Mills at Janet Norem and Joel Powell Designs.

Power Jewelry

The emergence of Margaret Thatcher as the first female Prime Minister of Britain was of both political and gender significance. She put accepted notions of power, control and femininity more transparently onto the cultural agenda and sparked much debate about the new executive women, not least about what she should wear. Enter the style guide. The most successful was written by fashion consultant John T Molloy with a stirring title ringing as a call to arms: *Women: Dress For Success* (1980). Molloy believed that a new set of rules was needed for women of power in the world of work and prescribed a diet of serious sober suiting in subtly neutral colors of navy and grey. Women had to blend successfully into the male environment without causing too much fuss and Molloy believed those with any common sense would do well to reject anything too frilly and overtly feminine. He had strong views on the use of jewelry in the workplace, which included 'The most useful piece of jewelry any businesswoman can wear is a wedding ring. A wedding ring announces to the world that you are there for business and nothing else' (see below for more of his advice for businesswomen).

Molloy's 'dress for success' look struck a chord across the world and was re-named 'power dressing.' In the early years of the 1980s the black or navy suit with padded shoulders and a crisp white shirt became *de rigueur*, but as the decade progressed the style was subverted; skirts got shorter, heels became higher and jewelry—brash, bright and sexy—flashed about the wrists and throat. In 1980 fashion maven Diana Vreeland commented 'everything is power and money and how to use them both. We mustn't be afraid of snobbism and luxury.' This 'greed is good' philosophy was neatly summed up in Versace and Bulgari's coin jewelry, an invention of the Romans and revived by Castellini in the nineteenth century. Bulgari placed coins, both ancient and modern, into gold frames that hung from heavy gold chains and in the high street the gold sovereign and gold ingot reached dizzying heights of popularity. Spending was recognized as a cultural as well as economic activity and, unlike in the previous decade, consumers didn't need to be quiet about it—it was literally time to flash the cash.

ABOVE Jewelry by Butler & Wilson, who responded with alacrity to the vogue for glitz and glamor in the 1980s. Faux gold was all the rage in this decade, and over-large collars and dangling earrings (aka power jewelry) were worn as daywear.

JOHN T MALLOY'S *DRESS FOR SUCCESS*

* Instead of buying four or five cheaper pieces throughout the year, buy one good piece.
* If you have expensive jewelry, don't wear it on the first meeting. Sneak up to people with it. Otherwise it will have the effect of artillery.
* A ring should not be a big bulge but should lie flat against the hand.
* Anything that clangs, bangs or jangles should be avoided.
* Dangling earrings are out.

LEFT During the 1980s, Bulgari, the iconic Italian jewelry house, moved from special-occasion jewelry to pieces designed for daywear. Their range of simple, modular designs that could be worn in combination included these rings of 1982.

ABOVE A fashion shoot from 1981 exemplifies the 'greed is good' narrative that was to define the ensuing decade. Model Rosemary McGrotha, in a white silk kaftan by Fernando Sanchez and diamonds by Harry Winston, reclines next to a briefcase filled with money in the Hotel du Palais in Biarritz.

Frankly Fake

The universal currency of credit helped in the dissolution of class boundaries in the 1980s and aspiration was neatly catered for with the new 'lifestyle' branding. An aggressive form of rather strident glamour entered fashion inspired by television rather than the cinema of old, in particular the long-running series *Dallas* and *Dynasty*. Joan Collins as Alexis Colby was a high-camp dominatrix of cartoon dimensions, wielding her flashy style as a formidable weapon in the war of the sexes. In her hands glamour found its original power, that of elevating the mundane reality of womanhood into mesmerizing fantasy, and her look suggested that with the right combination of hair, make-up, power suits and huge jewels any *femme fatale* could fool the eye into thinking it was seeing something utterly spectacular. Natural beauty no longer cut it.

Jewelry was the key to unlocking this supernatural power and the more fake and larger-than-life the better. The French couture houses enjoyed incredible success from residual products such as make-up, handbags and jewelry, which were a quick buy into a classy brand image. A city dealer might not yet be able to afford a Chanel suit, but she could buy a pair of logoed earrings that could be prominently on view with the new shorter haircuts or sport a chunky chain belt with the magical double-C logo. Most significantly, women with economic independence were no longer waiting around for the man in their life to buy them a bauble, they were doing it for themselves. Pendants were out, they were quite unsuited to the world of work, and neck-hugging looks were in—the short triple-strand necklace made a huge comeback but this time around it was obviously fake, with pearls the size of bird's eggs.

ABOVE AND LEFT In 1983 Karl Lagerfeld took over the fashion house of Chanel and rebranded it to chime with the times. He broadened its customer base with an injection of youthful vitality, wittily using the traditional symbols of the double-C logo and the camellia. This Chanel brooch, necklace and pendant earring set, cast in goldplated white metal, shows his bold and uncompromising approach with its quilted detail, wittily referencing Chanel's iconic 2.55 black, lambskin bag.

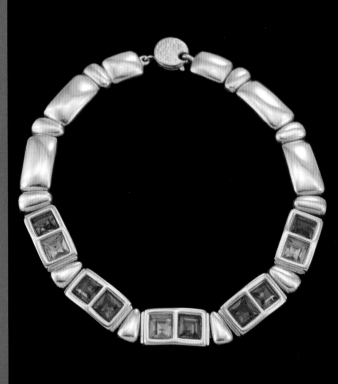

LEFT A 1985 ensemble by Karl Lagerfeld at Chanel. The black wool, sleeveless dinner dress and long black suede gloves with trompe l'oeil jewels and chains embroidered at the waist and wrists are worn with gold earrings and a gold chain necklace.

ABOVE Other couture houses, such as Yves Saint Laurent, followed Chanel's brash example and produced large pieces of fake-looking costume jewelry. This couture collar necklace, constructed of heavy links, is set with large, princess-cut rhinestones in emerald, amethyst and topaz and fastened with a spring ring closure.

Yves Saint Laurent showed oversized gem-cut glass costume jewelry in all of his collections and was renowned for his cuff bracelets, which models wore on both their wrists, each bracelet glittering with hand-set Swarovski crystals in his favorite combinations of red and green or fuchsia pink and persimmon. Fine jewelers also followed the trend for unusual color combinations: emeralds were placed next to bright orange garnets, the deep red of rubies clashed with the intense purple of an amethyst. When a deposit was discovered in Western Australia in 1979, pink diamonds became popular and available. In 1983 Karl Lagerfeld took over as Chanel's design director and expressed the new aesthetic perfectly by giving priority to the Chanel logo as a brashly dominant feature in his catwalk designs. Chanel jewelry was big and brassy; gold interlocked Cs appeared as clip earrings, on charm bracelets and caught up in huge ropes of chain and pearl. Poured red and green glass by Gripoix was set into massive gilt Maltese crosses and tassel necklaces. All the big French houses such as Givenchy followed suit with jangling charm bracelets, faux-pearl logo earrings and thick hip-hop chains, and in 1980 Paloma Picasso began designing bold and brilliantly colored graffiti-inspired jewelry for Tiffany. Perhaps most astonishingly, this hysterically baroque look was considered entirely appropriate for day as well as evening and women stalked the streets in spike heels wearing power suits in lime green or canary yellow with huge bouffant hair and enough jewelry to sink a battleship.

ABOVE Yves Saint Laurent jewelry created for the catwalk in 1985. The vogue for gold was at its height at this time.

FAR LEFT Goldplated clip earrings by Yves Saint Laurent, top, mix the abstract with the naturalistic in a brushed antiqued finish while goldplated, Swarovski crystal earrings, also by Saint Laurent, are reminiscent of Juliana's work in the 1950s.

LEFT Two Art Deco Revival pins by Yves Saint Laurent from the 1980s revive the monochromatic color palette of the 1920s.

ABOVE RIGHT A pink, red and fuchsia crystal clamper bracelet by Robert Sorrell, showing the designer's passion and homage to 1940s and 1950s costume jewelry.

RIGHT A pair of clip chandelier, opal earrings showing Sorrell's amazing craftsmanship and color sense. All his work is handcrafted using Swarovski crystals.

TOP Robert Sorrell's easily identifiable cartouche.

ABOVE An Art Deco-inspired brooch by Sorrell. The Art Deco style enjoyed a huge revival in the 1980s, and Sorrel is said to have derived inspiration from studying the catalogues of the great auction houses.

RIGHT A Sorrel mosaic bow brooch, very similar in style to the work produced by Larry Vrba in this decade.

Butler & Wilson

British antique dealers Nicky Butler and Simon Wilson specialized in Art Nouveau and Art Deco jewelry, which they sold from a stall in London's premier antique market Portobello Road in 1968, Chelsea Antiques Market in 1969 and Antiquarius in 1970. Vintage was undergoing its first foray into fashion as a generation of young style seekers discovered its alternative charms as a path into true individuality. The previously derided style of Art Nouveau began to enjoy a revival—the motifs of the dragonfly and cicada were both used in early Butler & Wilson work. Fashion editors such as Caroline Baker for *Nova* and Grace Coddington for *Vogue* began to use antique jewelry in fashion shoots. The demand for the original pieces became so high that the duo realized there was a market for vintage-inspired costume jewelry in the same way that Biba had produced pastiches of pre-war fashion in the late 1960s. In 1972 Butler & Wilson opened a shop in the Fulham Road where they created an astonishingly successful collection of Deco-inspired work, combining a 1920s feel with a modern Pop Art sensibility. The Art Deco image of the sad-faced Pierrot was revived with aplomb and proved an instant hit when re-created in black and white diamanté or painted porcelain, sometimes swinging from the crescent of a silvery moon and fashioned into a sweeping necklace. Surrealist clasped-hand brooches sat side by side with rhinestone-encrusted teddy bears or sparkling spiderweb pins and their look of exaggerated glamour was a perfect fit with the fashion feel.

The duo are perhaps best known for their figurative diamanté work, which in the 1980s included flora, fauna and insects of every imaginable size and shape, given instant fashion cachet after an advertising campaign featured stars such as Faye Dunaway, Jerry Hall, Twiggy and Catherine Deneuve, snapped by contemporary photographers such as David Bailey adorned in their glittering trinkets. In 1982 after Nicky Butler's excursions into Mexico, Butler & Wilson revisited the Navajo style of jewelry, so popular in the early 1970s. Chunky silver and turquoise pieces began to grace the shelves of the shop. As the fame of their name grew, so the pieces became more and more extravagant—some looked even somewhat threatening, such as the huge predatory spider brooches that looked poised to leap from the lapel of a jacket or sinuous serpents that coiled round the neck or wrist of an femme fatale clad in black jersey body-con. In 1986 their reputation was complete when Princess Diana attended a concert in Vancouver, Canada, wearing a black tuxedo suit accessorized with a massive diamanté and black glass brooch in the shape of a serpent, proving fabulous fakery could be worn by women from every echelon of society. The spirit of Chanel had returned.

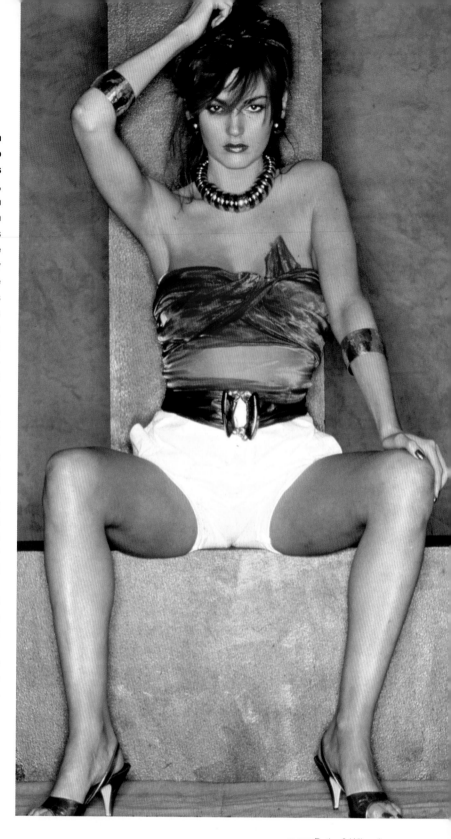

ABOVE Butler & Wilson's exaggerated jewelry designs typified the brash glamour of the 1980s and were incredibly successful. Here a model wears a mix of bronze and brass accessories by the design duo in 1980.

LEFT In the 1980s, a traffic-stopping series of huge billboards were put up along the Fulham Road in London showing glamorous film stars modeling Butler & Wilson jewelry. This iconic image of the American actress Faye Dunaway was seen on one of the billboards.

BELOW LEFT This Butler & Wilson lizard brooch, in prong-set Austrian crystal, is jointed down the length of the body and tail so that it can be articulated into different shapes and worn over the shoulder.

BELOW A bracelet by Erickson Beamon, in homage to great American jewelry designer Miriam Haskell, is crafted in deep red crystal and faux silvery grey pearls set in plaques.

Erickson Beamon

Detroit-born Karen Erickson and Vicki Beaman launched their company in 1983 after moving to New York where they had begun producing the intricately handcrafted crystal-and -beaded necklaces for which they are known and which are still meticulously hand-assembled by a team of artisans today. The pair have an international reputation as a result of collaborations with catwalk designers, including John Galliano and Zac Posen, for whom they create custom jewelry that interprets the theme of each collection—for example, they designed crystal devil horns for an Anna Sui catwalk show. Erickson says that 'the key is being able to pull out what the designers are thinking. They don't always have a definite idea. We have to dig into their brains and materialize what they're envisioning. The trick in working with designers and stylists is to keep our own integrity and not look like anyone else.'

The New Black

The color black—decadent and sexy, mysterious and rebellious—dominated this decade in fashion, interiors and jewelry. By the early 1980s black entered fashion with renewed vigor after an unsettling series of Paris shows by a group of experimental Japanese designers who were to change the face of fashion. Yohji Yamamoto and Rei Kawakubo had models walking resolutely down the catwalk appearing as if stoic survivors from some nuclear holocaust in crumpled and wrapped clothes that were asymmetrical, abstract and seriously monochromatic. Kawakubo worked 'in three shades of black,' as she put it, and Yamamoto used this non-color to explore new ways of dressing by synthesizing Western clothing archetypes and indigenous Japanese clothing. By mid decade black was back providing a backdrop for polished gold jewelry but also as a base color that could be offset by those of a more intense hue such as shocking pink, lime green or kingfisher blue. Women designers such as Paloma Picasso at Tiffany and Marina B perfectly understood the lure of this trend for the independent and successful global businesswoman who wore black, both as a uniform at work in the form of a sharp power suit, and at play in an LBD.

Marina B

Daughter of Constantino and granddaughter of Sotiro Bulgari, Marina B (1930–) has jewelry in her blood-stream. In 1979 she broke away from Bulgari and opened her own shop at 9 place du Molard in Geneva, where she began creating lines under the name Marina B. In 1980 she registered a new diamond cut, which was a mix of a triangle, heart and drop and gave a new vibrancy to the popular rock. Her sexy, vibrant designs caught the imagination of rich, yet independent women and were recognizable by their dramatic color combinations, which played on the drama created when black was used to offset vividly colored stones. The designer went even further by infusing her design with the adaptability and versatility women began to expect from their clothes, in particular the day-to-night concept. A working woman did not have the time to return home before changing for a dinner date so needed both clothes and jewelry that could transform her from an executive Cinderella into a soignée swan. The addition of the right piece of jewelry could make this transformation complete and Marina B's 'interchangeable' jewelry struck the right note. In 1980 the Pneu earrings had drops of jewels that could be taken out and swapped for others to match the color of an outfit. The interchangeable gems had different values too, so the most expensive could be saved for night. The success led to other designs such as brooches and matching earrings with reversible stones that could be rotated to show a discrete one for day and pavé-set with diamonds to dazzle at night.

OPPOSITE Paloma Picasso, daughter of the Spanish artist Pablo Picasso, is an acclaimed jewelry designer who rose to fame in the 1980s with her bold and beautiful creations.

ABOVE Paloma Picasso with an array of her 1980s designs using the favored color palette of the decade —white, black and gold.

LEFT The woman as the epitome of showy glamour was a popular 1980s figure in fashion editorial. Here, Yves Saint Laurent has accessorized a white mink fur bolero jacket with large pieces of jewelry.

The New Jewelry

Building on the aesthetic advances of the 1970s, studio jewelers in Britain, Holland and Germany in particular continued their experimentation into the relationship between jewelry and the body. Post-Modernism had profound effects in the making of avant-garde jewelry not least because it was another theoretical incursion into the 'art versus craft' debate. Post-Modernists argued that the value of any cultural artifact was not necessarily in direct correlation with intellectual weight, kitsch could have cultural meaning too; fine art, despite the posturing of bohemians, was not untainted by the pressures of the marketplace but clearly driven by it and was just as much capitalism's lapdog as fashion. Post-Modernism's questioning of boundaries and taste allowed for a critical re-evaluation of jewelry. Whether it was fashion, craft, design or sculpture, all had the same weight if there was no value system, or if that value system was entirely democratic. Michel Foucault was one Post-Modernist theorist who entered the debate writing:

When we establish a considered classification, when we say that a cat and a dog resemble each other less than two greyhounds do…what is the ground on which we are able to establish the validity of this classification with complete certainty? On what 'table,' according to what grid of identities, similitudes, analogies, have we become accustomed to sorting out so many different and similar things?

The New Jewelry movement was named after the publication of a landmark book written by Peter Dormer and Ralph Turner in 1985, *The New Jewelry: Trends and Traditions*. Turner had been involved in the curation of jewelry for decades and in the 1980s was head of exhibitions at the Craft Council in London. The premise of the movement was to expand the debate of what actually constituted a piece of jewelry design and to this end its practitioners such as Susanna Heron, Geoff Roberts and Swiss jewelers Pierre Degan and Otto Künzli played provocatively with the traditional vocabulary of personal adornment. Künzli's drawing-pin pieces of 1980 and wallpaper brooches of 1982 onwards caused many heads to shake in disbelief. New Jewelers also entered into the realms of performance art; for example, Tom Saddington welded himself into a huge stainless-steel can at the Arnolfini Gallery in Bristol, which was opened with a giant tin opener so that he could have 'an insight into the notion of getting inside a piece of jewelry to wear it.' Caroline Broadhead fashioned brooches and bracelets out of laminated wood, cotton threads, rope and dyed nylon filament, materials more suited to industrial design or textiles rather than jewelry; her 1983 nylon-filament Sleeve ran from the shoulder down to the wrist

of the wearer. Paul Derrez of Amsterdam and director of the Galerie Ra, which remains an important outlet for new jewelers, produced theatrical and sculptural work in silver such as the Pleated Collar of 1982 and Pebble Necklace of 1985.

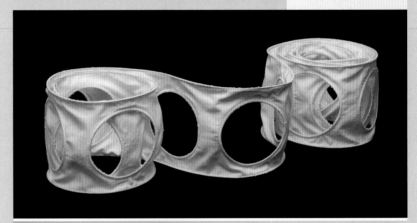

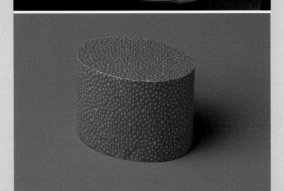

TOP As if in response to so much decadence, avant-garde jewelers created work with intellectual weight instead. Otto Künzli was one such designer who took the most mundane objects of culture and transformed them into jewelry, such as this thumbtack pin of 1980 in 22-karat gold and steel.

ABOVE Caroline Broadhead created uncompromisingly modern jewelry out of deliberately non-precious material, such as this arm-piece entitled 22 in 1 (1984) in cotton, nylon and monofilament.

LEFT Caroline Broadhead modeling her own silver and nylon thread necklace and filament tuft earrings.

BOTTOM An Otto Künzli wallpaper brooch of 1982 in fabricated wallpaper, polystyrene and plastic.

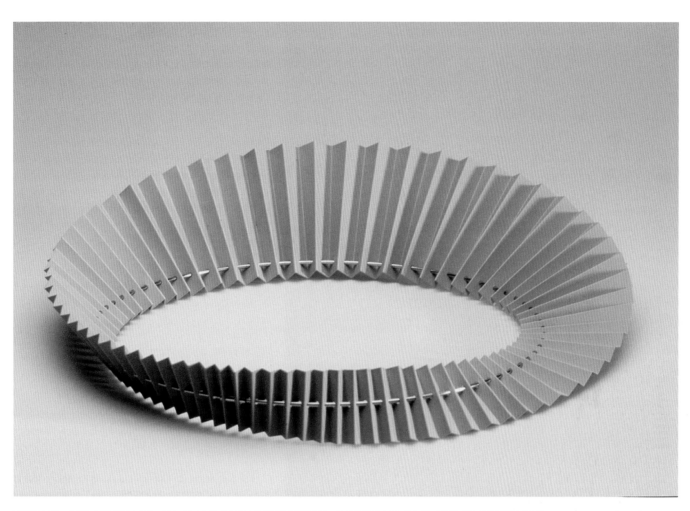

ABOVE Paul Derrez's Pleated Collar of 1982, rendered from plastic and steel. He remains a driving force in contemporary jewelry as director of the Galerie Ra in Amsterdam.

LEFT Pebble necklace in cork, 1985, by Paul Derrez. A trompe l'oeil piece that appears to be fashioned from beach pebbles, but has the lightness of cork. His work is the antithesis of mass-production.

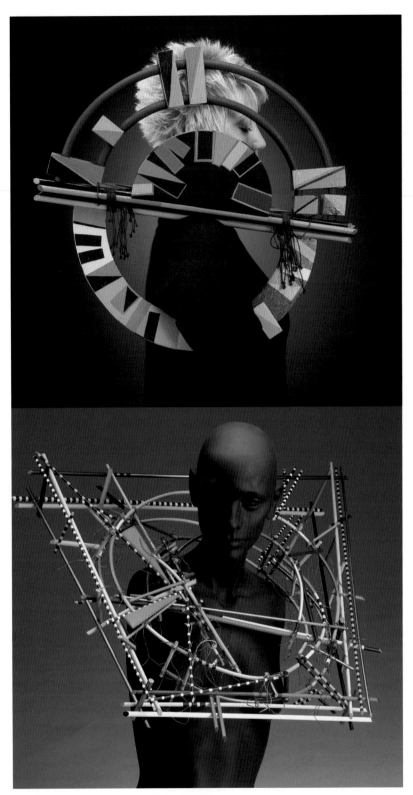

Marjorie Schick

Born in Illinois and raised by a single mother who was an art teacher, Marjorie Schick (1941–) studied jewelry at Indiana University with Alma Eikerman, a pioneer in the field of metalsmithing. Inspired by the large-scale metal forms of Abstract Expressionist sculptor David Smith she began building body pieces that blurred the boundaries between jewelry and sculpture to create a visually dynamic form of wearable art. In 1967 she was made professor of art at Pittsburgh State University, where she has remained ever since as an inspirational educator for generations of young jewelry designers.

Described as one of the most radical of American designers, Schick has always seen jewelry as a three-dimensional drawing that could function as wearable art. Her huge neckpieces extend the boundaries of the body, making the wearer look almost like a peacock with its tail feathers extended. She says,

My work is a sculptural statement which is complete when off the figure yet is constructed and exists because of the human body. I am intrigued by the idea that the human body is capable of carrying large objects, both physically and visually; therefore I often construct forms of a scale which puts the work into the category of body sculpture rather than jewelry.

For her, the body becomes a living sculpture that is then adorned with shapes, which are constructed out of a variety of materials on a massive scale. Brooches in metal and painted paper stretch from shoulder to shoulder, brilliantly colored ceremonial collars in wood and paper cover the face and head, causing the wearer to reconsider how he/she moves in the surrounding space. Schick talks of changing the way we feel about wearing jewelry, of becoming more conscious as consumers and wearers of how it interacts with our bodies in culture. The wedding ring, for instance, is what she calls a Thirty-Year piece—it is worn daily so has to be practical for mundane everyday tasks like washing up and driving a car; over time it becomes so perfectly in tune with the body it is forgotten. Three-Hour jewelry comprises the more expensive items that we may wear for a party to gain admiration and then take off and stow away safely when we get home, whereas her Thirty-Second designs are so monumental and some so heavy, that even short-term wear makes them unforgettable. Even once-simple activities like walking through a door becomes an action that has to be renegotiated—jewelry takes charge of the body and becomes the most controlling of personal adornment.

TOP Entitled For Pforzheim: Folding Collar Number 2, this painted wood, rubber and cord work was created in 1989 by Marjorie Schick.

ABOVE Not a Square: Necklace (1986) in painted wood, reed and thread by Marjorie Schick. Her jewelry extends the boundaries of the body and interacts with the surrounding space.

LEFT A Plane of Sticks, Sculpture for the Neck (1986). This painted wood sculptural piece by Marjorie Schick shows how her 1980s experimentation breached the boundaries between jewelry and fine art.

ABOVE Model Wanakee wears earrings by sculptor and jeweler Robert Lee Morris. Reclining on a sofa, she wears a sequinned sweater and white charmeuse pants, both by Oscar de la Renta, and a gold ring by Madeleine van Eerde for Boris.

Gold and glitz

The 1980s trappings of luxurious excess included jewelry that was bold, brash and showy. The cult of visible wealth meant settings and stones, whether real or faux, had to be large and were a focal point for any elegant black dress.

Crucifixes

Maripol's original rosary-inspired designs, as famously worn by Madonna in the 1980s, became one of the defining looks of the decade and were produced by fashion houses such as Christian Lacroix, who produced an elaborately designed version in rolled gold and on the high street.

Key looks of the decade
1980s

▼ Fluorescents

Fluorescent colors appeared as counterpoint to the sophistication of gold and was influenced by post-punk and 1980s hip-hop. Lime green and pink, once seen in the graffiti art of New York's Keith Haring and the city's subways, crossed over into pieces such as this 1985 collar necklace by Steven Rosen.

▲ Bracelets and cuffs

The cuff bracelet made a comeback after the thin discreet metal bangle designs of the preceding decade. With its intimations of body armor, the thick metal cuff, studded with huge faux stones, matched the vogue for power dressing as women entered the executive workplace as the equals of men.

◄ Ropes and chains

The influence of punk could be seen in the exaggerated and almost fetishistic effects created by 1980s jewelry. Ropes and chains were worn in multiples by stars like Madonna, whose influence was felt on the high street.

▼ Coin jewelry

The display of wealth through adornment was at its most obvious with the revival of coin jewelry, one of the most ancient types of adornment. Bulgari through Chanel, created coin jewelry for the high street. This 10-karat goldplated Chanel, quadrangle coin cluster earrings are typical of this decade.

▼ Geometrics

The geometry of Art Deco was revived and exaggerated on a much larger and dramatic scale. The elegance of Suzanne Belperron and Raymond Templier, pioneers of this aesthetic in the 1920s, was replaced with huge, abstract, gem-studded forms like this Yves Saint Laurent necklace and earrings.

Logos

The cult of visible wealth in the 1980s created a veritable logo-mania. Lagerfeld was one of the most successful at this overt branding and transformed the House of Chanel from a rather matronly label into one of youthful energy and joie de vivre. Double-C logos were fashioned into earrings, bracelets and pendants.

1990s to Now:
Future Collectables

If 1980s style is defined by its flamboyance, the early 1990s were the modicum of reticence and restraint. Designers responded to the so-called 'New Age,' the moniker given to a cultural moment that was expressed in a reawakened spirituality feared to have disappeared during the shopping frenzy of the previous decade. More and more people were becoming aware of the fragility of the planet; others consuming more stealthily in response to a global recession that made obvious expressions of wealth look vulgar beyond belief. The trappings of luxurious excess were anathema in a new decade that was calling for a change in consciousness. A minimalist aesthetic began to enter design, a new take on Modernism that made consumers both chic and environmentally aware and could be seen in the restrained designs of Prada and Jil Sander and the continued popularity of the work of jeweler Robert Lee Morris.

The renunciation of status dressing could only last so long. By the 2000s fashion began to move away from the sterility of 1990s minimalism to a look of luxuriant and decadent excess. Avant-garde designers John Galliano and Alexander McQueen showed models who embodied both siren seduction and sexual threat; post-millennium *femmes fatales* stalked the catwalk in shows of dramatic theatricality and future apocalypse, ushering in an era of maximalism.

In mainstream jewelry a similarly decadent flashiness could be executed on the cheap with the rise of the cubic zirconia, the cubic crystalline form of zirconium, which when synthesized becomes incredibly hard, flawless and clear and can be made transparent to resemble a diamond or colored to simulate precious stones. The cheapness of the faux diamond was well suited to the maximalism of the early twenty-first century, especially when marked under the rather glamorous title 'Diamonique.'

Themes in Jewelry

Fine jewelry remained reassuringly expensive but an understatement crept in—chains were finer, gems less overt and decorative motifs gave a nod in the direction of nature with a plethora of butterflies, dragonflies and aquatic themes. In 1991 Bulgari brought out its version of a New Age range—the Naturalia collection, while simultaneously supporting the World Wildlife Fund's Biological Diversity Campaign, and referenced both flora and fauna in its motifs and materials with the use of coral and pearl. Gold rings took the form of stylized ruby-eyed fish swallowing their own tails and one gem-set Naturalia pavé-set diamond, chevron, fish bangle comprised eight gem-set panels in red coral, chalcedony, amethyst, citrine and pink and green tourmalines, all mounted in 18-karat gold. Japanese designer Kaoru Kay Akihara, working under the name Gimel, took similar inspiration from nature that seemed poised on the brink of destruction—one pavé-set ring was shaped like a lotus flower in pink diamonds and green garnets with a tiny sapphire snail secreted inside, which could only be seen by the wearer. Gimel's painterly use of small pavé-set gemstones became a dominant feature of high-end jewelry into the 2000s, as it allowed for an incredible subtlety of color which, in the hands of the right jeweler, could be set to diffuse softly across the piece from one tone to another.

An awareness and response to multiculturalism became increasingly evidenced by the use of vernacular motifs and materials transplanted from non-western cultures, a prime example of which was the popularity of materials that mimicked ivory. Huge pieces of hand-made silver Tibetan jewelry such as turquoise-studded pendant prayer boxes found their way into the jewelry departments of stores such as Liberty's of London and Bloomingdale's in New York City and were mimicked on the catwalk by contemporary designers. This was jewelry for the *haut* hippie, a newly spiritually aware and artistic woman who lived in Notting Hill or Greenwich Village. Expensive ethnic jewelry became a folk costume for the ethical yet super-rich in the same way as it had in the early 1970s.

TOP RIGHT Concerns for the environment led to a revival of interest in both naturalistic forms and ethnic themes. This pair of silver earrings, with the Native American symbol of the thunderbird, are inset with turquoise and beadwork by Elizabeth Taliman, a jeweler of Navajo/ Cochiti descent.

RIGHT Thierry Mugler's usual cast of superheroes and *femmes fatales* were supplanted in his 1999 spring/summer collection by a tribal-inspired style that used body paint, masks and huge sculptural earrings to accompany the pared-down minimalism of the clothes.

PAGE 194 In 2003, Swarovski commissioned a number of cutting-edge jewelry designers to create collections of one-off jewelry pieces for a series of spectacular catwalk shows called Runway Rocks. Shaun Leane used his signature thorn motif to explore body modification and binding in 2004.

RIGHT Francis Mertens' body jewelry and earrings were created for Swarovski Runway Rocks in 2008. Based in Antwerp in Belgium, Mertens uses computer aided design (CAD) in his process, together with high-tech, lightweight materials like titanium, to create huge and detailed naturalistic designs.

'Real' jewelry began to be perceived as a little old-fashioned, more to do with connoisseurship and ostentation rather than fashion. However designer Marie-Hélène de Taillac sparked a revolution in jewelry by using real gems in a contemporary way, shaping briolette-cut stones; a faceted teardrop shape, previously only used for diamonds. The pavé setting became the trademark of what many consider to be the greatest living jeweler, Joel Arthur Rosenthal (aka JAR), who produces only 70 pieces a year, such is the quality of craftsmanship, and James de Givenchy, Nigel Milne, Catherine Prevost and Neil Lane began cutting expensive stones in modern ways.

LEFT CLOCKWISE A selection of jewelry by Neil Lane. Lane launched his jewelry business in 1989 in Los Angeles, after spending two years studying painting at L'Ecole des Beaux Arts in Paris. Lane's work shows a keen eye for color combined with a high deluxe style. Here are a pair of diamond and platinum chandelier earrings; a platinum and diamond ring; a white gold bangle set with studded rough-cut diamonds; an extravagantly ruffled cuff bracelet in a 'white-on-white' style that enjoyed a massive revival in the 2000s; a pavé-set diamond cuff bracelet with a flowerhead motif.

RIGHT CLOCKWISE Marie-Hélène de Taillac launched her Paris-based label in 1999. She is known for her elegant designs in fine gold settings, with brilliant color combinations of semiprecious stones. Here are a 22-karat gold, irregularly sized sequin necklace, first designed in 1999; a briolette rubelite pendant suspended from a handmade gold chain —the briolette cut was traditionally only used on the finest diamonds until Taillac applied the process to semiprecious stones in 2001; the Rainbow necklace of 2002; the 1001 Night hoop earrings, a modern take on the traditional hoop earring with a rainbow of briolette-cut stones.

Catwalk Collaborators

The mordant theatricality of fashion shows became more and more extreme as designers vied with each other to raise column inches and sell residual products—the couture customer base was quite literally dying out and jewelry was an important source of revenue. It was also a way of adding bite to a show by enhancing its effects—Naomi Filmer's gold vampire teeth for Hussein Chalayan, for instance, added just a little extra magic.

Jewelry designed for the catwalk is among the most edgy of contemporary jewelry. In Galliano's autumn/winter 1998–9 collection, the designer made parallels between the decadence of the *belle époque* and contemporary culture by drawing on photographs of La Belle Otero as an *objet de luxe*, specifically referencing her infamous Cartier diamonds. Designers such as Naomi Filmer and Shaun Leane experiment with age-old materials such as bone, human hair and bodily fluids in collaboration with fashion designers Hussein Chalayan and Alexander McQueen, fusing jewelry with art and sculpture to extend, confuse and mark the boundaries of the body. These pieces are not realized commercially, but are site specific in the way that certain works of art are geared to a specific gallery or architectural space.

However designers such as Irish jeweler Slim Barrett are not only leading and influencing commercial jewelry design but are creating their own ranges where the ideas formerly experimented with on the catwalk are given more commercial appeal. Barrett cleverly invests his very modern jewelry with cultural references of his Irish heritage and homeland as in his 18-karat gold Feronia Coronet. He says, 'I draw from a deep well of knowledge and culture.' Naomi Filmer, born in London in 1969, studied goldsmithing at the prestigious Royal College of Art before becoming a senior research fellow at Central Saint Martins College of Art and Design in London. Her work is fearless in its radical celebration of the body—in one series huge glass lenses capture and magnify isolated areas of a torso, elbow or back, creating unexpected shapes and shadows.

OPPOSITE Lesley Vik Waddell is known for large-scale conceptual pieces of body jewelry that reference the restriction of the body caused by corsets and neck braces or scold's bridles.

TOP Irish jeweler Slim Barrett moved to London in 1983 where he began catwalk collaborations with the House of Chanel and Galliano, among others. His most famous piece, this Celtic-inspired, gold and diamond coronet, was worn by Victoria Adams when she married footballer David Beckham in 1999.

CENTER The Aveta torque from Barrett's Celtic-Nouveau collection in goldplated, sterling silver.

BOTTOM A glamorous Gothic body piece, designed for the catwalk by Barrett.

ABOVE Jeweler Naomi Filmer focuses on ordinary parts of the body that are never really celebrated. She has collaborated with several catwalk designers, such as Anne Valerie Hash, for who she designed these Orchid neckpieces in 2008. Hash's clothes celebrated the erotics of the orchid's shape and were complemented by a carved gold necklace by Filmer.

RIGHT Another striking black metal neckpiece by Filmer for Hash, 2008.

OPPOSITE Ball in the Back of my Hand by Naomi Filmer for Alexander McQueen 2001. McQueen's constriction and manipulation of the body is reflected in Filmer's sculptural body pieces, which mirror and exaggerate the effects of the fashion designer's elegantly Sadeian cruelty.

Shaun Leane

The dark romance of Galliano and McQueen's fashion design had its counterpart in the jewelry of London-based Shaun Leane. At the age of 16 he underwent the most traditional of training as a goldsmith in London's Hatton Garden, where he focused on antique restoration before eventually set up his own workshop. In 1992 Leane was persuaded by fashion designer Alexander McQueen to create jewelry to accompany his second show Highland Rape, a collaboration that continued until McQueen's death in 2010. As McQueen's shows got bigger, so did the jewelry. With no commercial concerns to stifle him, the jeweler could let fly with his imagination. Leane caught the macabre feel of McQueen's fashion aesthetic perfectly with designs that embraced the notion of *memento mori*—the idea that behind the fashionable facade lay death 'as all things must pass' which was also being explored by artist Damien Hirst. For McQueen's Dante collection of 1996–7 Leane encircled the models' arms with silver thorns, which were also used as faux face piercings; for his spring/summer 1998–9 collection Leane cast an aluminium corset from a living skeleton, its silver ribcage encircling the living model's own, harbinging the death that lies at the heart of life by drawing attention to the earthly pleasures of the flesh. McQueen's fascination with love, pain and death found exaggerated expression in Leane's coil corset of 1999, which took nearly three months to make as every coil was made by hand using a concrete body cast. For the catwalk show the model had to be screwed in by a series of metal brackets affixed to the side of this huge body piece.

Leane's Gothic-erotic aesthetic forms the basis of his own internationally successful work that has been worn by clients such as Sarah Jessica Parker and Daphne Guinness. As he describes it:

I fuse inspirations from different styles and cultures, often total opposites, like tribal and Art Deco, with elements of Victorian sentiment, and this creates a certain modernism I think. When I was first given a platform with McQueen, I felt let loose, free to push boundaries and this was where I found my style, and first created my signature Tusk motif. The simple lines, proportions, the provocative touch of darkness, have followed through in my work, seen at best in my iconic Hook My Heart motif, playing with the concept of love.

This indisputably modern yet darkly romantic style can be seen in the Luna collection, made up of sculptural pieces reflecting the contours and luminous light of the moon by using amethysts and purple sapphires mixed with grey moonstone and diamonds. Leane's Cherry Blossom, Entwined and Nightingale collections have all been described by Sotheby's auction house as the 'antiques of the future.'

ABOVE Model Stella Tennant wears a Shaun Leane coiled corset, 1999. It was handmade using a concrete body cast and shown at Alexander McQueen's autumn/winter 1999 collection, entitled The Overlook.

LEFT A group of Luna rings by Shaun Leane in white gold; white gold, moonstone and pavé-set silver diamonds; and amethyst and purple sapphires set in white gold. These sculptural pieces echo the contours and luminous light of the moon.

FAR LEFT Shaun Leane for Alexander McQueen at Swarovski Runway Rocks, Moscow, 2007. Leane has recreated the Victorian star-shaped brooch on a large scale and pavé-set it with blue topaz crystal.

LEFT Shaune Leane for Alexander McQueen in 2007. Leane takes another popular Victorian jewelry motif, the crescent moon, and turns the object of whimsical fantasy into a Gothic masterpiece that appears to pierce the neck. Cabochon moonstones give a luminous and eerie effect.

BELOW LEFT Leane was inspired by the Japanese fable of the origins of cherry blossom, said to come from the clouds over Mount Fuji after it was sprinkled with seeds by a goddess. These three pieces interpret the different stages of blooming: the pearl ring represents buds and the last ring, with the enamel flower, represents full bloom. All are in gold with enamel and pearl accents.

Frank Gehry

American architect Gehry (1929–), of the famed titanium-clad Guggenheim Museum in Bilbao, Spain, began designing for Tiffany in 2006, the first new artist to be introduced to the firm since Paloma Picasso in 1980. Gehry uses sterling silver, platinum and black gold with opal, ebony and granite, studded with raw-cut diamonds and crafted into amorphous abstract shapes that echo the organic Modernism of his buildings. Gehry's architectural projects, such as Disney Hall, Los Angeles, were in reaction to the historicism of Post-Modernism. Rather than taking refuge in nostalgia, Gehry introduced a sensual organic feel into architecture with his swooping curvilinear forms that gave the graphic starkness of Bauhaus Modernism a new lease of life. This soft yet minimalist feel can be seen in the jewelry ranges Torque and Orchid for Tiffany & Co., which concentrate primarily on the use of dynamic shape and unusual materials such as cocholong stone and pernambuco wood rather than individual gemstones. For Gehry,

Jewelry is an art form and it's an interesting one in that it is a very personal expression of the wearer's style and personality. I've always looked at fashion and thought of it as a measure of what people—and women in particular—are thinking about. So I was always conscious of jewelry as an important aspect of fashion. Once I started creating jewelry, and observing women wearing the designs, the pieces came to life in the same way a building literally becomes part of life. When I finish a building and it's filled with people, it's an extraordinary feeling. And I had the same experience with the jewelry.

Kazumi Nagano

Born in Japan, Nagano (1946–) graduated at the Tama University of Art, Tokyo, with a masters degree in fine art, during which time she learned the technique of *Nihonga*, a traditional Japanese painting. Based on thousand-year-old traditions, *Nihonga* employs pigments derived from natural ingredients such as minerals, shell, coral and semiprecious stones bound together with *nikawa*, a glue made from animal hide. *Nihong's* aesthetic concerns include the attempt to inspire feelings of calm and contemplation in the viewer and in 1996 Nagano began applying this technique to jewelry design. Bracelets are woven from strands of silver and gold or fashioned out of painted paper and nylon thread with incredible dexterity and delicacy of touch and the softly supple and tactile shapes that result have proved internationally successful.

LEFT Three jewelry designs by Japanese-born Kazumi Nagano: a paper, red lacquer and gold brooch, 2009; a Japanese paper, 18-karat gold, nylon thread, Chinese ink and silver pin brooch, 2009; a superbly crafted woven bracelet using 18-, 14- and 10-karat gold and nylon thread, 2009. Formerly a fine artist, she uses a combination of exquisite handmade paper, gold, nylon thread and lacquer in her quietly contemplative work.

ABOVE In 2003, Tiffany & Co. collaborated with architect Frank Gehry to design exclusive jewelry collections. The first collection debuted in 2006 in New York; the abstract aesthetic of his fine jewelry echoes the concerns of his radical architecture.

BELOW Kazumi Nagano weaves strands of silver, gold and Japanese paper thread to create different colorways and textures in her softly organic and very delicate work. These two brooches combine woven gold, nylon thread and diamond beads.

RIGHT A necklace constructed of beads, individually woven from 14- and 10-karat gold and palladium, by Nagano.

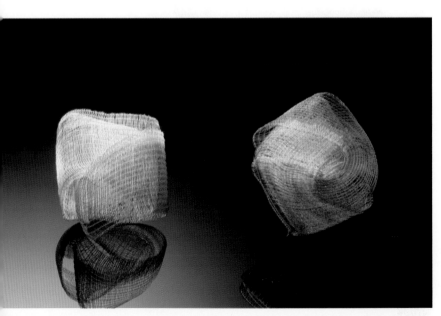

Theo Fennell

Having grown up in a traditional military family, Fennel was educated at Eton. He then went to art college, the first pupil from Eton to do so for ten years, and on graduation took up an apprenticeship in Hatton Garden. Around this time one customer bought in a 1920s champagne glass of 18-karat gold which was engraved with the message, 'Good morning, Diana.' It's quirky design fired his imagination and he began to see a career in making whimsical objects for the pure pleasure of his wealthy clients, who included Elton John, drawn to the jeweler's dramatic style of modern ostentation or 'bling' combined with classical jewelry techniques. He is one of the few jewelry designers to cater successfully to male as well as female clients.

Fennell's company was formed in 1982 with the first shop opening in the Fulham Road, London, and the jeweler found himself being referred to as the 'King of Bling' or the 'Jeweler to the Stars' with customers such as Elle Macpherson, P Diddy and Victoria Beckham sporting his work—David Beckham hit the headlines when he bought one of Fennell's huge diamond-encrusted crucifixes for a reputed £40,000. Designs such as a solid silver lid for a marmite pot, jewel-encrusted key pendants and bespoke rings at £250,000 a pop chimed with the maximalism of the times, although could come across as a little garish. After stepping down from the company that bore his name in 2008, Fennell has recently regained the helm and is back producing witty and expensive designs for the next generation of oligarchs. Recent designs appear to be less overt in their extravagance and include *touché-bois* necklaces fashioned from reclaimed wood from the Theatre Royal, Drury Lane, and antique poison bottles found on the banks of the Thames. Fennell says, 'beautiful jewelry is not about saying, "Look at how rich I am." It's about saying, "I love this—don't you?"'

RIGHT Theo Fennell's work exemplifies modern 'bling' at its finest, with ostentatious work that chimes with the decadence of post-millennial celebrity culture. Clockwise from the top: an 18-karat white gold aquamarine and pink tourmaline Bombe ring; an 18-karat white gold ruby and diamond cross pendant, one of his best-known designs; an 18-karat white gold diamond and black diamond skull ring; and an 18-karat rose gold pink sapphire and diamond key pendant.

Solange Azagury-Partridge

Azagury-Partridge sees her lack of any formal training as an absolute bonus saying, 'The advantages of being self-taught are that I have no preconceptions or received opinions about the rules of jewelry.' After studying French and Spanish at university the designer took a part-time job with Nicky Butler of Butler & Wilson. After a year she went on to work for antiques dealer Gordon Watson, from whom she learned the history of fine jewelry and the work of the great designers of the twentieth century including Suzanne Belperron, who still inspires her work.

After becoming engaged in 1987 and finding it impossible to source a ring that suited her tastes, Azagury-Partridge designed her own ring—a simple gold band set with an uncut diamond. This use of a stone that appeared to have been hewn roughly from the earth became a mark of her oeuvre—she deliberately ignored the brash sparkle of an intricately faceted gemstone in favor of a style with more subtlety and spiritual meaning. Her engagement ring was so roundly admired among her friends and acquaintances that the budding designer set up her own company and in 1995 opened her first outlet in London's Westbourne Grove. Azagury-Partridge's designs are known for their idiosyncrasy, such as the best-selling Heart of Gold that is literally a miniature, anatomically correct human heart fashioned out of gold and hung on a chain. Her huge exuberantly sculptural rings set with unconventional combinations of multicolored stones and enamel form a key part of themed collections, which are launched every year, and include Cosmic, 1999; Seven, 2002; and Platonic, 2007, her first all-diamond collection with bead-set diamonds in blackened gold. In 2001 she was handpicked by designer Tom Ford to be creative director for Boucheron where she stayed for three years before returning to London. As she succinctly puts it, 'I just want my jewels to add a bit of joy to life.'

RIGHT Solange Azagury-Partridge has injected new energy into contemporary jewelry as a result of her unusual color combinations and wittily subversive shapes. The infamous Heart of Gold pendant, is an anatomically correct miniature human heart.

BELOW Random necklace from 2010 in blackened white gold, sapphire, diamond, emerald and ruby with fire opal.

CLOCKWISE FROM LEFT An enamel 18-karat gold Pope ring with rubies; Days of the Week ring in gold, ruby, diamond and enamel; Cosmic Eye ring in gold with diamond, ruby, onyx, lapis, turquoise, mother-of-pearl and chrysopase; Adam and Eve ring in enameled gold with emerald, ruby and coral; blackened white gold and diamond Platonic ring; the Bi-Di white gold and diamond ring.

Shopping and Collecting

Collecting vintage is the most sustainable way of consuming fashion—it's a perfect example of recycling and a key to creating your individual look. Stars of the past used jewelry to create a trademark: Gloria Swanson, grande dame of 1930s film, always sported a selection of thick, gold, slave cuffs on her left arm, while Audrey Hepburn was often seen wearing a bracelet of dangling charms. Interest in style icons such as these also has the effect of making such pieces increasingly collectable. Think of the future, too, as today's jewelry will be the vintage of the future: buy modern costume jewelry of quality, treat it with care and you will have heirlooms to pass down to your grandchildren.

The market for vintage jewelry remains buoyant and the key to buying well is quality and condition. Vintage costume jewelry by famous names such as Elsa Schiaparelli, Marcel Boucher and Miriam Haskell always holds its value and many fabulous pieces went unsigned, so bargains are still to be had. Look for corroded or worn plating, cloudy rhinestones, missing or cracked stones and chipped enamel. Though scratches in silver and gold can be repaired, blisters, cracks or holes cannot be restored. Fastenings should be tested to see if they still work effectively and avoid any pieces with obvious soldering because this probably means they have been repaired at some point.

Where to Buy

There are obvious outlets for buying vintage jewelry such as specialist jewelry fairs, retro fashion markets like Portobello Road and Bermondsey Market in London and the bustling flea markets in Clignacourt in Paris and Brooklyn, New York. Lille holds Europe's largest flea market during the first weekend of September. Along miles of pavement, two million stallholders lay out their wares—the atmosphere is amazing, with an incredible array of vintage jewelry at bargain prices. Charity and thrift shops can also be great for vintage jewelry and bargains are still to be had out there. Most major cities have a gem of a vintage jewelry store, such as Linda Bee, a long-established dealer in London's Grays Antique Market (who specializes in feline-related items), Miriam Haskell, Joseff of Hollywood and Schiaparelli. Pippin Vintage Jewelry in New York has baubles covering almost every inch of the store with prices ranging from $5 for kitsch costume jewelry to $800 for the finest antique pieces.

How to Spot Fake Costume Jewelry

As the demand for vintage costume jewelry has taken off, so many fakes have appeared on the market. One trick by some disreputable dealers is to amalgamate all the old rhinestones from broken pieces into a new setting. Vintage settings are usually smooth and rhodium plated; fakes may have a textured finish or an attempted 'antiqued' or oxidized look. Genuine rhinestone jewelry must be at least 40 years old, so if the brooch you are perusing looks pristine, then it's probably new.

Check for any dust around the stones that could indicate age and look at the style of clasp—is it compatible with the date of the piece? Feel the weight of the jewelry and familiarize yourself with the trademark signatures and stamps of the key designers documented in this book. The American firm Weiss, for instance, always prong-set their stones, so if you see an item purporting to be Weiss and the stones are glued, you will recognize that it's a fake. Avoid more expensive pieces such as Trifari Jelly Bellies until you have developed your 'eye'—remember it will be a process of trial and error at the start of your collecting bug. The best advice is to always question anything, particularly online, that looks like a real bargain—it most probably isn't. There are plenty of sites online providing information about specific styles, such as Miriam Haskell, that are being faked at any given moment (see http://imageevent.com/bluboi/haskellfakes), so be sure to do your homework before you make a bid.

Spotting a Fake Diamond

When buying a diamond, bear in mind the four 'Cs'—color, cut, carat and clarity—and always go to a reputable dealer/appraiser if you intend to invest a lot of money. It is highly recommended that you obtain a certificate from the Gemological Institute of America (GIA). Generally speaking, the larger a diamond, the rarer it is; a 4-carat diamond is worth considerably more than two 2-carat diamonds of the same quality.

- Always pay great attention to the quality of the setting—a diamond is an expensive stone so the setting will never be in poor-quality metal.

- Real diamonds do not sparkle like rainbows; their light is grey and white.

- If the diamond is not in a setting, turn it upside down over a piece of newspaper. If you can easily read the print, it's a fake.

- Breathe over the diamond—the fog from your breath should disappear instantly. If it stays for more than two to three seconds, it's a fake.

- If a drop of water is put on the facet of a diamond it will remain a drop and not spread over the surface. If it does, the stone is glass or crystal.

OPPOSITE Model wears a two-piece blue blouse and skirt in the 1960s, accessorized with a coral bead necklace by David Webb. The beads are gathered together with gold and emerald cabochons.

Spotting a Fake Pearl

There are so many different kinds of pearls that identifying whether a pearl is real, cultured or fake can be a bit of a minefield. Even dealers have difficulties and it has been said that the only true test is to slice the pearl in half to see the layers of natural nacre or submit it to X-ray!

There are other less destructive or time-consuming ways to determine a real pearl from a fake, but they are by no means conclusive.

- Take the pearl and gently rub it over the surface of your teeth—a natural pearl should feel slightly gritty. Cultured pearls are a little smoother but should still retain a slight bumpy or gritty feel. Don't rush for your credit card yet, though, as fake pearls are sometimes given a faux natural surface to fool prospective buyers.

- Hold the pearls under a bright light, either indoors or outdoors. Study them for variations in color and iridescence—if the pearls are identical in shape and color, they are fake.

- Use a magnifying glass to look for irregularities such as bumps or pits over the surface and carefully inspect the drill hole. If you can see layers, they are probably the real deal.

- Go for quality. Real pearls are heavier than fake, tend to be knotted between each pearl and have sterling-silver catches with safety chains.

Caring for Fine Jewelry

Jewelry that contains precious gemstones such as diamonds should be stored individually because even the hardest stones can chip. Individual cloth pouches may be purchased from most jewelry stores and will prevent stones from accidentally scuffing one another in your jewelry box. Antique diamonds must be cleaned by a professional as both stones and settings may be delicate and need expert attention. For cleaning other gemstones the following tools are recommended:

- Shallow dish—never clean in a sink as an unstable plug could lead to disaster! Presoak your jewelry here.

- Soft bristle toothbrush to remove dirt from your jewelry with no abrasion

- Mild detergent

- Lint-free cloth—those used for cleaning glasses are perfect.

Step 1: Remove any fibers affixed to the prongs of settings with tweezers.

Step 2: Place the piece in a mild solution of detergent and water then scrub lightly with the toothbrush, changing angles as you go.

Step 3: Rinse carefully in fresh water and finally, dry and buff with a soft cloth.

LEFT An ornate costume 'Parrot' bracelet by Canadian jeweler Alan Anderson. Anderson specializes in making new pieces with unusual vintage stones from his collection.

Caring for Pearls

Pearls are delicate and prone to damage from pollution; they are also susceptible to staining from cosmetics, perfume and hairspray so make them the last thing you put on before you go out. They should never be cleaned with any kind of solvent or abrasive but merely wiped with a soft, lint-free cloth. Keep away from the beach or pool when wearing pearls—the silk string on which they are usually strung deteriorates quickly when wet and pearls should never be exposed to chlorinated water or sunscreen. Wipe with a lint-free cloth after wear because the more that pearls come into contact with the skin, the quicker they lose their luster. Keep out of the sunlight and avoid cooking when wearing pearls—they are organic and can become dehydrated and damaged when exposed to too much heat.

Bakelite or Fakelite?

An enormous amount of fake Bakelite (or Fakelite) is on the market at the moment, much of it produced in India. Watch out for large multicolored polka-dot bangles, figurative rings with motifs such as Scottie dogs and obviously 'antiqued' hinges. Martha Sleeper pieces are being reproduced in this way—if an item looks cheap with no obvious signs of wear, avoid it, as all her work is old and extremely rare. To test for the real thing give a brisk rub with your thumb on a piece of Bakelite and then quickly smell it—it should have a resinous or camphor-like odor. Or, if at home with a flea-market find, place under hot running water for 30 seconds and, again, sniff it to detect the smell of phenol. If the phenol aroma swiftly disappears to leave a plastic smell, it's Fakelite.

- With so much fake Bakelite about, it's best to visit a reputable dealer rather than to buy from the Internet—leave that to the experts.

- No Bakelite is produced today. Dealers may refer to 'new Bakelite' but it is, in fact, polymer.

- There is no such thing as 'white' Bakelite; it darkens and turns slightly yellow with age.

- Study the fastening and hinges and how they have been attached to the piece. Old Bakelite pieces have small holes drilled into them with pins, rivets or screws for findings—they will not be glued.

Caring for Bakelite

Bakelite is sensitive to sunlight, which causes it to discolor or fade, so keep it out of direct light and store by wrapping in a soft cloth. It does not respond well to changes in temperature and can occasionally craze or crack in contact with a radiator or air-conditioner, or when stored in plastic. Wash by hand with soapy water, dry with a towel and then apply a polish such as Turtle Wax or Simichrome to buff and remove minor scuffmarks.

Buying Online

Be canny if you decide to buy online—as recommended earlier, it is best to do this only if you are very experienced collector. If a seller produces a number of pieces of vintage jewelry from one well-known designer such as Schiaparelli, its authenticity could well be dubious—it's highly unlikely that anyone would dispose of a whole collection all at once. It's also easy to research the seller by looking carefully at their feedback. If it's a private sale it's advisable not to buy—you will have no idea of their reputation. Read the details in the item listings carefully because if the piece you buy has been misrepresented then you may be able to get your money back.

Be sure to take the delivery charges into consideration and check that your item is insured if it's to be shipped —also be aware that you may incur quite hefty import charges if you purchase from overseas. If you buy from anyone other than through eBay you will not be covered should anything go wrong; never pay for any item using an instant cash wire transfer service—it can be extremely unsafe with a dealer you do not know. If you buy through eBay using Paypal, the seller will never be given any bank or credit card details about you apart from your address, and if you have PayPal Buyer Protection, your purchase can be covered up to $1,000.

ABOVE A citrine ring and drop earring set, circa 1920s. Buying a vintage piece in its original box will help authenticate its provenance and therefore its value.

Museums and Collections

UNITED KINGDOM

Brighton Museum & Art Gallery
Royal Pavilion Gardens
Brighton
East Sussex BN1 1EE
Tel: 01273 292882
Website:
www.brighton-hove-rpml.org.uk/
Museums/brightonmuseum
A good collection of Art Nouveau jewelry, including pieces from several countries.

British Museum
Great Russell Street
London WC1B 3DG
Tel: 020 7323 8000
Website: www.britishmuseum.org
The collection includes jewelry from about 5,000 BC to the present day. Much is on public display, while more is accessible via the museum's online collection.

Cheltenham Art Gallery & Museum
Clarence Street
Cheltenham GL50 3JT.
Tel: 01242 237431
Website:
www.cheltenhammuseum.org.uk
Outstanding permanent collection including Arts and Crafts silver and jewelry by Charles Ashbee's Guild of Handicraft.

The Fashion Museum
Assembly Rooms
Bennett Street
Bath BA1 2QH
Tel: 01225 477 173
Website:
www.museumofcostume.co.uk
Small collection of costume jewelry dating from the eighteenth to the twenty-first century. Includes hatpins, buckles, brooches, necklaces, earrings, bracelets and tiaras. Although the costume jewelry is not on display in the museum, an active study facility enables access to the collection.

Museum of London
London EC2Y 5HN
Tel: 0870 444 3851
Website:
www.museumoflondon.org.uk
This fine jewelry collection includes groups assembled by such notable collectors as Dame Joan Evans, Baroness D'Erlanger, Lady Cory and Queen Mary. Includes the Cheapside hoard—the greatest hoard of Elizabeth and Jacobean jewelry in the world.

Museum of the Jewellery Quarter
75–79 Vyse Street
Hockley
Birmingham B18 6HA.
Tel: 0121 554 3598
Website: www.bmag.org.uk/
museum-of-the-jewellery-quarter
The story of the Jewellery Quarter and Birmingham's renowned jewelry and metal-making heritage. The Earth's Riches gallery showcases jewelry made from materials from the natural world, including whale tooth, coral, diamonds and platinum.

Tower of London
London EC3N 4AB
Tel: 0844 482 7777
Website:
www.hrp.org.uk/toweroflondon
Be dazzled by the 23,578 gems that make up the Crown Jewels, including the world's most famous diamonds.

The Ulster Museum
Botanic Gardens
Belfast BT9 5AB.
Tel: 028 9044 0000
Website: www.nmni.com
Particularly strong in eighteenth-century paste, nineteenth-century jewelry and Art Nouveau pieces. Includes the most complete collection of nineteenth-century Irish jewelry in existence, also a collection of pre-historic and early medieval Irish jewelry.

Victoria and Albert Museum
Cromwell Road
London SW7 2RL
Tel: 020 7942 2000
Website: www.vam.ac.uk
The William and Judith Bollinger Jewellery Gallery displays 3,500 jewels from the V&A's jewelry collection, one of the finest and most comprehensive in the world.

Whitby Museum
Pannett Park
Whitby
North Yorkshire YO21 1RE
Tel: 01947 602908
Website:
www.whitbymuseum.org.uk
One of the best collections of jet artifacts in the world with over 500 examples.

UNITED STATES

American Museum of Natural History
Central Park West at 79th Street
New York NY 10024-5192
Tel: 212 769 5100
Website: www.amnh.org
Twenty-five dazzling diamonds are on display in the Morgan Memorial Hall of Gems.

Brooklyn Museum
200 Eastern Parkway
Brooklyn
New York NY 11238-6052
Tel:718 638 5000
Website:
www.brooklynmuseum.org
One of America's largest museums with collections that include jewelry from Ancient Egypt to the present day.

Luce Foundation Center for American Art
Smithsonian American Art Museum
8th and F Streets, N.W.
Washington DC 20004
Tel: 202 633 5435
Website:
www.americanart.si.edu/luce/
A storage and study center, with public space, that holds a large collection of antique and more contemporary jewelry.

AUSTRALIA

The National Opal Collection
Level 1
119 Swanston Street
Melbourne
Tel: 613 9662 3524
Website: www.nationalopal.com
Retail showroom and museum that displays a huge variety of Australia's national gemstone and explains how they were formed and mined.

BELGIUM

The Diamond Museum
Koningin Astridplein 19–23
B-2018 Antwerpen
Belgium.
Tel: 32 (0) 3 202 48 90
Website: www.diamantmuseum.be
Antwerp is the diamond center of the world. This museum covers every aspect of diamonds, including a collection of diamond jewelry from the sixteenth century to the present day.

DENMARK

The National Museum of Denmark (Nationalmuseet)
Frederiksholms Kanal 12
DK 1220 Copenhagen K
Tel: (45) 3313 4411
Website: www.natmus.dk
Danish pre-historic and Viking jewelry; some Amager and north African traditional jewelry.

FINLAND

The National Museum of Finland
Mannerheimintie 34
Helsinki
Tel: (35) 894050 9544
Website: www.nba.fi/en/nmf
Finno-Ugric traditional jewelry from Finland, Estonia and Russia.

FRANCE

Musée des Arts Décoratifs
107 rue de Rivoli
75001 Paris
Tel: 00 331 4455 5750
Website: www.lesartsdecoratifs.fr
Around 1,200 jewels are exhibited in the Galerie des Bijoux.

Musée d'Orsay
1 rue de la Legion d'Honneur
75007 Paris
Tel: 00 331 4049 4814
Website: www.musee-orsay.fr
Fine collection of jewelry and
goldsmiths' work from the 1860s.

Musée du Louvre
36 Quai du Louvre
75001 Paris
Tel: 00 33 4020 5760
Website: www.louvre.fr
Collection of jewelry ranging
from ancient to mid-nineteenth
century; includes the magnificent
French Crown jewels display in
Galerie d'Apollon.

**Musée Lalique (Musée
de France)**
29 rue de Zitersheim 67290
Wingen sur Moder
Bas-Rhin
Tel: 03 88 890814
Website:
www.cc-paysdelapetitepierre.fr/
The only museum in France
dedicated to the work of Art
Nouveau master jeweler and
glass worker, René Lalique.

GERMANY
Fabergé Museum GmbH
Sophie Strasse 30
76530 Baden-Baden
Tel: 49 (0) 7221 970890
Website: www.fabergemuseum.de
Dedicated solely to the life and
work of Carl Fabergé, including
exquisite jewelry.

Schmuckmuseum Pforzheim
Jahnstrasse 42
D-75173 Pforzheim
Tel: 07231 392126
Website: www.schmuckmuseum.de
One of the few dedicated
jewelry museums in the world.
A permanent exhibition from
Antiquity to the present day,
plus a rolling schedule of
temporary exhibitions.

GREECE
**The Ilias Lalaounis
Jewellery Museum**
Kallisperi 12 and Karyatidon Street
Acropolis 11742
Athens
Greece
Tel: 30 210 9221044
Website:
www.lalaounis-jewelrymuseum.gr
The only museum worldwide
dedicated to contemporary
jewelry with over 4,000 pieces of
jewelry and micro-sculptures.

National Archaeological Museum
44 Patission St
Athens
Tel (30) 210 8217724
Website: www.namuseum.gr
Classical jewelry including the
treasure from Mycenae.

HUNGARY
Museum of Applied Arts
IX. Ulloi ut 33-37
1450 Budapest Pf.3
Tel: 06 1 2175222
Website: www.imm.hu
Includes a number of outstanding
Art Nouveau jewels, such as
works by Rene Lalique and
Oszkár Tarján (Huber).

ITALY
Museo degli Argenti
Uffizi Gallery
Florence
Tel: 055 238 8709
Website: www.uffizi.com/museo-
degli-argenti-florence.asp
Over 500 pieces from the
seventeenth century to the
present day.

NETHERLANDS
Galerie Marzee
Lage Markt 3
Waalkade 4 6511
VK Nijmegen
Tel: (31) 243229670
Website: www.marzee.nl
The largest gallery for modern
jewelry in the world: hosts four or
five exhibitions at any time with
new openings every two months.

POLAND
The Amber Museum
Main Town Hall
Ul Dluga 47
Gdansk
Tel: (48) 587679100
Museum dedicated to amber,
including the achievements of
contemporary amber artists.

Stores and Boutiques
UNITED KINGDOM
Blackout II
51 Endell Street
Covent Garden
London WC2H 9AJ
Tel: 020 7240 5006
Website: www.blackout2.com
Vintage costume jewelry.

Cenci
4 Nettlefold Place
London SE27 OJW
Tel: 020 8766 8564
Website: www.cenci.co.uk
Vintage fashion, accessories
and jewelry from the
1930s onwards.

Circa 1900
Upstairs
6 Camden Passage
London N1 8ED
Tel: 0771 370 9211
Website: www.circa1900.org
Specialists in Arts and Crafts, Art
Deco and Art Nouveau jewelry.

Electrum Gallery
21 South Molton Street
London W1K 5QZ
Tel: 020 7629 6325
For unique contemporary jewelry
from Tone Vigelund, Wendy
Ramshaw, Gerda Flöckinger, and
more.

Linda Bee
Grays Antique Market
58 Davies Street and
1–7 Davies Mews
London W1K 5AB
Tel: 020 7629 7034
Website: www.graysantiques.com
Long-established dealer in
London's Grays Antiques Market.

Obsidian, Harry Fane
Tel: 020 7930 8606
www.harryfane.com
A world authority on vintage
Cartier and Verdura.

Palette London
21 Canonbury Lane
London N1 2AS
Tel: 020 7 288 7428
Website: www.palette-london.com
Eclectic mix of quirky vintage
jewelry from the 1920s to
the 1990s. There is also a
finder service.

Rellik
8 Golborne Road
London W10 5NW
Tel: 020 8962 0089
Website: www.relliklondon.co.uk
Clothing and accessories from
the 1920s to mid-1980s.

Rokit
42 Shelton Street
London WC2H 9HZ
Tel: 020 7836 6547
Website: www.rokit.co.uk
Vintage and retro clothing
and jewelry from the 1920s
to the 1980s.

Tadema Gallery
10 Charlton Place
London N1 8AJ
Tel: 077 1008 2395
Website: tademagallery.com
Specialists in late nineteenth and
early twentieth-century jewelry:
Art Nouveau, Jugendstil,
Skonvirke, British Arts and Crafts,
Egyptian Revival, Art Deco and
Mid-Century jewelry.

Van den Bosch
123 Grays Antique Market
58 Davies Streeet
London W1K 5LP
Tel: 0207629 1900
Website: www.vandenbosch.co.uk
Jewelry from the Arts and Crafts,
Art Nouveau, Jugendstil and
Skonvirke movements.

UNITED STATES
Annie Cream Cheese of Las Vegas
3327 Las Vegas Boulevard
Las Vegas NV 89109
Tel: 702 452 9600
Website:
www.anniecreamcheese.com
High-end designer vintage clothing that also stocks a large selection of vintage jewelry.

Decades Two
8214 Melrose Ave
Los Angeles CA 90046
Tel: 323 655 1960
Website: www.decadestwo.com
Vintage couture boutique with a carefully edited selection of vintage designs from the 1930s to the 1990s that often appear on the red carpet during awards seasons.

Keni Valenti Retro-Couture
155 West 29th Street
Third floor, Room C5
New York NY 10001
Tel: 917 686 9553
Website: www.kenivalenti.com
Vintage boutique with a selection of vintage designer jewelry.

CANADA
Deluxe Junk Company
310 Cordova Street
Vancouver
British Columbia V6B 1E8
Tel: 604 685 4871
Website: www.deluxejunk.com
Vancouver's oldest vintage clothing and accessories store.

Divine Decadence Originals
136 Cumberland Street
Upper Floor
Toronto
Ontario M5R 1A2
Tel: 416 324 9759
Vintage clothing and jewelry.

AUSTRALIA
Rokit
Metcalfe Arcade
80–84 George Street
The Rocks
Sydney
Tel: (02) 9247 1332
Website: www.rokit.com.au
Large range of fine antique and vintage clothing and jewelry.

Vintage Clothing Shop
7 St James Arcade
80 Castlereagh Street
Sydney 2000
Tel: (02) 9238 0090
Website:
www.thevintageclothingshop.com
Unusual and eclectic selection of quality original vintage clothing and jewelry.

Antiques Markets
Most cities have weekly, or even daily, antique or flea markets where time and patience can be rewarded with some lucky finds.

UNITED KINGDOM
Bermondsey Market
Bermondsey Square
Tower Bridge Road, London
Every Friday 4am–1pm.
This historical market needs an early start, but it's worth the effort.

Portobello Road Market
Portobello Road, London
Website:
www.portobello road.co.uk
Market every Saturday, shops are open six days a week.
Europe's largest market with plenty of vintage jewelry finds.

UNITED STATES
Antiques Garage
112 W 25th between Sixth and Seventh Aves
Tel: 212 243 5343
Website:
www.hellskitchenfleamarket.com
Saturday and Sunday, 9am–5pm.
More than 100 vendors, located in a Manhattan parking garage.

Hell's Kitchen Flea Market
39th Street, between 9th and 10th Avenues
Tel: 212 243 5343
Website:
www.hellskitchenfleamarket.com
Every Sunday 9am–6pm.
Small second hand market that gets busy quickly, so arrive early.

FRANCE
Clignancourt Market
Avenue de la Porte de Clignancourt
Website: www.marchesauxpuces.fr
Mon–Sat, 9am–6pm.
A grouping of 2,000–3,000 stalls on the northern fringe of the city.

Lille Flea Market
First week of September.
For two days a year the streets of Lille are transformed into a bargain hunters dream, with 62 miles (100 km) of stalls and 10,000 exhibitors.

Charity/Thrift Stores
Keep and eye on your local charity or thrift stores for lucky finds; visit their websites to find your local stores.

UNITED KINGDOM
Barnardo's
www.barnardos.org.uk

British Red Cross
www.redcross.org.uk

British Heart Foundation
www.bhf.org.uk

Cancer Research UK
www.cancerresearchuk.org

Marie Curie
www.mariecurie.org.uk

Oxfam
www.oxfam.org.uk/shop

Save the Children
www.savethechildren.org.uk

Sue Ryder
www.suerydercare.org

UNITED STATES
Arc Thrift Stores
www.arcthrift.com

Goodwill Industries International
www.goodwill.org

Salvation Army
www.salvationarmyusa.org

CANADA
Goodwill Industries International
www.goodwill.on.ca

AUSTRALIA
Society of Saint Vincent de Paul
www.vinnies.org.au

Salvation Army
salvos.org.au

Brotherhood of St Laurence
www.bsl.org.au

Online Stores
www.affordablevintagejewelry.com
www.agedandopulentjewelry.com
www.anniesherman.com
www.bagladyemporium.com
www.bejewelledvintage.co.uk
www.chicagosilver.com
www.circa1900.org
www.decogirl.co.uk
www.druckerantiques.com
www.enchantiques.nl
www.heirloomjewellery.com
www.heritagejewellery.co.uk
www.jacksonjewels.com
www.laurelleantiquejewellery.co.uk
www.modernity.se
www.morninggloryjewelry.com
www.magpievintage.co.uk
www.pastperfectvintage.com
www.penelopespearls.com
www.rubylane.com
www.scandinaviansilver.co.uk
www.thejewelrystylist.com
www.vintagecostumejewels.com
www.vintagecostumejewellery.co.uk
www.vintagejewelryonline.com
www.v4vintage.com
www.wartski.com

Auction Houses

UNITED KINGDON

Bonhams
101 New Bond Street
London W1S 1SR
and
Montpelier Street
London SW7 1HH
Tel: 020 7447 7447
Website: www.bonhams.com

Christie's
8 King Street
St James's
London SW1Y 6QT
Tel: 020 7839 9060
and
85 Old Brompton Road
London SW7 3LD
Tel: 020 7930 6074
Website: www.christies.com

Sotheby's
Tel: 020 7293 5000
Website: www.sothebys.com

UNITED STATES

Bonhams
220 San Bruno Avenue
San Francisco CA 94103
Tel: 415 861 7500
and
7601 Sunset Boulevard
Los Angeles CA 90046
Tel: 323 850 7500
and
580 Madison Avenue
New York NY 10022
Tel: 212 644 9009
Website: www.bonhams.com

Christie's
20 Rockefeller Plaza
New York NY 10020
Tel: 212 636 2000
Website: www.christies.com

Sotheby's
Tel: 212 606 7000
Website: www.sothebys.com

AUSTRALIA

Bonhams
Level 57 MLC Centre
19–29 Martin Place
Sydney
NSW 2000
Tel: 612 9238 2395
Website:
www.bonhams.com/australia

CANADA

Bonhams
20 Hazelton Ave
Toronto M5R 2E2
Tel: 416 462 9004
Website:
www.bonhams.com/canada

Contributors

Many thanks to the below online shops for their archive resources, information and advice. Please see individual listings for vintage jewelry-buying information.

Affordable Vintage Jewelry
www.affordablevintagejewelry.com
Contact: Polly Curtiss
Tel: (001) 203 558 8281
Vintage, antique and estate jewelry with an emphasis on vintage sterling silver.

Aged and Opulent Jewelry
www.agedandopulentjewelry.com
Specializes in high-end vintage costume jewelry.

Bag Lady Emporium.com
www.bagladyemporium.com
Contact: Marion Spitzley
bagladyemporium@gmail.com
Bakelite and plastic jewelry, as well as signed and unsigned.

Butterfly Blue
www.rubylane.com/shop/
butterflyblue
Contact: Patricia Howard
Tel: (001) 604 948 8686

Chicago Silver
www.chicagosilver.com
American Arts and Crafts, focusing on the Kalo Shop.

Decogirl
www.decogirl.co.uk
Contact: Wanda Ingham
decogirl@sky.com
Tel: (44) 07525 203928
Specializing in Bakelite and plastics, especially Lea Stein.

Drucker Antiques
www.druckerantiques.com
Contact: William Drucker
bill@druckerantiques.com\
For Georg Jensen.

Enchantiques
www.enchantiques.nl
Contact: Erna Kager
info@enchantiques.nl
For vintage 1950s and 1960s, including Eisenberg Originals.

Green's
www.rubylane.com/shop/greens
Contact: Susie Green
Tel: (44) 020 7435 4085

The Jewelry Stylist
www.thejewelrystylist.com
Contact: Melinda Lewis, stylist at thejewelrystylist.com
Tel: (001) 707 751 1665
Costume jewelry, included parures and individual pieces by Haskell, Schreiner, Trifari, Schiaparelli, YSL and Chanel.

Looluu's
www.rubylane.com/shop/looluus
Leslie Sturt

Lets Get Vintage
www.letsgetvintage.com
mrgvintage@optonline.net

Little Shiny Objects
www.rubylane.com/shop/
littleshinyobjects
Tel: (917) 488 7555

Melange-Art
www.rubylane.com/shops/
melange-art
Linda Sweeney
Tel: (001) 520 825 4005

Modernity
www.modernity.se
info@modernity.se
Tel: (46) 8 20 80 25
For Scandinavian Modern, such as that by Torun Bülow-Hübe.

Morning Glory Antiques and Jewelry
www.morninggloryjewelry.com
Costume jewelry, including Juliana, Haskell, Trifari, Swarovski, Coro, Eisenberg and Weiss, as well as plastic.

Past Perfect Vintage
www.pastperfectvintage.com
Contact: Holly Jenkins-Evans
montyholly@insightbb.com
Tel: (001) 502 718 9190

Penelope's Pearls Vintage and Antique Jewelry
www.penelopespearls.com
Contact: Nancy Bohm
Tel: (44) 519 773 3587

Two Silly Magpies
www.rubylane.com/shops/
twosillymagpies
Contact: Patti Williamson

Glossary of Jewelry Terms

A jour: Opening in a gemstone setting that allows light to pass through the stone from both sides.

Aguette: Gemstone, often a diamond, cut in a narrow, rectangular shape. Small diamonds cut in this way are often used as accents.

Aigrette: Very popular in the early twentieth century, this hair ornament was often decorated with feathers or glitter.

Ajoure: Design with holes punched, cut or drilled into a piece of metal rather than wires, which have been bent or formed into the design, as with filigree.

Alloy: Metallurgical term for a mixture of two or more metals. In jewelry, most metals are alloyed together, either to alter the color of the metal or to give it greater strength.

Amulet: Object or a talisman to protect against danger and the unknown.

Anodizing: Technique used to dye and/or modify the surface of a metal (usually titanium) using electrolysis.

Art Deco: Popular during the early twentieth century from the 1910s, the style originated in France and is characterized by geometric designs and angles.

Art Nouveau: Designs from the late nineteenth and early twentieth century which made their way into jewelry making, often characterized by curved, flowing, asymmetrical lines. Many designs feature leaves, flowers, insects and *femme fatales*.

Aurora borealis: Name for a particular type of rhinestone with an iridescent finish; a process created by Swarovski and Christian Dior in 1955.

Baguette: Small, rectangular-shaped stones with facets.

Bakelite: Synthetic resin invented in 1909. Made from phenol and formaldehyde, it is characterized by its hardness and was used extensively in jewelry of the 1960s.

Bar brooch or pin: Long, narrow brooch or pin often set with gemstones.

Baroque pearl: Sometimes also referred to as a 'potato pearl,' this is an irregularly shaped pearl or stone and favored by Miriam Haskell.

Basse-taille: Translucent enamelling applied over an engraved metal surface; popular with mid twentieth-century Scandinavian silversmiths.

Bevel cut: Where the surface has been cut at an angle of less than 90 degrees.

Bezel: A band with a groove or flange. A setting that involves a metal band (bezel) that encircles the gemstone and extends slightly above it and holds the gem in place.

Brilliant cut: The most popular cut shape for diamonds, its shape resembles a cone and is intended to maximize light return through the top of the stone.

Briolette: A drop-shaped stone with triangular or diamond-shaped facets all the way around.

Butterfly wing jewelry: Jewelry made from real butterfly wings. Often a picture depicted by reverse painting, the whole thing is then encased in plastic or glass.

Cable chain: Style of chain whose links are round and uniform in size.

Cabochon: Gemstone cut with a rounded, domed surface, with no facets. Usually round or oval, but can be other shapes. Denser semiprecious stones such as turquoise or tiger's-eye are mainly given the cabochon cut as they do not need as much light to penetrate their beauty.

Cameo: Carving in which the surrounding surface of a design is cut away, leaving the design in relief.

Cannetille: Wire filigree braided to form a cone-shaped scroll or spiral. Used as a gem setting framework.

Carat: Unit of weight used to describe diamonds and other precious gems. The metric carat of 200 milligrams was adopted by the USA in the early 1900s and is now universally used.

Cartouche: Decoration characterized by swirls and scrollwork in a symmetrical design.

Catalin: Early form of phenol plastic material sometimes referred to as Bakelite, although the composition is a little different.

Champlevé: An enameling technique where grooves are cut into the metal and filled with enamel.

Channel setting: Two strips of metal (gold, platinum or silver) are used to hold gemstones in place at the sides, with no metal between the stones. It is better than a prong setting for small stones.

Chaton setting: This setting holds a stone in place through a series of metal claws around a metal ring; also referred to as a coronet or arcade setting.

Chatoyancy: Strip of light reflected onto the surface of a stone that glints back and forth, resembling a cat's eye.

Claw setting: Often employed so that the back of the stone can be open to allow more light to pass through, this is a setting in which the stone is held in place by a number of metal prongs (claws).

Clip-back/Clip-on: Earrings designed for non-pierced ears.

Cliquet: Also known as a jabot pin, or *sûreté*, this is a fastening device that uses a pin-and-snap closure.

Cloisonne: Multistep process whereby filigree is inlaid with enamel to produce a glassy sheen and a wide variety of colors.

Collier de chien: Wide, ornamented, jewelled necklace worn tightly round a woman's throat, also known as a 'dog collar.'

Confetti Lucite: Form of plastic Lucite which is transparent with chips or glitter encased inside.

Crown: Top half of a gemstone.

Cushion: This can be a type of diamond cut incorporating both a round and square shape. Also refers to a style of signet ring stamping.

Damascene: Process of applying gold or silver onto iron or steel to produce intricate patterns. Damascene jewelry often comes from Spain or Japan.

Decoration etched: Very faintly carved surface decoration.

Demantoid garnet: Sub-variety of andradite; the rarest and most expensive of garnets, the color ranges from dark- to yellowish-green.

Diadem: Ornamented band, often with gemstones, worn around the brow. More recent examples were made in Art Nouveau style.

Diamanté (rhinestone): A diamond substitute made from rock crystal, glass or acrylic.

Duette: Combination two-part pin on one pin back, made famous by Coro.

Electroplating: Method of finishing a metal in which an electric current puts a layer of metal on another alloy.

Emerald cut: Often but not always an emerald, this is a stepped, normally rectangular gemstone cut with cropped corners.

En esclavage: Bracelet or necklace containing similar metal plaques connected by rows of swagged chain ("enslaved").

Enamel: Glass-like, decorative surface produced by fusing colored powdered glass "paste" to metal (usually bronze, copper or gold).

Engrave: Gouging out a design in metal with engraver's tools, or embellishing metal or other material with patterns using a stamping tool or drill.

Facet: The polished face of a gemstone.

Faceted: Small, flat-cut surfaces that make a sparkling effect on transparent stones. Diamonds, rubies and sapphires are nearly always faceted (the opposite of cabochon).

Fakelite: Modern, mass-produced product; neither true Bakelite nor vintage (also known as French Bakelite).

Ferronière: Headdress featuring a thin metal band adorned with a single large gemstone.

Festoon: Design motif consisting of a garland or string of flowers, ribbons or leaves.

Filigree: Technique used to produce delicate, intricate patterns in gold or silver wire twisted into patterns. Often used for metal beads and clasps.

Fox tail chain: A type of woven chain made from many individual, interlinked links.

French backs: An earring back for non-pierced ears where the earring is tightened against the earlobes by means of a screw. Also referred to as a screwback earring.

Fruit Salad jewelry: Also known as 'tutti frutti' and made of glass or plastic stones in the shape of fruits or leaves.

Garland style: Popular in the early twentieth century and made possible by the widespread use of platinum. Characterized by lightness and delicacy that employed motifs such as garlands, ribbon bows, swags and tassels.

Girandole: Chandelier-like brooch or earrings with three pear-shaped pendants hanging from a larger central setting.

Givre stones: Stones made of transparent glass fused around a translucent core to give a frosted appearance.

Gold filled: Looking like karat gold and often referred to as rolled gold, gold-filled pieces must be at least one twentieth by weight in gold to be classified as such.

Gold-plated: Finish where a very thin layer of gold is applied to the surface of a piece, usually by electroplating; often marked GEP, gold plated or gold electroplate.

Grain: Unit sometimes used to measure pearls—a metric or pearl grain is equal to 50 milligrams or a quarter of a carat.

Grooved: Routed out in a line.

Guilloché: Machine-turning technique for engraving a repetitive decorative pattern onto a metal surface.

Guilloché enamel: Translucent enamel is applied to metal, which has detailed engraving on it.

Habillé: Refers to the image in a cameo of a woman wearing some form of gem-set jewelry.

Hallmark: Official stamped mark applied to metal items by the Assay Offices of Britain as a guarantee of authenticity and to indicate metal content.

Hammered finish: Indented hammer marks on a metal's surface.

Inclusion: Particle of solid, liquid or gaseous foreign matter contained within a stone.

Inlaid: Technique where a space is routed out of metal and a contrasting material fitted into that space. Bakelite polka-dot bracelets are an excellent example.

Intaglio: Opposite of cameo, this is a carved gem from which the design is engraved or carved into the object.

Iridescence: Optical phenomenon in which the hue on the surface of the stone changes according to the angle from which the surface is viewed.

Jabot pin: Tie pin accented with jewels, popular in the early twentieth century.

Jarretière: Type of metal bracelet with a strap and buckle on one end and a mordant at the other.

Jelly Belly pin: Style of figural brooch made famous by Trifari and Coro with a clear lucite cabochon that forms the "belly" of the piece.

Juliana: Style of jewelry, not a maker, these pieces were designed by the DeLizza and Elster factory and are highly collectable. The jewelry itself is never marked, only with paper hanging tags.

Karat: Usually abbreviated to the letter 'K,' karat refers to the purity of gold: 24K is 100% pure gold, 18K is 18 parts gold with six parts other alloyed metals.

Lariat: Long necklace with open ends (no clasp) kept in place by knotting or looping the ends.

Lavaliere: Pendant which has a dangling stone below it.

Liberty style: A style associated with the famous London store that epitomized the Art Nouveau look of the early twentieth century.

Limoges: French technique for enamelling and firing to create a pictorial image, usually a portrait, to be used as a brooch.

Lobster claw: Clasp resembling a lobster's claw with a spring mechanism that can be opened to attach to the other end of the chain.

Loupe: Magnifying glass used by jewelers to see the inclusions and imperfections inside gemstones with a ten-times magnification.

Lucite: Thermoplastic acrylic resin (strong plastic) patented by the DuPont company in 1941; lucite has a specific gravity of 1.19 and is clear. Due to its transparent nature it was easily colored or more interestingly mixed with glitter or other small pieces of material, which is known as 'Confetti Lucite'.

Maltese cross: Cross with four arms of equal length; the width of each arm widens, the further it gets from the center.

Manchette: Wide bracelet tapering into the shape of a shirtsleeve.

Marquise cut: Elongated, faceted oval cut tapering to a point. Similar to a navette cut (see below), but slightly more rounded.

Matinée length: Single-strand necklace 22–23 in (56–58 cm) long.

Metal inlay: Imbedding or insertion of sheet metal or wire into an indentation or groove in the surface of a finished piece of metal.

Millegrain setting: Where a gemstone is secured with tiny beads that are fashioned from metal.

Mirror finish: Highly reflective surface with no visible abrasion pattern. Created with rouge, muslin or a flannel buffing wheel.

Mohs scale: Comparison chart developed in the early part of the 1800s. It tells us how hard minerals are in comparison to others—useful when buying or storing gemstones.

Mother-of-pearl: Hard, smooth, pearlized inside linings of abalone and other shellfish scraped off and used as an inlay.

Navette: Oval stone which is pointed at both ends.

Navette cut: Oblong, tapered slender cut similar to a Marquise, although more slender.

Négligée: Necklace pendant with two unevenly suspended drops.

Nickel silver: Also referred to as 'German silver,' this alloy contains no actual silver but mainly copper, with approximately 20% nickel and 20% zinc.

Opalescence: Named after the appearance of opals, a material appears yellowish-red in transmitted light and blue in scattered light.

Open-backed: Use of a setting for a stone where the stone is set in a metal frame with an open back, which allows more light to pass through.

Opera length: Single-strand necklace 30–35 in (76–89 cm) in length; it hangs to the breastbone.

Ormolu: Refers to gilded bronze or brass mounts.

Pampille: Graduated row of articulating set gemstones that taper to a point.

Parure: Matching set of jewelry; usually a brooch, necklace, earrings and a bracelet, though can be larger. Part of a parure is called a demi- or semi-parure.

Paste: Brilliant-cut glass stone made to resemble a genuine gemstone.

Paste diamantés: Beautifully crafted, PD stones are made from high quality cut crystals that can be open or foil-backed.

Patina: Chemical film formed on the surface of metal through wear, corrosion or oxidization; often deliberately added by metalworkers.

Pavé: The process of setting stones, where a number of small stones are set as closely together as possible. Better pieces employ a claw setting.

Pavé cut: Pinpoint gemstones or diamonds set close together to create a field of color.

Pavilion: Lower half of a gemstone.

Pendeloque: Pear-shaped gemstone cut, or a pear-shaped drop earring suspended from a circular or bow setting.

Piqué: Gold or silver inlay design pattern (pricked). Also a carbon diamond inclusion.

Plique-à-jour: Translucent enamelling technique with the look of stained glass.

Princess length: Single-strand necklace, which is 18 in (45 cm) long.

Prong: Setting with a series of metal prongs that grip around the side of stones. Better rhinestone jewelry is prong set rather than glued.

Repoussé: French for 'to push back,' repoussé is a technique for creating a relief design by pressing or hammering the inside or back of a metal surface.

Reticulation: Giving a metal surface a rough or wrinkled texture with a naturally formed appearance. Also known as Samorodok, this process was popularized by Russian artists such as Fabergé.

Rhinestones: Cut-glass stones usually small and circular, often foil-backed to increase their reflectivity and sparkle. Rhinestones may be used as imitations of diamonds.

Rivière: Necklace of ascending graduated gemstones or diamonds.

Rondelle: Usually comprizes two circular discs, often decorated with rhinestones on their outer edges—which Chanel uses as decorative spacers in more elaborate necklaces.

Rose cut: This standard rose cut for diamonds, also known as the Dutch rose cut, has 24 triangular facets: six star facets meet at a point at the top and 18 cross facets.

Rose recoupée: Style of cutting a diamond (or other transparent gemstone) in the basic rose-cut fashion but with a 12-sided base and 36 facets cut in two horizontal rows.

Rose montee: A rhinestone that comes pre-mounted in a metal cup with holes in it.

Sautoir: Long necklace of beads or pearls, often ending in a tassel, and very popular in the 1920s.

Sawing: Technique developed in the early twentieth century for dividing a rough diamond before bruting and faceting.

Schiller: Flecks in the iridescent color display found in labradorite and moonstone.

Scroll piece: Component used in the manufacture of earrings for pierced ears, it holds the earring onto the ear by attaching to the pin. Also known as "butterfly."

Seed pearl: Very small round pearl.

Shank: Portion of a ring that encircles a finger.

Shot ball: Using tiny shot balls fused to the metal's surface to create a pattern or design and add texture.

Snake link chain: The links actually made of wavy metal plates joined together to form a tube.

Solder: Fusible metal alloy (gold solder: gold mixed with lower melting metals) with a melting point below 840°F (450°C), which is melted to join two metallic surfaces.

Step cut: Term used for stones which are rectangular and whose facets are parallel to the edge of the stone in a "stepped" effect and with a flat top.

Sterling silver: Alloy that is 925 parts pure silver and 75 parts copper.

Sûreté: Also known as a cliquet or jabot pin, this is a fastening device that uses a pin-and-snap closure.

Taille d'epargne: Enamelling technique where outlines or shallow channels are engraved into the metal, then filled with opaque black, blue or red enamel.

Tiara: Of Persian origin, a decorative, flowered or jewelled headband worn in the front of the hair for special occasions.

Tiffany mounting: Solitaire mounting with a four- or six-prong head to hold the diamond. The shank is usually simple and narrow.

Torsade: Necklace comprising many strands twisted together instead of left to hang loosely.

Translucent: Allowing light to pass through, but the light is scattered. Translucent stones include moonstones, opals and carnelian.

Transparent: Permitting light to pass through without scattering so that it is possible to see right through. Transparent stones include diamond, sapphire, emerald and ruby.

Trombone clasp: Usually used on a brooch or pin, this is a metal 'stopper' that is pulled out along the back of the pin to release a prong.

Tutti Frutti: See Fruit Salad jewelry.

Verdigris: Green patina that can develop over time on costume or fine jewelry. Its presence means there is metal damage underneath.

Vermeil: Sterling silver with a layer of gold applied on top; the gold must be at least 10 carat.

Index

Figures in italics indicate captions.

Picture Credits

The publishers would like to thank the following sources for their kind permission to reproduce the pictures in this book.

Key: t=Top, b=Bottom, c=Center, l=Left and r=Right

Affordable Vintage Jewelry: /Courtesy Polly Curtiss: 168tl, 168tr **Aged and Opulent Jewelry:** /www.agedandopulentjewelry.com: 9l, 112tl, 112cl, 112bl, 130bl, 130br, 132tr, 132br, 133l, 133br **AKG Images:** /CDA/Guillemot/©ADAGP, Paris and DACS, London 2010: 52r, /Sotheby's: 27r
Alamy: /Antiques & Collectables: 82bl, 104b, 105c, /David Gee: 120t
Alinari Picture Library: /Fratelli Alinari Museum Collections-Nunes Vais Archives, Florence: 30 **Arkitekturmuseet:** /The Swedish Museum of Architecture/Sune Sundahl: 144l, 144r **Bag Lady Emporium:** /Courtesy Marion Spitzley, www.bagladyemporium. com: 8r, 28l, 43t, 67 (all images), 68bl, 69b, 83t, 86 (all images), 87bl, 87br, 91tr, 91cr, 91br, 92tl, 92bl, 93bl, 105tr, 126 (all images), 127t, 127cr, 127b, 131b, 146t, 149tl, 150tr, 151t, 154t, 154bl, 158bl, 158br, 172t **The Bridgeman Art Library:** /Hermitage, St. Petersburg, Russia/Pendant brooch from the Faberge workshop, St. Petersburg, c.1900 (gold and diamonds): 34, /Kremlin Museums, Moscow, Russia/Giraudon/Easter Egg in the Form of a Vase Containing Flowers, 1899 (metal & enamel), Faberge, Carl (1846-1920): 35, /Private Collection /Photo ©Christie's Images/A Belle Epoque keyless pendant watch with gold and diamond set fob by Tiffany, from C.H. Meylan and Black Starr & Frost (platinum, pearl & diamond), American School: 20t, /Private Collection/ Photo ©Bonhams, London, UK/A collection of silver, enamel and gold Art Nouveau and Arts and Crafts brooches, including designs by Charles Horner, Murrle Bennett and William H. Haseler, c.1908-11: 24, /Private Collection/Photo ©Bonhams, London, UK/A selection of Jewellery: 37, /Private Collection/©ADAGP, Paris and DACS, London 2010/Hair ornament by Lalique and pendant by Philippe Wolfers (1858-1929), Lalique, Rene Jules (1860-1945): 15r, /Private Collection/© 2010 Calder Foundation, New York/ DACS London/Jewellery (silver), Calder, Alexander (1898-1976): 102b **Butterfly Blue:** 185bl ©**Carlton Books Ltd:** /Jewellery Courtesy Caroline Cox: p169 (all images), 172cr, /Jewellery Courtesy Lisa Dyer: 213 **Chicagosilver.com:** 8l, 22 (all images), 23t, 23c **Corbis:** 40l, /Ainaco: 196t, /Bettmann: 81, 112r, 114r, 162t, /Blue Lantern Studio: 68t, /Christie's Images: 20b, 29r, 154br, 156t, /Condé Nast Archive: 4, 44, 46l, 46r, 57, 62, 64r, 65t, 71, 74t, 80, 84, 88-89, 90, 92r, 105br, 106, 109, 111, 117, 118, 119, 128, 131tl, 132l, 137 (main), 138, 141, 143, 150bl, 152, 155, 159, 160, 174, 177, 179t, 179b, 181l, 187b, 191t, 192bl, 192br, 210, /Philippe Eranian: 32, 127cl (panther), /Ric Ergenbright: 158t, /The Gallery Collection: 40r, /Hulton-Deutsch Collection: 10, /John Springer Collection: 70, /Douglas Kirkland: 146b, 173br, /Odile Montserrat/Sygma: 186, 187t, /Mucha Trust: 14, /Genevieve Naylor: 100t, /Thierry Orban/Sygma: 196b, / Swim Ink: 42tr, /Sygma: 43br **Christie's Images Ltd:** 110t, 110b
David Watkins: 164 **Decogirl:** /decogirl.co.uk/Photography ©Carlton Books: 9cl, 149 (all images except tl) **Courtesy of Drucker Antiques:** 13bl, 13br, 29t, 121 (all images) **Enchantiques:** /Courtesy Erna Kager/www.enchantiques.nl: 113r, 127cl (red brooch), 135t **Gerda Flöckinger C B E:** 6–7 (all images) **Getty:** 207t, /AFP: 98t, 98b, / Chicago History Museum: 23b, /General Photographic Agency: 60bl, /Hulton Archive: 33, 43bl, 100b, 101, 102t, 115, 145t, 150br, /Imagno: 26, 27l, /John Kobal Foundation: 83c, 120b, /Lipnitzki/Roger Viollet: 77t, /Terry O'Neill: 185t, /SSPL: 38t, 151b, /**Time & Life Pictures:** 114l, 150tl **Green's:** /Susie Green/www.rubylane.com/shops/greens: 161c, 185br **The Jewelry Stylist:** /Courtesy of Melinda Lewis, The Jewelry Stylist/ Photographic Editor Darrel Chua: 1, 116t, 135c, 135b, 136 (all images), 137tl, 137cl, 180 (all images), 181r, 182cr, 182br **Joseff Hollywood Archive:** 72-73 (all images)
Kazumi Nagano: /Mr Mitsuo Shimada: 206 (all images), 207bl, 207br **Leslie Sturt:** 87l, 87cl, 87cr **Lets Get Vintage:** /www.letsgetvintage.com: 116b, 133cr, 139b (all flower brooches) **Little Shiny Objects, NYC:** /Marcy Drexler, Email: sunshinegirlmd@ yahoo.com: 87c (Horse & Pig)
Marie-Hélène de Taillac: 199 (all images) **Marjorie K Schick:** /Photo: Gary Pollmiller: 190 (both images), 191b **Mary Evans Picture Library:** 29l, 48, 49tr, 130t, /Illustrated London News: 36t, 49tl, 55, /Imagno: 42tl, /National Magazine Company: 64l, 65b, 66t, 66b, 82br, 108, 147, 151c, /Rue des Archives/Tallandier: 12 **Melange-Art, Tucson:** 182t, 182cl, 182bl, 193c, 193b **Modernity:** /www.modernity.se: 122-125 (all images) **Morning Glory Antiques & Jewelry:** /www.morninggloryjewelry.com: 8cr, 74c, 74bl, 74br, 75 (all images), 88, 93tl, 93c, 93cb, 93br, 94-95 (all images), 133tr **Museum of Arts & Design, New York:** /Gift of Donna Schneier, 1997/John Bigelow Taylor, 2008: 188tr, 188cr, 188b, Gift of the artist 2008/John Bigelow Taylor: 161t, 161b, /Gift of the artists, 2001: 140b, /Gift of the artists, 2001/John Bigelow Taylor, 2008: 166t, 166b, /Museum purchase with funds provided by the Collections Committee, 2000/ John Bigelow Taylor, 2008: 162b **Naomi Filmer:** /Anne Valerie Hash: 202l, 202r, / Photographed & Produced by Chris Springhall & Gavin Alexander: 203 **Neil Lane:** 198 (all images) **Collection of the Oakland Museum of California:** /Gift of Eugene Bielawski, The Margaret De Patta Memorial Collection: 103 (all images) **Past Perfect Vintage:** /www.pastperfectvintage.com/Courtesy Holly Jenkins-Evans: 8cl, 8c, 38b (all images), 60tr, 60cb, 60br, 61c, 61b, 68br, 83b, 113l **Paul Derrez:** /Galerie Ra: p189 (both images) **Penelope's Pearls Vintage & Antique Jewellery:** /Nancy Bohm: 9c, 168cl, 168cr, 168bl, 168cb, 168br **Picture Desk/Art Archive:** 58, /Alfredo Dagli Orti:

41, 59t, 59b, 104cl, 105bl, 116c, /Alfredo Dagli Orti/Beaux Bijoux/Eileen Tweedy: 69t, / Gianni Dagli Orti: 49b, /Gift of Mrs Edward C Moen/Museum of the City of New York: 21, /Museum of London: 28r, /Musée Carnavalet Paris/Gianni Dagli Orti: 19t, /Rue des Archives/Tallandier: 13t, /Victoria & Albert Museum/Eileen Tweedy: 53 **RMN:** / Jean-Gilles Berizzi/©ADAGP, Paris and DACS, London 2010: 54 **Rex Features:** /Ken Towner/Evening Standard: 204t, /Roger-Viollet: 139t, /**Sipa Press:** 176, /Unimedia International: 163, 173bl **Scala, Florence:** /White Images: 39 **Shaun Leane:** 204c, 204b, 205cl, 205cr, 205b **Slim Barrett:** 201 (all images) **Solange Azagury-Partridge:** 209 (all images) **Swarovski:** /Shaun Leane for Alexander McQueen for Swarovski Runway Rocks: 205tl, 205tr, /Shaun Leane for Swarovski Runway Rocks: 194, /Francis Mertens for Swarovski Runway Rocks using Swarovski Gems™: 196-197, /Lesley Vik Waddell for Swarovski Runway Rocks: 200 **Theo Fennell:** 9r, 208 (all images)
Topfoto.co.uk: 82t, 134, 142t, 142b, 148, 156b, 157, 167, 171l, 171r, 172cl, 178, 184, 188cl, 193t, /Art Media/HIP/©ADAGP, Paris and DACS, London 2010: 16r, 17, / The Granger Collection: 18, 96, 99, 104tr, /John Hedgecoe: 170, /Land Lost Content/ HIP: 172b, /PA: 192t, /Ullsteinbild: 78, 79 **Two Silly Magpies Inc.:** 2-3, 9cr, 183 (all images), 212 **Photo Courtesy Verdura:** /Copyright David Behl: 76l, 76r, 77b **Victoria & Albert Museum/V&A Images:** 15l, 25l, 25r, 36b, 42b, 47, 50, 51r, 56, 61t, 91l, 145b, /©ADAGP, Paris and DACS, London 2010: 16l, 19b, 51l, 52l, /Roger Doyle: 173t, / Ornamentum: 165br, /Schiaparelli France SAS: 97, /©David Watkins: 165t, 165c, 165bl, /©David Watkins & Wendy Ramshaw: 140t

Every effort has been made to acknowledge correctly and contact the source and/or copyright holder of each picture and Carlton Books Limited apologizes for any unintentional errors or omissions, which will be corrected in future editions of this book.

Further Reading

Art Deco Jewelry, Laurence Mouillefarine and Evelyne Possémé, Thames & Hudson, 2009.

Art Nouveau Jewelry, Vivienne Becker, Thames & Hudson, 1998.

Charmed Bracelet, Tracey Zabar, Stewart, Tabori & Chang, 2004.

A Collector's Guide to Costume Jewelry, Tracy Tolkien and Henrietta Wilkinson, Thames & Hudson, 1997.

Costume Jewellery, Judith Miller, Dorling Kindersley, 2007.

Jewels and Jewellery, Clare Phillips, V & A Publications, 2000.

Rough Diamonds: The Butler & Wilson Collection, Vivienne Becker, Pavilion Books, 1990.

Understanding Jewellery, David Bennett & Daniella Mascetti, Antique Collector's Club, 2010.

Vintage Costume Jewellery: A Passion for Fabulous Fake, Carole Tannenbaum, Antique Colllector's Club, 2005.

Author Acknowledgments

Thanks to the wonderful three 'Ms' Marnie, Maggie and Mary, Katy Lubin for her insight into pearls, genius Sheila Ableman, lovely Lionel Marsden, the ever-dapper Khalid Siddiqui, my mates at Sassoon and Lisa Dyer and all at Carlton Books.